To my Dad, Sandy King
And to Skooby, Chi, Caz and Simon,
for helping me find the strength and courage to fly

Sandra Lean © Copyright 2007

All rights reserved

British Library Cataloguing In Publication Data
A Record of this Publication is available
from the British Library

ISBN 978-1-84685-704-1

First Published 2007 by
Exposure Publishing,
an imprint of
Diggory Press Ltd
Three Rivers, Minions, Liskeard, Cornwall, PL14 5LE, UK
and of Diggory Press, Inc.,
Goodyear, Arizona, 85338, USA
WWW.DIGGORYPRESS.COM

CONTENTS

Acknowledgements

Perhaps the saddest realisation is that this book only exists as a result of tragedy. It arises from the suffering of ordinary people thrust into extraordinary circumstances.

Nothing can take away from the horror of those families who have lost a loved one to murder, and I can only express my deepest sympathy for the families whose loved ones' murders form the basis of this book.

It is not, and never has been, my intention to cause these families any further suffering.

However, the suffering and distress caused to the victims of miscarriage of justice and their families is also very real, and it is this which has led to the extensive investigation of the cases highlighted in this book.

The courage and determination of the victims themselves, and their families and friends is an inspiration. The strength and belief it takes to keep on fighting, in the face of such dreadful injustice, is enormous, yet each of them carries on, utterly committed to proving their innocence, and having their convictions overturned. Sadly, much of the rest of us go about our business, completely unaware of their plight, and oblivious to the fact that it could happen to any one of us.

There are others, much closer to home, without whom this book would simply never have made it into print.

Skooby and Chi, my entire inspiration for everything I do. Between you, you bring the greatest wisdom and understanding in my life – you taught me the real meaning of unconditional acceptance.

Caz, who wouldn't let me off the hook, not even for a minute, who pushed even when I thought I could do no more, and who never stopped believing in me.

Simon, who forces me to keep discovering myself anew, to keep questioning the truth, and to really find out what I believe in, by putting it to the test.

Kyle, who, aged just 10, took on the responsibility of making sure the page numbers tallied properly.

Betty, for absolutely everything!

Louise, who told me all those years ago, that it's ok to be me.

Fran and Mark, Phil, and all of the others, too numerous to name, who have joined me at various stages on this long journey.

Thank you all – none of this would have happened without you.

The author wishes to convey her deepest sympathy to the family of Sally Clark, who died on March 16th 2007.

Introduction

"All research on the subject {of the Criminal Justice System} agrees that the public is, in fact, profoundly ignorant of the system, and... there is a duty to promote access to clear information and understanding that has, unfortunately, been lacking."
JUSTICE's Response to the Auld Review, January 2002.

THERE is a general feeling in the UK that our justice system, whilst not perfect, is one of the best in the world. It is perceived as open and fair; a process of thorough investigation, culminating with an outcome which is most likely to be correct. Miscarriages of justice, we believe, are few and far between, and when they do occur, there is often still a faint whiff of suspicion, a sense that there is no smoke without fire. This is partly because it seems so difficult to believe that in a system where a case has to jump through so many hoops, involving so many different people, they somehow *all* got it wrong. There is also the negative connotation of "getting off on a technicality" – the person claiming miscarriage of justice is perceived to have actually committed the crime, but has used a clever lawyer to find some legal loophole with which the conviction can be deemed unsafe.

It comes as quite a shock, then, to realise that our perception of the system and its reality are vastly different. Miscarriages of justice are not occasional unfortunate (or manufactured) events. In the decade 1989 – 1999, the Court of Appeal overturned more than 8470 criminal convictions – that is 770 successful appeals **every year.** At the Crown Court, in the same period, around 3500 convictions made earlier in the Magistrates Courts were also quashed **every year.** These figures, from the Lord Chancellor's Department's statistics, show quite clearly that miscarriages of justice are an everyday occurrence – more than 10 people, every day, of every week, of every month of every year are wrongfully convicted. And these are just the ones we know about. How many other people might there be, languishing in jail for a crime that they did not commit? For many people, the response to this question is "who cares?" The perception that miscarriages of justice occur only rarely, and involve people who are generally seen to be guilty of *something* anyway, is so strong, and so regularly and routinely reinforced, that public sympathy is virtually non-existent.

In the 10 years covered by the Lord Chancellor's statistics, more than 42,000 people had convictions against them overturned. That they were wrongly convicted in the first place is a tragedy for them, for their families, and for the British Justice system. Yet nothing of any real merit seems to have been learned from this enormous failure of the system. In 1997, the Criminal Cases Review Commission was set up to investigate alleged miscarriages of justice. Currently, they receive around 800 cases per year, of which approximately one in 25 is referred to the Court of Appeal. It does seem a rather small number – just 32 cases per year, in light of the previous figure of nearly 800 per year. Has the system improved so drastically in just over 5 years (from 1999)? If so, how did that happen? What were the causes of such high incidence of wrongful conviction, and how were they rectified to the extent that we appear to be witnessing a 96% improvement rate?

In the space of just six weeks in 2006, four high profile cases hit the headlines in succession. On February 9th Sion Jenkins, accused of murdering his foster daughter, Billie-Jo, was acquitted, following three trials and two appeals. On February 7th, Shirley McKie, a police officer who had been accused of leaving a fingerprint at the scene of a crime was finally cleared, after 9 years, of any wrong doing. Steven Johnston had his murder conviction quashed on March 17th, and evidence of "serious mistakes" in the trial and prosecution of Nat Fraser, who had been imprisoned for the murder of his wife (whose body had never been found), was revealed on March 14th, leading legal experts to claim "it could be difficult to convince an appeal court that he has not been the victim of a miscarriage of justice" (Scotsman March 14th 2006).

What is startling about three out of these four cases is the manner in which suspicion is still being encouraged as to their innocence. In Shirley McKie's case, for example, a spokesperson for the Scottish Criminal Records Office (who were shown to have mis-identified the fingerprint they claimed was Shirley's, then gone to great lengths to cover up this mis-identification) stated in a television interview that the officers involved *still stood by their original findings.* Pushed to agree that she was effectively saying Shirley McKie was lying, in complete contradiction the official outcome of the investigation, the spokeswoman simply repeated her statement that the original officers believed their finding on the fingerprint to be correct. Press coverage of both Nat Fraser and Sion Jenkins carries the unmistakable hint that although technically, they have not been found guilty, neither have they been proven innocent - and this, in a country whose judicial system is based on the premise that an individual is "presumed innocent until proven guilty." Quite simply, it is not required of any citizen to *prove their innocence*. It is the responsibility of the system to prove *guilt*. Only in the case of Steven Johnston has there been acceptance that police and the prosecution appear to have been guilty of cover-up, with-holding evidence, and manufacturing the case against Mr. Johnston and an inquiry has been set up (although it is to be carried out by Lothian and Borders Police, rather than an independent body).

Sadly, there has still been no justice for the victims – Billie-Jo Jenkins, Margaret Ross, Arlene Fraser and Drew Forsyth. Their murders remain un-solved, their murderers still at large, and free to strike again.

These four cases, however, bring us back to the questions raised earlier. What went wrong? And where else might the same things be happening? The tendency for fingers still to be pointed, even after a case has been completely discredited, means that the opportunity to examine how miscarriages occur, and what can be done to prevent them, is lost. If the majority of people have reason to believe that the guilty person has somehow managed to "wriggle out" of their conviction, they will also tend to believe that it's unfortunate, and perhaps even call for changes to the law which would prevent such "wriggling out" in the future. If people don't know what's broken, they can't know how to fix it – or even that anything needs fixed in the first place!

Until two years ago, I had no idea that anything was broken. I believed in the justice system, although I knew it had its faults. A chance meeting with someone who believed that a family member was a victim of a miscarriage of justice was to change all that. At the time, I was merely intrigued. Perhaps, like many people, I had an assumption that the relatives of almost everyone convicted of a serious crime don't want to believe that one of theirs could do such a thing, and will tend to convince themselves that there has been a mistake. What I found left me shocked and sickened. The information was there, easily accessible, for me, or anyone else to see. Because it had simply never occurred to me to ask the questions (perhaps because I believed there *were* no questions to be asked), I had never been exposed to the answers. The more I delved, the more apparent it became that something is terribly wrong with our system, but hardly anyone seems to know, or care.

As my investigations progressed, I found another curious phenomenon. Not only were people reluctant to discuss the issue of miscarriages of justice, and the suggestion that there may be some very serious flaws at the heart of our justice system, they would vigorously (and sometimes with hostility) defend their position that I was mistaken – *even with pages of documented evidence before them*. It reminded me of the children's story of the elephant in the sitting room. Everybody knows you don't find elephants in the middle of the sitting room floor, so everyone acts as if there is no elephant there, even though they can all see it. Why? In the absence of back-up from anyone else, each individual assumes the others really *can't* see the elephant, otherwise they'd say so. Secondly, it's an *elephant* for goodness sake! If there was really an elephant there, then everyone would be talking about it. So we ignore the evidence of our own senses, for fear of looking stupid, or being judged by others.

The elephant in the sitting room of our justice system is definitely there. But until more people are prepared to look at it, and admit its existence, thousands of innocent people will continue to be convicted of crimes they did not commit.

In order to highlight the extent of the problem, consider the following:

Imagine we are asked to vote for a new justice system, with the following rules:

1. The guilty verdict must be as a result of purely circumstantial evidence
2. There must be glaringly obvious "reasonable" doubt
3. There must be **no** DNA/forensic evidence linking the suspect to the crime
4. The suspect must not have been identified by formal means at or near the crime scene
5. There must be some suggestion of another person or persons being present at or near the crime scene (against whom no charges are being pursued)
6. There must be over-reliance on "expert" testimony, to the detriment of the suspect
7. Crucial, unsubstantiated evidence must have been given by someone with a vested interest in the suspect being convicted
8. There must be serious questions about timescale/ ability of the suspect to have been physically possible of carrying out the crime
9. Clothing must be a strong part of the prosecution's case
10. Character assassination must be a strong part of the prosecution's case
11. There must be evidence of pathologists/ forensic scientists selectively interpreting evidence to the prosecution's own ends
12. The suspect must be seen to have been of previous good character, and have no convictions/psychological conditions

Obviously, no-one with an ounce of sense would agree to such a justice system. **Yet all of the cases highlighted in this book have at least 10 out of the 12 items listed above, as critical features.** In every single case documented here, at least 10 of these points are present within the investigation and subsequent prosecution. This book exists as an attempt to answer the question of *how* these prosecutions could possibly be secured, beyond reasonable doubt, when the presence of many of the above factors, even on their own, introduce such doubt. Taken together, we find ourselves back with the elephant in the sitting room. If, for example, there is no DNA or forensic evidence linking the suspect to the crime, the suspect has never been identified at or near the crime scene, there are other people who have been identified at the scene, and crucial but unsubstantiated evidence is given by someone with a vested interest in seeing the suspect convicted, can we honestly conclude that the conviction is safe beyond reasonable doubt?

If, in the absence of more concrete evidence, the prosecution opts for character assassination of the suspect or defence witnesses, "expert" testimony of a highly technical and difficult to understand nature is a central part of the prosecution's approach, forensic data is presented in a selective and biased manner, and there are serious questions about the suspect's ability, either physically, or within the suggested time-scale, to have carried out the crime, can we rest easy that guilt has been proven beyond reasonable doubt?

This book will look at how these convictions are secured – at how the system itself is flawed, and how these flaws are exacerbated by personalities, the media, unexamined assumptions, and the inherent difficulty of asking "ordinary people" to make judgements on specialised or technical subjects about which they may have little or no knowledge or understanding.

A criticism leveled at most people who begin to investigate what may be miscarriages of justice is that we appear to have "forgotten" the victims. This, of course, is not the case. It serves no-one, least of all the victim, to have the wrong person convicted and, unpalatable as it is, impartial, unemotional examination of all the facts is a necessary factor in getting to the truth.

Also, there is a tendency for politicians and the media to emphasise a legal system which somehow favours offenders and ignores the needs and rights of victims, which, in turn, makes it much more difficult to objectively examine wrongful convictions. Where the public in general is led to believe that, in the vast majority of cases, only the guilty are imprisoned, investigations such as this one are seen to be the work of "do-gooders," who are standing up for the rights of people who have done bad things. Yet the cases highlighted in this book, and the many, many more which formed the basis of its research, all involve people who have not been proven to have done anything wrong. This is not an issue of technicalities or semantics. As a civilised society, we absolutely **must** ensure that we have satisfactorily proven that a person is guilty of the crime for which we are taking his or her liberty.

Also, the choice of which cases have been highlighted and which have been left out should not be taken as any sort of indication that some cases are more "worthy" than others. I reviewed literally dozens of cases; it would not have been possible to include all of them in one volume, so some sort of criteria had to be decided upon, in order to select. Quite simply, those with the largest number of points from the list above were chosen, since they highlight the most extreme examples of unsafe convictions, in that there is so much evidence to the contrary, it would, at first glance, appear to be well nigh impossible to secure any conviction.

As you, the reader, examine each case, and discover the similarities which crop up within police investigations, judges' directions, expert testimony, the role of the media, and so forth, I invite you to bear in mind just one thought:

This could happen to any one of us

References:
Michael Naughton, Dept of Sociology, University of Bristol, Observer Crime and Justice Debate July 28th 2002 Reproduced at www.portia.org
Miscarriages of Justice www.onlineinfo.org
BBC Scotland News Saturday June 24th 2006
The Role of Juries in the British System, Dr Zakaria Erzincliogu, reproduced at www.innocent.org

Chapter One

The British Justice System

THERE are so many threads woven into the fabric which produces miscarriages of justice and unsafe convictions that it is difficult to find a starting point. It is not just a case of finding the bits that have gone wrong, and fixing them – like the knots in a fisherman's net, every piece you pick up is inextricably linked to all of the others. Singling out "the justice system" for example, misses the point – the system is not a faceless, feeling-less machine, because its component parts are human beings, with their own thoughts, beliefs, prejudices and influences. Indeed, part of the problem is that we have shared beliefs and unexamined assumptions which can often prevent us from being able to take the necessary step back and realise that something is amiss in the first place. As is the case generally, unless something affects us directly and personally, we tend to take a face value approach. Since the majority of us will have little to do with the criminal justice system as a whole, and failures within that system in particular, we will have little reason or motivation to look any deeper into what appears to be a functioning, effective apparatus. The whole negative connotation of being involved with the criminal justice system serves to keep us from delving too deeply – quietly hidden in the depths of many of our belief systems is the idea that those who *do* become involved with the criminal justice system must have done something to become involved – and that something has to be something that the wider population would regard as wrong. This reasoning actually helps maintain the status quo, by making it very difficult for the general public to accept that there are many, many people caught up in flaws and failures in the criminal justice system, people who have not done anything wrong. Our prejudice against those who have been imprisoned blinkers us from the truth, and this prejudice is sustained by social, moral and political influences, as well as the media. In order for the system to function at all, a "them and us" mentality needs to be fostered – "we" are right because we obeyed the law, and the proof of this is that we have had no dealings with the criminal justice system, and have not been imprisoned. Therefore, "they" *must* be wrong, because they have gone all the way through the criminal justice system and have landed up in jail. (Of course, this also uncovers the assumption that the system works, in that someone who has not done anything wrong will be exonerated by the system – if they are not, then it is they, and not the system, who must be at fault.) Murder cases, particularly high profile cases with intense media coverage, bring sharply into focus all of our assumptions and prejudices.

We have a tendency to believe, in general, that we know what happens in the event of a murder. We assume that there are specific practices and procedures which swing into action, following a logical, prescribed path, and that those involved are working within specified rules and guidelines. In essence, most people assume the process goes something like this:

The Investigation

A body is found. The police arrive and seal off the area, and begin a painstaking search for evidence. Modern science allows for detailed forensic and DNA analysis, so, we presume, even the tiniest piece of evidence may yield rich information. The "murder squad" – officers trained specifically to be part of this elite team - keep the scene in a sterile condition, ensuring that nothing is allowed to contaminate it, whilst the evidence is collected. Meantime, other officers are out asking questions, trying to get a picture of the who, where, when, what and why of the case. Everything is collected, everything is analysed, in a logical, impartial manner. As the pile of evidence increases, certain factors begin to piece together, creating a picture of what has happened, and who might be responsible. Once this logical, rational, procedure has been carried out, the police are likely to have their suspect, and an idea of what other evidence, if any, they will need to prove that person's guilt. Eventually, with all the required evidence in place, the suspect is arrested and charged, and a date is set for the court case.

The Trial

All of the evidence collected during the police investigation is made available to both the prosecution and the defence. (Note the unspoken assumption that all of the evidence collected during the police investigation is *not* available to either defence or prosecution prior to this point.) Each side agrees to let the other know what evidence and witnesses it intends to use during the trial.

A jury is selected randomly – aside from the obvious consideration that jurors must not have any information about the defendant or the case, and must not be prejudicial in any way. Both the prosecution and the defence present their cases to the jury, using witnesses and evidence to back up their claims. The witnesses can be cross-examined to test the validity of their testimonies. Independent expert witnesses can be called to give testimony on areas which are beyond the scope or experience of ordinary people. Forensic evidence, DNA evidence, and pathology reports are presented by court or governmental authorities, such as Home Office Pathologists, and so on. The judge may advise the jury on points of law, but remains impartial, in that he or she does not lead the jury in favour of the arguments presented by either the prosecution or the defence.

Finally, after all the evidence has been heard, the main counsel for prosecution and defence each sum up their case, the judge sums up the whole case in an impartial manner, and the jury retires to consider its verdict. The jury, throughout, has not been allowed to discuss the case with anyone other than other jurors, and is not allowed access to anything which may interfere with the evidence as it has been presented in court. After careful consideration of all that has been presented in court, the jury comes to its decision, based on a logical, rational assessment of the evidence. In a murder case, this should be unanimous, or at least a very large majority.

And there we have it - the perfect case.

This view of the legal system is strongly supported by television and film depictions of crime fictions – everything is crystal clear, the truth is uncovered by meticulous, untarnished investigation, and there is a logical progression from one stage or point to all of the others.

We use terms such as "presumed innocent until proven guilty" and "beyond reasonable doubt," confident that we know exactly what they mean, and equally confident that they have concrete, definitive specifications – that there is a common measure that quantifies the "reasonable" in reasonable doubt, and that "proven" in this context carries the same meaning as it does in its scientific context. The "burden of proof" we assume has an identifiable, recognisable property, that can be clearly seen to have been "discharged." Evidence is exactly that – information, people or objects which provide proof to back up claims made in court. The main purpose of a court case, we believe, is to get to the truth of the matter, to decide whether or not the accused person carried out the actions of which he or she is accused.

Yet even a superficial examination of some of the terms used begins to uncover the reality – that this perfection which we perceive in our justice system exists nowhere but in our imaginations:

"Independent expert witnesses" are not independent, in the context we understand. They are independent, in that they do not belong to the case, but that is as far as it goes. Both prosecution and defence bring in their own "independent" expert witnesses, and these witnesses are paid by whichever side brought them in. Clearly, the prosecution, for example,

17

is not going to pay for a witness whose findings are going to undermine the prosecution case, and the same is true for the defence. Immediately, the whole concept of independent expert witnesses as *impartial* expert witnesses is compromised.

The same is true of forensic scientists – there is no state employed body of forensic scientists who are wheeled out to give evidence in court cases. With the exception of Home Office accredited pathologists, they are all private institutions, their fees paid by either the prosecution or the defence. Of course, they are as liable to cross-examination as any other witness, but their standing as expert independent witnesses can make such cross-examination more difficult, and possibly less credible – how does the average person know, for example, what significance lividity marks on a body suggest, without guidance from an expert? If that expert's guidance is then questioned, and alternatives are suggested, how does the average person know which to rely on?

The unchallenged acceptance that independent witnesses have no vested interest in the evidence they give leads us to trust such evidence as dependable and true. Indeed, the suggestion that these witnesses are paid because their particular opinion weighs more heavily to one argument than another seems almost offensive, bordering on claims of corruption, and we have a very strong belief that our justice system, one of the best in the world, could not possibly be corrupt. As a result, we are left with an uneasy stand-off – on the one hand, we cannot escape the reality that these witnesses are, indeed, paid for their findings, and that they are chosen specifically *because* their findings support the theory being floated by one side or the other, yet on the other hand, we have a very real need to continue to believe that our system is fair, moral and transparent. At best, we console ourselves with the acceptance that at least each side has a chance to acquire "independent" witnesses whose evidence supports its own particular stance. We can regain some comfort from the understanding that scientific findings can draw different conclusions from the same initial data, and that is the nature of scientific investigation. Yet even this, in itself, is an indicator of our tendency to selectively embrace or reject information, dependent on our objective – there is a widely held belief that that which is proven, scientifically, is irrefutable. Logically, then, if different conclusions are being drawn from the same data, scientific *proof* has not been attained, and, as a result, the "evidence" of these witnesses is still in its experimental or investigative phase. Even though this is the case, there is still a tendency to trust it, because of its assumed link with the scientific.

So much for the independent, but what of what we understand by the term "expert?" The Oxford dictionary defines an expert as "one with specialist skills or knowledge representing mastery of a particular subject." Mastery of a subject, one would presume, goes beyond the experimental or investigative, to a place of certainty. If that were truly the case, then it would make sense for the prosecution and defence to share the cost of expert witnesses, since the evidence given by these witnesses would be truly impartial.

But who decides what constitutes mastery? Surely only another expert can decide if someone else is an expert? This is not just a matter of mere semantics – whereas, in the not too distant past, "expert" appeared to be limited to a small number of highly trained, well qualified individuals whose output displayed their expertise, the modern application of the term 'expert' is much broader, and, as a result, much more difficult to define. Take, for example, an expert in facial expression or body language. It is far less easy to measure such a person's expertise by their output. There is no set–in-stone science which proves irrefutably that someone moving their eyes in a certain way, just before answering a question, is always lying, or that someone crossing their arms across their chest is always defensive. Yet because these people are coated with the veneer of authority afforded to experts, their opinions (and, at the end of the day, that is often all they are – there is little genuine scientific proof to back them up) are given a great deal of credence in courts.

Another fantasy that feeds our perception of the validity of the investigative/judicial process is the concept of "all of the evidence." We accept, pretty much without question, that all of the evidence which has been collected during the investigation is (a) all of the evidence that could possibly have been collected, and (b) all of the evidence that is used during the trial. Neither, in fact, is true. What evidence is collected is a decision taken by the officers carrying out the investigation. If they decide that something is not worth pursuing, or simply fail to notice something, that is *available* evidence that will never make it into the courtroom. Of course, such decisions are critical at the early stages of an investigation, since a decision not to pursue something, or a failure to notice something, can drive the investigation in a specific direction, whether or not that ends up being the correct direction. This raises the question of what, exactly, constitutes the "correct direction." The answer to that question is dependent on the real, rather than the assumed objective of the investigation itself. We are minded to believe that the investigation is driven by a search for the truth – that no prior decisions are taken as to what may or may not be significant in determining that truth. However, if the investigation is driven by the requirement to find someone to prosecute, then the decisions as to what to pursue, or not, take on a wholly different dimension. Something which may lead to the truth, but is unlikely to lead to a prosecution, may be discarded in favour of that which may not be "the truth" in the bigger picture, but fits more neatly with that which is likely to secure a prosecution. This is an uncomfortable factor, and one which we often overlook, because, once again, it calls into question the fairness, morality and transparency of the whole justice system. It is easier to believe that any investigation will always be driven by a search for the truth, but, in reality, this is just not the case. Too many other factors come into play – financial considerations, media attention, public pressure, the image of the police force involved, the length of an investigation – there are many, many inputs which will impact on just what truth, exactly, is sought in an investigation.

Once the evidence is collected, the "disclosure officer" then lists what evidence is deemed to be relevant, both for the prosecution and for the defence. This is an extremely important factor, because the disclosure officer works for the police. Therefore, if the disclosure officer deems a piece of evidence irrelevant, that evidence is simply recorded in separate a list or schedule. But obviously, what the prosecution deems relevant will not necessarily be the same as what the defence might deem relevant. The defence can request full details of anything on the list or schedule, but to do so, must give details of their client's defence, and their reasons for requesting the item. Having disclosed their defence (which is recorded) this can actually later be used against them – if, for instance, the client's defence changes before the case, negative inference can be drawn from this change. Further, the defence having "revealed their hand," the police are now in a position to reconsider their case, and gather any extra evidence, or approach defence witnesses. All of this, however, is quite often academic, since items recorded on the schedule are routinely labeled in such a way that their significance cannot be ascertained, leading, in some cases, to crucial evidence being lost to the defence in this manner.

Another question is this – to whom, exactly, is the "distribution officer" answerable? The answer is, initially, to the chief investigating officer, and ultimately, to the Crown Prosecution Service. In essence, the editor of the distribution officer's output is the chief investigating officer in the case. Part of a "new Crown strategy towards major trials" involves closer cooperation between an allocated QC, the Crown Prosecution Service, and the senior investigating officer "at the earliest possible stage," according to the government's recent new "Justice for All" legislation. This raises some uncomfortable issues with regard to the distribution officer – since the objective of the Senior Investigating Officer and the allocated QC is to secure a conviction, is it possible that they may inadvertently influence the disclosure officer's decisions as to what is deemed "relevant" or not?

Finally, there is the belief that both sides will reveal to each other all of the evidence they intend to use during the trial. In reality, this very often does not happen. Once one side or the other has sprung evidence, or a witness, without prior notice, the judge may rule it as inadmissible but it is too late – the jury has heard the evidence, and nothing to refute it. Being told that it is inadmissible actually counts for nothing, in that the jury does not have to give reasons for its verdict – if the jury thinks the inadmissible evidence is of some worth, or carries some persuasion, it is as likely to give as much weight to that evidence as to any other admissible evidence.

Even just on these few examples, it becomes apparent that our justice system bears little resemblance, in reality, to our perception of it. But that leaves us in a difficult position, because it is a system on which we rely to ensure criminals are properly apprehended and punished, and it is a system on which we rely to be fair, impartial, and ultimately, effective.

For the majority of us, it is easier to believe that there are some quirks and anomalies in the system, but that it basically does what we need it to do. The stark truth is that there are more than just a few quirks and anomalies – the entire system is flawed throughout, and, in many, many cases, it does not do what we need it to do – in fact it does quite the opposite, leaving those who have committed some of the most awful crimes free and undetected, whilst imprisoning completely innocent people.

The police investigation is supposed to provide enough evidence to convince the Crown Prosecution Service that the case should proceed to court – that there is enough evidence to secure a conviction, otherwise, it would be a complete waste of time. This should be a safeguard against cases getting into court with insufficient evidence, yet the reality, again, proves that it is not the safeguard it appears to be. With the advances of technology, many cases appear, on the surface, to have evidence, but the quality does not match the quantity. Several pages of analysis of fibres, or composition of rock, or whatever, may be interesting, but unless they provide evidence relevant to the case, they are worthless. Yet, in many of the cases highlighted here, it is precisely that type of evidence which has swung the balance between a case having enough evidence or not. The existence of the Crown Prosecution Service safeguard can actually have the opposite effect, once the case reaches the courts. Since the jurors know that they would not be sitting on the case at all if the Crown Prosecution Service had not decided that there was enough evidence to proceed, the jury sets out from a slightly biased position – the belief that there is, theoretically, enough evidence to convict the person in the dock. Just how we manage to fit this comfortably with the notion that a person is "presumed innocent until proven guilty" is not clear. How can we accept, on the one hand, that the person in the dock is to be presumed innocent when we know, on the other, that a large investigative body has decided that there is enough evidence to prove that he or she is not?

Again, in an ideal world, the jury would simply weigh up the evidence in its own right, and decide whether or not it provides the necessary proof. But we cannot escape the fact that they begin from a standpoint that an authority with a great deal of experience in these matters has *already* examined all the evidence they are about to hear, and decided that it is sufficient to convict.

As with every other aspect of the system, the Crown Prosecution Service itself is made up of human beings, who are making decisions not only on the evidence presented to them, but through the filter of their own beliefs and persuasions. This may go some way to explaining how so much technical data comes to be accepted as sufficient evidence, especially in those cases where such data is extremely complicated or detailed. The tendency to rely on what appears to be scientific evidence is not confined to the judicial system – as a society in general, we have come to place a great deal of faith on the scientific and logical. The irony is, the two do not always go hand in hand – perfectly reasonable scientific information may have no logical connection with a case, but because, in our minds, the two are inextricably linked, we make the mistake of assuming that there *must be* some logical connection, otherwise that information would not be presented. This is another elephant in the sittingroom scenario – where several people are all required to evaluate data about which they may have little real knowledge, and where their continued employment depends on that evaluation, if everyone else seems to think the data is there for good reason, each individual is then under pressure to "find" the connection, or at least accept its existence. It is only when individuals are freed from this pressure, or have no reason to accept or believe one thing or another, that this institutionalised flaw becomes apparent. Confined by the parameters of their job, and the expectations of their organisation, other avenues of possibility are effectively closed off to those employed within such a system. Again, staff at the Crown Prosecution Service begin their investigation from a slightly biased standpoint – the underlying assumption is that the police are not going to present a case unless they feel it is strong enough to proceed to court, so, in effect, it becomes something of a "box ticking" exercise, particularly in view of new legislation which encourages the involvement of the Crown Prosecution Service in the police investigation from an early stage.

This drip down effect from the jury relying on the Crown Prosecution Service to have checked that there is sufficient evidence, to the Crown Prosecution Service expecting the police to provide sufficient evidence, places the responsibility for providing sufficient evidence squarely at the feet of the police. While, at first glance, this might seem obvious, in that it is, after all, the police who carry out the investigation, it reveals yet another underlying assumption. The police are responsible for providing sufficient evidence to secure a *conviction*. That is not the same as the police being responsible for getting to the truth, and this is a critical factor. The pressure on the police to make an arrest, especially in high profile cases, is enormous. When an investigation is ongoing, the pressure mounts, and it does not take too large a leap of the imagination to see how this is likely to affect investigative procedures. Someone, somewhere, has to make a decision about which lines of enquiry to follow up, and which to leave. It is here, at this particular stage, that many investigations are dangerously narrowed down. Having cut out several limbs of possible enquiry, the investigative team is now left to find its answers from the remaining available information. Rather than continuing to gather information, the process becomes one of examining a limited number of factors and asking "where does this piece fit." That it might not fit anywhere is no longer a consideration – the narrowing down of investigations in this manner demands that sense be made from the "now available" evidence.

The result is often a form of self-fulfilling prophecy. Assumptions are drawn regarding what is most feasible or likely, in order to narrow down the investigation. On many occasions, these assumptions reveal an underlying prejudice on the part of the officers making them – one common reference is that "85% of victims are murdered by someone known to them." The pertinent question is, of course, what percentage of investigations is run on this assumption? In every one of the 15% of cases where the killer is *not* known to the victim, this assumption will automatically lead the investigation in the wrong direction, and close off avenues of enquiry which are more likely to lead to the murderer. At the same time, vast amounts of police time will be wasted trying to piece together data which cannot be pieced together. However, where an investigating team is convinced that it is on the right track, it will try extremely hard to "make those pieces fit;" - along with a narrowed down field of enquiry comes a narrowed down form of reasoning. This is not limited simply to police enquiries, of course – it exists in almost every field of human activity. Because we do not have unlimited access to everything available, we are required to work with, and make sense of, that to which we *do* have access.

However, in police investigative procedures, the results of coming to believe that this narrowed down field of enquiry is the *whole* field of enquiry, can have devastating results.

It is not just a case of understanding police investigations in their own right, of course – as has already been pointed out, no one part of the system exists independently of the others – police investigations are shaped and driven by other authorities and institutions, and themselves impact on other authorities and institutions. The following chapters attempt to trace the interplay of the various aspects which lead to wrongful convictions, and to examine just how they continue to influence the outcomes of court cases to the present day.

Firstly, we will examine the actual cases themselves, the facts and details which led to these convictions. Then, with a wealth of examples to hand, we will look at the wider picture.

References:
"Expert witnesses aren't what they seem – and I should know," Dr Theodore Dalrymple, Telegraph February 2ⁿᵈ 2003, reproduced at www.portia.org, Chapter 14. Alex Ward, Guardian, London October 3rd, 2004, quoted at www.justice4simon.koncept07.net
"Dr Paul Ekman" by Stephen Juan, National Post, Canada, November 28th 2005
"A Conversation with Paul Ekman," New York Times, August 5th 2003
"Unfair Legislation." www.portia.org, Chapter 6.
"Justice for All," cjsonline.gov.uk, and Criminal Procedures and Investigations Act 1996
"Justice Without Science Isn't Justice," Frank Ward, www.portia.com, Chapter 14 Science and the Law, Dr Zakaria Erzinclioglu, at www.innocent.org and www.justice4simon.koncept07.net

Chapter Two

The Case of Derek Christian

"This is such a strange and obscure story that it is difficult to recommend any punitive term with complete confidence." Lord Bingham, Lord Chief Justice, 1998.

WITHIN the details of this first case emerge the roots of several strands which will repeat in many of those to follow. From this starting point, we begin to recognise patterns, common to so many cases, which, in themselves, give rise to "reasonable doubt."

Of course, this is not to say that Derek Christian is the first person to whom these things have happened – far from it. But this book had to begin somewhere, and the case of Derek Christian provides some of the most clear, solid and astonishing examples that it almost suggests *itself* as the first case to be examined.

Background.

On February 9th, 1995, at around 3.30 in the afternoon, 66-year-old grandmother Margaret Wilson was walking along a country road towards her home in Burton Fleming, East Yorkshire. Two men, working on tractors in an adjacent field, saw a car draw up in the country road, close to Mrs Wilson. The driver got out, walked "briskly" towards Mrs Wilson, and for a few minutes, he and Mrs Wilson disappeared from view. Just moments later, the driver sprinted back to his car, and sped off – the men on the tractor estimated that he may have reached up to 80 mph on the country lane.

Their suspicions raised, the two men ran towards the spot where Mrs Wilson had last been in view, to find her lying in a pool of blood. Her throat had been slashed twice, killing her instantly. This was a completely senseless, motiveless, pointless killing, an apparently random attack without rhyme or reason.

Unfortunately, from their original vantage point in the adjacent field, the tractor drivers had been too far away to provide an accurate description of the car driver, but both agreed that the car had been large. One was quite adamant that the car had been a white Montego; the other could only say that it was a large car, either white or silver in colour.

Police investigating the scene of the murder found two footprints in the verge at the side of the road, beside Mrs Wilson's body, and some tyre marks on the road, where the car had sped away. The following day, a blood-covered knife was found discarded at the scene; police identified it as a "J Adams industrial knife," a type common to local food production industries.

The police investigation immediately swung into action. Appeals were launched for witnesses to come forward, checks were initiated on cars matching the description from the two eyewitnesses, and an investigative survey of industrial knife availability in the area was begun.

On February 12th 1995, three days after the murder, Derek Christian was interviewed by police, in common with every other owner of a Montego car in the area. However, as other witnesses began to come forward, it became clear that Derek was not the man police were looking for – several women had reported a man acting suspiciously in the area, all of them describing a large, clean shaven man in a white car. Derek's car was silver, and, more importantly, he had a beard. The police officer who questioned him just three days after the murder noted this information on a standard enquiry form, and described the beard in court as a "pronounced goatee" beard – certainly not the type that would have been grown in just three days.

Furthermore, Derek Christian could easily have been either eliminated from the enquiry, or positively identified, by one of these early witnesses, who "believed she would recognise the assailant if she were to see him again." By that stage, Derek Christian's involvement or otherwise could have been clearly and categorically ascertained.

In order for evidence to be acceptable in court, it must be corroborated from two independent sources, especially in cases which lean heavily on circumstantial evidence, as Derek Christian's case did. Police officers at the time describing a bearded man with a silver car, and an eyewitness able to make a positive identification should have provided those two independent, corroborative elements – that is, they provided proof that Derek Christian did not fit the description of the suspect.

Here we uncover our first failure of the system we believe to be so incorruptible – eventually, one of the main elements of the prosecution case would be that Derek and his car "broadly fitted the description of the assailant and his vehicle," in spite of this early, concrete evidence to the contrary.

Initially, the police investigation was frustratingly non productive. In spite of claims to have taken thousands of statements, and to be following numerous leads, the police had little to go on. The murder weapon, although distinctive, was not unique in the area – the same type of knife was used by literally thousands of people in local factories and farms, and was on sale to the public via Boots, the Chemist. No fingerprints were recovered from the murder weapon.

For reasons which were never properly explained, a scene of crime officer decided not to take photographs or casts of the tyre marks on the road, on the basis that they would be evidentially "worthless," yet casts of two footprints found in the verge beside Mrs Wilson's body *were* made, but, it seems, were never properly followed up. There is, quite simply, no consistency to these decisions.

Feelings were running high in the area – this was an apparently motiveless, yet extremely vicious attack on a popular, elderly lady, and people naturally wanted the killer caught immediately.

What the police *did* have to go on were statements from several people who had come forward following appeals for information.

Identification and Witnesses

(1)   Marie Cundall had been walking her dog near the murder scene just five minutes before Mrs Wilson was attacked. She told police that a "large man" with "frenzied eyes" had pulled up alongside her in his car. She estimated that she had looked at him for 20 – 30 seconds, describing how he was "sitting upright in a white estate car." This witness was quite sure that she would have recognised the man, had she seen him again.

(2)   Karen Holloway described a man standing next to white car, which was parked on a verge close to Mrs Wilson. Although she did not see his face, she thought he looked "like a sales rep."

(3)   Louise Grey described a man who had driven past her in a white car.

Marie Cundall's recollection of the man was very clear, and she assisted police in producing an identikit picture of him. Louise Grey (statement No 3) agreed that the Identikit picture was "a good likeness." All of these women were very clear on one factor – the man they saw was clean shaven.

A further two women came forward – Wendy Price had been out riding her horse some 10 miles away from Burton Fleming between 1pm and 1.30pm on the day of the murder, when a man in a car followed her down a track, drove past her, then pulled in and waited. She explained that she had no doubt that he meant her harm:

"His eyes just glared right through me and my defence mechanisms told me to get the hell out of there."

Ann Matson described being "stalked" by a man matching the same description two days previously, at around 10.30am, some 11 miles from the murder scene.

Since the case against Derek Christian was purely circumstantial, it seems fair to examine other circumstantial, but perhaps more compelling possibilities: – what appears to have emerged from these early statements is a picture of a man stalking, or frightening women, on country paths, or lurking in country areas, within a 10 mile-or-so radius, in the days leading up to the murder of Mrs Wilson. It cannot be emphasised clearly enough that this was not a big city, or a busy metropolitan area. This was a small village area in East Yorkshire, where *one* man behaving suspiciously would have raised alarm – the idea of several men behaving in the same way would, most likely, have created a degree of panic in the area.

The first incredible anomaly in this case arises from these witness statements.

Marie Cundall, Louise Grey and Wendy Price all had a very good view of this man, and were able to accurately describe him, yet none of them were asked in court if the man in the dock (Derek Christian) was the man they had seen that day. No identity parade was ever held, nor were any of the witnesses asked to pick him out from a series of photographs.

In fact, Wendy Price told the BBC's "*Inside Out*" programme in January 2004, (some 5 years after conviction)

> "They never asked me in the court whether I could identify Derek Christian, they never said, Is this the gentleman that followed you? – I was never asked that."

She continued, *"**I know the gentleman I saw in the court that day was not the gentleman I saw out riding.**"*

According to "*Inside Out*," this leaves two possible explanations –

> "either the man who followed Wendy Price was *not* the killer {of Margaret Wilson}, but a different man out to do harm in the same vicinity, on the same day, or he *was* the killer, and he was not Derek Christian."

Once the statements of the others are taken into account, the balance of probabilities shifts even further.

In the space of two days, three women have reported a man "lurking" or "stalking" on secluded country roads – all three describe a very similar person. Within minutes of the murder, a further two women report driving past someone driving away from the scene, one describing a similar car, the other describing the driver himself, again similar to the descriptions given by the other women. If there was a "different man out to do harm in the same vicinity," was he the same man who alarmed Ann Matson and Marie Cundall? Was he the same man seen driving away by Louise Grey? Was it the same car that was seen by Karen Holloway and the two tractor drivers?

The fact is, we will never know, because none of these witnesses attended an identity parade, and none of them was asked if Derek Christian was the man they had seen. Such an oversight seems almost unbelievable, especially since every single description of the man had him as "clean shaven," and Derek Christian had a "pronounced goatee" beard.

The double irony here is that it is the police, themselves, who initially eliminated Derek because of his "pronounced goatee."

Yet, the omission of what should have been standard police procedure in conducting an identity parade robbed Derek Christian of the chance of being formally eliminated from the enquiry.

Furthermore, the sightings by Ann Matson and Wendy Price were at times when Derek had a substantiated alibi – another important element of the prosecution case would be that Derek did not have an alibi which could be substantiated.

Since it is clear that Derek Christian was not convicted on eyewitness testimony, it would be reasonable to assume that other, much stronger evidence was used to secure the conviction.

Sadly, that is just not the case.

The Car

The conduct of the police officers who originally interviewed Derek on February 12th 1995 raises several questions. Firstly, both officers made very similar entries in their police notebooks on the same date – February 28th **1996** – more than a year after the event.

DC Stevens stated in court that he was asked by DC Marsden to supply a statement (on that date in 1996), and also that he had an "idea" that DC Marsden was making a similar statement at the same time. The statement was to the effect that the car in Derek's driveway "looked white" when they first saw it. In fact, there was a silver Montego on Derek's drive that day, and it was one of *two* cars parked there.

However, one of these officers then went on to state, in court, that he had not seen a silver car in the drive at all, never mind one that may have looked white.

The reference to Derek's silver car "looking" white appears to have come about as a way of trying to make the pieces fit. Of all of the witness statements who had described the man or the car, only three (out of a total of fourteen) did *not* describe the car as white – those three descriptions were "white or silver," "dirty, probably grey," and "light coloured." Within 12 months (certainly by February 12th 1996) the police had come up with an explanation for this discrepancy- they claimed that a silver car, in sunlight, could look white. This explanation studiously ignores the fact that Mrs Wilson was murdered at 3.30pm, on a February afternoon, when the sun would have been very low. It also ignores the evidence of Marie Cundall, who had looked, close-up, at the clean shaven man with the "frenzied eyes" just five minutes before the murder. She was quite certain that the car was white – estimating that she had looked at it for some 20 – 30 seconds. It was Ms Cundall's vivid recollection which led to the Identikit picture, which Louise Grey would describe as "a good likeness." Surely, if Ms Cundall's recollection was accurate enough to produce such a good likeness, it was also accurate enough to recall the colour of the car?

Why did it take a whole year for the investigating officers to decide that Derek's silver car "looked white" on his driveway? Indeed, can it really be acceptable that police officers can add retrospective notes in this manner, suddenly "remembering" new detail which was not logged at the time? It is important to realise that similar, and completely innocent behaviour on Derek Christian's part was used to devastating effect *against* him by the prosecution, with regard to his witness statement, as you will discover later. Quite bizarrely, Andrew Campbell, QC, prosecuting, would attempt to suggest in court that silver actually *is* white!

The basis for the continuing police focus on Derek appears to be the fact that his name appeared more than once, in different areas of the investigation.

Derek worked for McCains, where knives of the type used to murder Mrs Wilson were used, and he owned a Montego, which was one (partial) description of the attacker's car. On March 14th 1995, (less than a month after the murder) full forensic testing was carried out on Derek's car, but nothing was found to link him to the victim, or to the murder scene.

During the initial interview regarding the car, Derek had been asked to account for his whereabouts at the time of the murder (3.30pm on February 9th, 1995). He told police he had finished work at 3pm and driven home, as he did most days.

Some months later, on June 1st, he was interviewed about the murder weapon, (as the knife was of a type used at his workplace), and on September 12th, he completed a "knife project" questionnaire. On February 20th 1996 (eight days before the two police officers amended their notebooks to contain statements regarding Derek's car "looking" white), Derek's car was once again thoroughly examined by forensics experts, and once again, there was absolutely nothing found to link him to the crime. By this stage, it becomes apparent that continued police interest in Derek is unfounded. Although most of us would generally agree that investigations need to follow up every lead, we would also expect that there would be a degree of continuity and common sense. Even though Derek's name had come up a few times, given the "thousands" of interviews carried out by police, this should not have been either surprising or significant – the probability of Montego owner/white/silver/light coloured car owner with links to McCains/ Walkers/ Jacobs/ Boots in the area must have turned up dozens, if not hundreds of suspects. Yet the investigating team does not seem to have pursued any of these others with the same diligence or enthusiasm that they employed in the pursuit of Derek Christian.

Arrest and Alibi

On March 24th 1996, Derek Christian was arrested. He had separated from his wife Diane by that time, and was living at his parents' home. He was questioned for thirty six hours, and a number of items were removed from his parents' home, before he was released without charge. During this questioning, he had repeated his alibi that he had finished work at 3pm and driven home, although by that stage, some 13 months later, the details were unclear.

It is important to remember at this point that on the first occasion that police had spoken to him, just three days after the death of Mrs Wilson, Derek told police he had followed his usual routine – finished work at 3pm, and driven home by 3.45 to be home in time for his children coming home from school. (Derek's close relationship with his children was never disputed throughout the investigation or trial). When his car was tested for forensics, just one month after the death of Mrs Wilson, Derek gave the same account of his movements that day, as he did in the 36 hour questioning one year later in March 1996.

However, police investigators had discovered that Derek had made a withdrawal from a cash dispenser at 16.06 that same afternoon, suggesting that this could not have been a "normal" afternoon. Derek was then released on unconditional bail, having been exposed to the suggestion that something was "not quite right" about his statement. Rather than the obvious acceptance that he had simply forgotten his trip to the cash dispenser that afternoon, the implication was left weighing on Derek Christian that police were looking for a much more substantial explanation.

After his release, Derek and his in-laws, Jean and George Green, remembered that they had been moving boxes and furniture at the time, and eventually concluded that it had been that afternoon. Derek returned to the police, with his solicitor, and gave a new statement, accounting for his movements that afternoon. However, the police investigation uncovered telephone records, just weeks before the trial was to begin, which utterly destroyed Derek's new alibi. A telephone call was made from the Greens' home at 16.15 – they agreed they must have been in their home at the time, and not, as they had stated, in the car with Derek. As it transpired, the moving of the boxes *had* taken place, but the following afternoon. Derek had, quite simply, forgotten about his visit to the cash dispenser, but these two factors taken together (that he had forgotten the visit to the cash dispenser, and that the furniture moving had taken place on a different day) gave the prosecution grounds to claim that he would have come to court and "lied and lied and lied." The implication to the jury, of course, was that since he had "lied" so consistently about his whereabouts between 15.01 and 16.06 that day, he must be lying about everything else as well. The Greens were not called to give evidence that they, too, had been mistaken about the date, and even the police agreed that it had been a genuine and honest mistake. Unfortunately, the jury were unaware of this.

This fateful 65 minutes, from 15.01 to 16.06, when Derek had no substantiated alibi, would be used to devastating effect by the prosecution.

Timing and Psychology

However, on closer inspection, this timeframe raises some difficult questions. The journey from Derek's place of work to his home takes around 35 minutes. In the remaining 30 minutes, it has to be accepted that Derek drove off his normal route into Burton Fleming, drove around looking for a victim, found Mrs Wilson and carried out the brutal attack, cleaned off all of the blood from his clothes and his car, then calmly went to the cash dispenser. He also drove his wife to work that evening, stopping off at Kwik Save to do some shopping, before returning home to look after the children. Is it really feasible that he could act so perfectly normally within literally minutes of carrying out such a dreadful murder?

Police psychologists who examined Derek could find nothing psychologically wrong with him. There was nothing in his background to suggest he was in any way capable of such behaviour. The police themselves had stated that they were looking for a man capable of a "ferocious and frenzied" attack, someone who was "pathological."

Professor Keith Bottomley, a crime expert, stated that "a no-motive killing suggests the murderer has some form of mental history." Derek Christian had no such history. Indeed, he had been in the armed forces for fifteen years – to suggest that he would have been able to "hide" such psychotic or pathological tendencies, is absurd. The police were looking for someone who was a clear psychopath or psychotic, and it was abundantly clear that Derek Christian was neither. Further, the prosecution were unable to offer any plausible explanation as to why, on this particular day, on his way home from work, Derek suddenly decided to drive to a nearby village, where he was known, in broad daylight, murder a woman in a particularly brutal fashion, then carry on as normal. There is no suggestion of any abnormal behaviour in the immediate run-up to the crime, and certainly no unusual behaviour immediately afterwards.

The Murder Weapon

Following a BBC *Crimewatch* appeal, metallurgist Allan Wirth, from Sheffield University, came forward and asked to examine the murder weapon. He concluded that a dark stain on the knife "almost certainly" resulted from cutting up potatoes. Mr Wirth never gave evidence in court, presumably because the information that the knife had been used to cut up potatoes did not prove anything other than that fact itself – both McCains, where Derek Christian worked, and the Walkers Crisps factory had hundreds of knifes being used to cut up enormous quantities of potatoes. However, the link to McCains, however tenuous, was another link to Derek Christian for the police investigation.

Questioned about the knife, he denied ever having used a knife of that type, and stated that he did not recognise the knife that was shown to him. Although many workers at McCain's *did* use that particular type of knife, it was not required for Derek's duties.

More than 1800 knives of that type had been supplied to McCain's in the two year period spanning the murder (staff often stole them), and police discovered that Derek had been involved in a clear out of lockers in 1994, during which 50 – 60 knives were found. The prosecution claimed that Derek must be lying (again) when he said he had never seen "such a knife," but this is, of course, a matter of semantics – Derek said he did not recognise the knife that was *shown to him* – ie, the murder weapon. Not a single witness could be found to testify that Derek had ever been seen with a J Adams knife. Claims by the prosecution that Derek could have taken a knife during the locker clear-out count for very little, since the same could, of course, be true of the other six members of staff involved in the clear-out, and, indeed, any of the 1000 plus factory workers at McCains who use these knives daily.

There were no fingerprints on the murder weapon, so the murderer must have been wearing gloves. In spite of the heavy reliance on "fibre evidence" from Derek's clothing, which would come later, these gloves were never traced.

There was never, at any time, a single piece of forensic evidence to link the knife with McCains, and there was definitely no evidence, forensic or eyewitness, to link Derek Christian with the murder weapon, or even a similar type of knife.

"Fibre Evidence" and Second Arrest

During the March questioning and search, police had taken many items from Derek's parents' home, including clothing which they intended to have forensically tested. They had already examined his car on two separate occasions, one within a month of the murder, and found it to be clear of any traces of blood, or any other forensic evidence or fibres that would have linked it to the murder. Given that the main thrust of the prosecution case would be that Derek's clothes had deposited fibres onto Mrs Wilson's clothes, and that he had picked up a single fibre from hers, it does seem rather strange that, with such close proximity, he did not deposit a single trace of blood, or any other particulate, in the car.

When the police originally took clothing from his parents' home, Derek pointed out that the joggers they had were *not* the ones he had been wearing that day, and told them exactly where to get the correct "working" joggers. It was, in fact, from these joggers that some of the "fibre evidence" would emerge, yet Derek's behaviour raises some interesting questions. If he *had* been the murderer, then he would have known that the first joggers taken by the police *could not possibly* link him to the crime, since only he, himself, knew that he had not worn them on that day. Yet, rather than simply remain silent, and let them take the wrong clothing, Derek led them to the exact items he was wearing that day. Is this really the behaviour of a murderer trying to cover his tracks? Indeed, if he was the murderer, it begs the question, why did he keep any of the clothing at all? The gloves were never traced – if he had disposed of these, why not the other clothes as well?

It was, however, the results of forensic testing on Derek's clothing which brought the Chief Investigating Officer, DCI Midgeley, to the conclusion that they now had solid, conclusive evidence with which to arrest Derek Christian. Up to that point, everything had been circumstantial, and nowhere near substantial enough to build a case. Although not a single trace of blood was found on Derek's clothing, DCI Midgeley, seized on the phrase "microscopically indistinguishable," referring to fibres found on both Mrs Wilson's clothing and on Derek's, as the direct link between Derek and Mrs Wilson that he had been searching for. At first glance, it seemed he may be correct – fibres "microscopically indistinguishable" from three items of Derek's clothing were found on Mrs Wilson's clothing, and one fibre "microscopically indistinguishable" from the fabric of Mrs Wilson's skirt was found on Derek's joggers.

However, the phrase "microscopically indistinguishable" is extremely misleading. In fact, this type of evidence has been used in several distinctly dubious convictions, as will become apparent later in this book.

Under cross-examination, Robert Falconer, the Crown's expert on the matter, conceded that "microscopically indistinguishable" does not mean "the same." There were, for example, many other fibres on Mrs Wilson which had not come from Derek Christian. Also, the jogging bottoms Derek wore on the day of the murder were distributed in their "tens of thousands" through discount stores and market stalls. (Fibres from all of these would also be "microscopically indistinguishable" from the ones shed by Derek's joggers). Mrs Wilson's skirt had come from cloth manufactured in Germany, with at least 3000 metres being bought by a skirt manufacturer in Manchester. Derek's "Regatta" jacket was one of around 250,000 sold each year, of which about 50,000 were green. All 50,000 of these jackets could well have shed fibres not only microscopically indistinguishable from those shed by Derek's jacket, but also from those shed by *all* of the others as well. It becomes plain, therefore, that the term "microscopically indistinguishable" becomes virtually meaningless in the context used in court.

Mr Falconer went on to admit, under cross examination, that he had searched for a "highly distinctive population of fibres that may prove useful," but no such population existed. He also stated that no single fibre or group of fibres can be attributed to one garment to the exclusion of all other garments, concluding "Garments are not unique." He went on to state, quite emphatically, "The findings cannot produce an unequivocal link between {fibres from} Derek Christian's clothing and those found on the victim's clothing." In other words, the fibres on Mrs Wilson's clothing could have come from virtually anywhere. Indeed, to highlight this point, other items of clothing were tested for elimination purposes. These tests showed that the green cotton in Derek's sweatshirt was found to be microscopically indistinguishable from the green cotton in a sweatshirt belonging to a PC Lee, a polo shirt, DC Marsden's own rugby shirt, a partly grey sweatshirt and a green and yellow rugby shirt. If "microscopically indistinguishable" was, as claimed by Andrew Campbell, "conclusive," then we would surely be forced to conclude that PC Lee and DC Marsden were also somehow implicated – how can we be certain that of the thirteen such fibres found on Mrs Wilson's clothing, none of them came from either of these officers? Furthermore, fibres found in the body bag into which Mrs Wilson had been put did *not* match either Mrs Wilson or Derek Christian. It was discovered that the scene of crime log book had not been properly maintained, so it was unclear exactly who had put the body in the body bag. This, of course, leaves wide open the possibility that other fibres found on Mrs Wilson's clothing may have come from whoever put her body in the body bag, but because of poor police procedures, there is no way of checking.

The "conclusive proof" as it turned out, was nothing more than circumstantial evidence which, in the event, proved nothing of note, yet Derek Christian was arrested in November 1996, and held on remand until his trial a year later, in November 1997.

<u>The Trial</u>

Although the fibre evidence, lengthy, extremely detailed, and probably very confusing for the jury, (at one point, a juror was actually seen to nod off), was central to the prosecution's case, other factors were led which require examination.

Evidence regarding the footprints in the verge beside the body was never brought to court, as no shoes belonging to Derek Christian had ever been found to fit the prints. There is nothing to suggest police ever tried to find any other explanation for these footprints, yet unanswered questions of this type must surely raise some sort of reasonable doubt? Either the prints belonged to the murderer, to an officer at the scene, to one of the two tractor drivers who ran to the scene, or to the victim herself? According to Crown admissions (statements with which neither the prosecution nor the defence disagree), "the footprints were not attributable to Derek Christian, nor any of the persons *known* to have been present at the scene of the crime," and also, significantly, "**None** of the footprints at the scene of the crime were attributable to Derek Christian." Someone left those two prints on the verge, and that someone was not Derek Christian. Although it is not absolutely clear whether others present at the scene of the crime left footprints, it has to be concluded that if they did, it would seem fairly certain that Derek, had he been at the scene, would also have left prints.

A local newspaper, published on February 7th 1996 (almost exactly a year after the murder) was taken from Derek's parents' home in March 1996. The prosecution claimed that he had kept this newspaper as a "trophy" on the "anniversary" of the murder. No mention was made of the fact that other newspapers, which did not mention the murder, were also found.

The late Simon Regan, in his article, "Beyond Reasonable Doubt?" 'The Rather Doubtful Case of Derek Gordon Christian,'" pointed out the "human fallibility throughout the entire judicial system – from lawyers and judges to the jury itself – is often all too prominent," and there are many factors in Derek's case which bear this out.

His defence team appeared to make unfortunate mistakes and omissions, weakening his case. For example, he was advised to appear in court with a full beard and long hair, wearing a suit. His appearance was subsequently described as "appalling" by those who knew him. One can only guess what the jury made of his appearance.

He did not cope well during questioning on the stand, and the prosecution tore him to pieces.

The first defence witness, after Derek himself, was a woman who claimed to have seen a man driving around the village at times when Derek was at work. Her testimony would support later witnesses who would also describe the clean shaven man driving around at times when Derek had an alibi which *could* be substantiated. The day after giving her evidence, this woman returned to the witness box and retracted all of her previous evidence.

The defence requested that the jury be dismissed, and a re-trial ordered, given that the actions of this woman would surely have an extremely negative impact. This one unfortunate event alone, following on from Derek's own "poor performance" would almost certainly have affected the "human fallibility" of the jury – how easy would it be for them to maintain an open mind as to the credibility of the remainder of the defence evidence. The jury was not dismissed, and the trial continued.

Although Wendy Price had given her statement to police on February 28th 1995, the defence was only informed of this statement a matter of weeks before the trial in November 1997. In a rather strange turn of events, the day after this witness had testified, the prosecution asked for her to be recalled, so that she could be asked some questions which had been omitted the previous day. Bear in mind that the prosecution had

had access to this woman's statement for more than two years, but the defence had only known of it for a few weeks, yet the *prosecution* requested the recall. In spite of defence objections, the judge ruled that the woman could be recalled if she could appear quickly. At that point, the prosecution admitted that she was actually in the building, having been contacted by police the previous evening and asked to return to the court the next day. Derek's supporters have long claimed that this behaviour on the part of the prosecution was an attempt to undermine this "very credible witness."

A further witness, again testifying to confronting a lurking man in the area two days before the murder (and again, at a time where Derek Christian had an alibi which could be substantiated) was unable to give evidence. She had had an asthma attack as she was due to take the stand, and was brought into court in a wheelchair. In the event, her statement, made to police in 1995, was read out to the jury. Once again, the description was of a clean shaven man in a white car, parked on a country road near the scene of the murder. There was, of course, no opportunity to further question this witness due to her medical condition, and, as with the other witnesses, she was not asked if Derek Christian was the man she had seen.

In spite of the heavy emphasis on the "fibre evidence" by the prosecution, Derek's defence team did not call their own forensic expert in this field, relying, instead, on cross examination of the Crown expert.

The later BBC "*Inside Out*" programme used another fibres expert, Alison Duberry, to explain that "microscopically indistinguishable" does not mean "the same." She explained "In terms of their colour, their appearance, and how they look down a microscope, it doesn't mean they definitely came from the same garment."

It appears that not enough was made of this definition by the defence. It was the central plank of the prosecution's argument, yet proper examination leads to the irrefutable conclusion that it proves *nothing* - fibres from many garments would have come back as "microscopically indistinguishable" from those found on Mrs Wilson's body, as the elimination tests had shown, therefore it could not be concluded that those fibres had come from Derek Christian's clothing.

The prosecution also tried to fit the image of psychotic or psychopathic tendencies to Derek Christian's personality, despite being unable to produce a single shred of evidence to support this. Indeed, Andrew Campbell, prosecuting, went as far as to suggest that the fact that there was *nothing* in Derek's past to suggest psychotic or psychopathic tendencies was a very good reason to suspect they were there! With no basis whatsoever in the evidence presented, he told the jury:

> "Don't be misled by his behaviour. Pathological killers don't wear a sign on their heads or have five ears. They are as, in appearance, just like you and me. Don't be misled that because Christian did not attract suspicion in the days afterwards, the killer can't be him."

Perhaps, had the defence provided a proper psychiatric report, and used testimony from the likes of Professor Keith Bottomley, who claimed the evidence "suggests the killer has some form of mental history," the prosecution's baseless claims may have carried less weight. As it stood, the jury was left with the absurd, but not very strongly contested opinion (of Mr Campbell) that because Derek had shown no pathological tendencies, that was no reason whatsoever to conclude that he could not be the killer.

Summary

The jury deliberated for just over two hours before returning their guilty verdict. The judge in any murder trial is duty bound to warn the jury in his summing up, that if any one of them feels that there is any dispute concerning the facts, or that an alternative, perfectly plausible explanation exists, they must find for the defendant – i.e., return a not guilty verdict.

Yet not a scrap of real evidence exists against Derek Christian. Despite several witnesses claiming to have seen a white car, with a clean shaven man, in and around the area, a man who owned a silver car and sported a "pronounced goatee beard" has been convicted.

There is no DNA or forensic evidence to link Derek or his car to the victim or to the murder scene. The timescale for him to have been the murderer remains dubious, and there is, and never has been, any evidence whatsoever to link him to the murder weapon.

His shoe prints do not fit the prints found at the scene of the crime, and several witnesses reported the clean shaven man in the white car behaving suspiciously at times where Derek had a substantiated alibi. The so-called "fibre evidence," even by the Crown expert's own admission, proves nothing of relevance to the case – it cannot, for example, prove that fibres found on Mrs Wilson came from Derek Christian, or vice versa.

The question remains, how could the jury have believed that there was no "reasonable doubt" when even a basic analysis of the evidence presented in court shows precisely the opposite? Simple facts, such as the police officers who added "similar" entries to their notebooks a year after the event must raise some questions, especially as one of these officers then went on in court to completely contradict what was written in his notebook? The existence of fibres *inside* the body bag which did not belong to either Mrs Wilson or Derek Christian was never adequately explained. To whom did they belong, and how did they get there? Since the scene of crime log book was flawed and incomplete, these questions cannot be answered, along with the question of why casts and photographs of the tyre marks were never taken. The shoddiness of these aspects of the police investigation alone raises doubts.

The fact that no identity parade was ever held, and no witnesses were asked if they recognised Derek Christian, means that two crucial opportunities to have him eliminated from enquiries (or at least to cast serious doubts on him being the "lurking man" seen by so many witnesses) were lost. It is important to note, therefore, that Derek Christian was brought to trial, not only with no evidence against him, but also never having been identified at or near the scene by *anyone*.

If we return to the imaginary Twelve Points for a new justice system, in the introduction to this book, we are left with some very uncomfortable facts:

- Derek Christian was convicted on purely circumstantial evidence.
- Reasonable doubt, as shown here, was glaringly obvious.
- There was no DNA or forensic evidence linking Derek Christian to the crime.
- Derek was not identified at or near the scene of the crime.
- There were several suggestions of another person or persons being present at or near the scene (against whom no charges were pursued).
- There was clear over-reliance on "expert" testimony to the detriment of Derek Christian.
- There were serious questions about the ability of Derek to have carried out the crime within the timescale suggested.
- Clothing constituted a strong part of the prosecution's case.
- Character assassination constituted a strong part of the prosecution's case.
- There was evidence of forensic experts selectively interpreting evidence to the prosecution's own ends.
- Derek Christian was a man of previously good character, with no psychological conditions or previous convictions.

Eleven of the Twelve Points raised apply to the case of Derek Christian.

Given the purely circumstantial nature of this case, it seems pertinent to include some other "circumstantial" matters:

Two days after the start of Derek's trial, 14-year-old Kate Bushell was murdered in Devon. Just short of a year later, in October 1998, one week after the nationwide broadcast of the *Crimewatch* special on Derek Christian's conviction, Lynda Bryant was murdered. Both of these murders bear several similarities to the murder of Margaret Wilson:

- All the murders took place on secluded country roads/paths
- All three victims had their throats slashed Marie Cundall, who had seen the assailant just 5 minutes before Mrs Wilson was murdered, was walking her dog, as was Lynda Bryant
- There was no attempt to conceal the murders
- There is no apparent motive for any of the murders
- A scarf worn by Mrs Wilson is still missing. Lynda Bryant's spectacles also went missing, but were later returned to the crime scene.

The most worrying issues in Derek Christian's case are:

- Reasonable doubt is established, yet the conviction stands
- There is *no* concrete evidence
- The prosecuting counsel used extreme methods to convince the jury
- "Expert testimony" was protracted and confusing
- The police appeared to "home in" on him, even when there was clear evidence to the contrary. (In fact, DCI Midgeley was quoted in an interview after Derek's conviction as saying, curiously, that Derek "didn't protest his innocence enough.")
- Police records were altered, poorly constructed, and evidence appears to have been manipulated to "fit."
- Police failed to follow other leads.

Many of these issues turn up in the other cases highlighted in this book. The following is a reply received by Derek's family from Mr John Townend, MP, to whom they had appealed for help. This letter is included as evidence of the extent to which bias and prejudice is institutionalised, and to emphasise the difficulties faced by those trying to overturn wrongful convictions:

Letter from Mr John Townend MP to K C Christian:

Thank you for your letter of 22 February 1999. Whilst I appreciate your feelings, as the brother of Derek Christian it is very difficult for you to deal with this matter dispassionately. I very much believe in British justice and I am afraid that I cannot comment on the case, other than to say that the jury, according to your papers, brought in a unanimous verdict. They sat through and heard all the evidence, and were therefore in a much better position to come to a correct verdict than reading papers which have been produced by friends of the defendant.

With regard to your second request about Derek Christian's prison sentence, my view is that if he is not guilty, then he should not be in prison at all and clearly the judiciary thought the trial had been correct otherwise they would not have refused grounds for appeal, but if he is guilty, as you say, it was a heinous crime and I think a term of imprisonment of 20 years is not excessive. Indeed, speaking generally, for the worse crimes I have consistently voted to bring back the death penalty.

I know my letter will be a disappointment to you but I am sure you will appreciate the position I take.

References:
BBC Inside Out, Yorkshire & Lincolnshire, Monday January 26th 2004
"Beyond Reasonable Doubt?" The Rather Doubtful Case of Derek Christian by Simon Regan
Exhibit 81 – Personal Descriptive Form, Derek Christian 12/02/95
Exhibit D1 Photofit by Marie Cundall
Exhibit D3 Photofit by Louise Grey
Excerpt from Marie Cundall's statement
Crown Admissions, Nos 1 and 3
Letter of complaint to the BBC 15th January 1999, and response from Fraser Steel, BBC 03/06/1999
Letter from John Townend MP
Transcript, Statement of Robin J Falconer 21/09/1995
Transcript, Statement of Robin J Falconer 13/09/1996
Transcript, Statement of Robin J Falconer 04/07/1997
"Justice Without Science Isn't Justice," Frank Ward 17/09/03, reproduced at www.portia.org

Chapter Three

The Case of John Taft

ON Sunday 9th October, 1983, Cynthia Bolshaw was found dead in her bath at around 10.30am. Mrs Bolshaw lived alone, and there was no sign of forced entry to her home. At the time her body was discovered, Mrs Bolshaw's car was not on her drive, although it had been seen there by a neighbour at 11.30pm the previous evening. Pathologist examination suggested that Mrs Bolshaw had been strangled, her death occurring sometime between 3 and 6am, most likely around 4am. For sixteen years, the murder remained unsolved.

Although Mrs Bolshaw had an active sex life, and was involved with several men, a fingerprint on the frame of an open bedroom window was never identified. A semen stain on her negligee was also unidentified, as the technology for DNA testing was, at the time, not sophisticated enough.

Mrs Bolshaw's car was seen some distance from her home, at approximately 4.30 on the morning of Sunday 9th October, firstly by a member of the public, and later, at 5.45am by a police officer on his way to work. The member of the public, a Mr Dawson, reported that he had seen a man with the car, and gave a detailed description, but the man was never traced.

The case remained open until 1999, when John Taft was arrested and charged with the murder of Mrs Bolshaw. This followed what police claimed was new evidence – a DNA match of the semen stain, and evidence given by Barbara Taft, John's ex-wife.

The case against John Taft, as with the others highlighted in this book, was flimsy, completely circumstantial, and in a most bizarre twist, the prosecution's own evidence provided John with an alibi, yet John Taft was convicted of murder, and sentenced to life imprisonment on November 24th 1999.

The prosecution claimed that John was involved in a casual sexual relationship with Mrs Bolshaw, and had killed her after having sex with her, possibly in "a drunken rage." He had then stolen items of jewellery, and deposited them in a telephone box some fifty miles away (near to a place where he had once worked) to make it look as if the killer was not a local man. The evidence used by the prosecution to support their case was, in many instances, evidence of nothing in particular, but rather was introduced either to discredit John's character and believability, or to confuse or mislead the jury.

At the time of the murder, John Taft, was, indeed, involved in a sexual relationship with Mrs Bolshaw. He was also married at the time. When he heard on the news that she had been murdered, he became very anxious, as his infidelity would have been disclosed, and his marriage jeopardised. Also, he was afraid of being wrongly accused of her murder. As a result, he told his wife that he had been at Mrs Bolshaw's house doing some work outwith his normal paid employment. He had asked his wife to provide him with a false alibi, but after discussion, they had realised this was not really an option, as it would be too easily recognised as such. At first glance, the case against John Taft *seems* quite convincing, but on closer inspection, it becomes very apparent that it was simply portrayed that way; the facts actually point to John Taft being innocent, and his conviction unsafe.

Evidence

There are several strands of the prosecution's evidence which are either misleading, unsubstantiated, or easily explained. John was not treated as a suspect in 1983. It was only following a statement from his ex-wife in 1999 that the case against John Taft was constructed. Barbara Taft was a student in October 1983, studying away from home. As a result, she only returned home every second weekend. The weekend Mrs Bolshaw was murdered, Barbara Taft was not at home, but she told police that the following weekend, when she returned home, her then husband told her about the murder of Mrs Bolshaw, and that he had been at the house doing a "foreigner" (a job outwith his normal paid employment). It was at this point he had asked her to provide him with a false alibi, as he was afraid of being wrongly accused of the murder. She also told police that he had removed distinctive "go faster" stripes from his car, to avoid it being recognised, that he had been spoken to at his place of work about a business letter and a business card found in Mrs Bolshaw's house, that he had ripped pages out of a works diary to conceal the link between him and Mrs Bolshaw, and that the man in the police photofit picture must have been "the man who gave Mrs Bolshaw a black eye" and returned later to murder her.

There are some serious anomalies in Barbara Taft's account of events – the photofit picture was not released until around 4 months later, the interview at John's place of work did not take place until the November, and the link with the business card was not discovered until 1999, after she had spoken to the police. When these discrepancies were pointed out, she simply stated that after such a long period of time "the mind can play funny tricks." Barbara Taft also said in court that John had *told* her that he had burned clothing and shoes, and buried them in the garden, but in an earlier statement, said that she had "gained the impression" that he had done these things.

With the statement from his ex-wife, and more up-to-date DNA testing providing a match between the semen on Mrs Bolshaw's negligee and John, the basis of the case was established.

Witnesses were produced who pointed out that a page ripped out from the works diary would definitely have been noticed, but no witnesses could be produced to say such a thing had happened. One witness, a Ms Hignet, told the court that she remembered seeing Mrs Bolshaw's name in the works diary, with John's initials next to it, so the contention that he had attempted to conceal the link by ripping out the page is clearly not the case. John had initially met Mrs Bolshaw whilst delivering a quote for some work from his employers to her home (this was standard practice within the firm, whereby employees who lived near to potential or existing customers would deliver such documents on their way to or from work.) In an attempt to maintain the "ripped diary page" story, the prosecution then tried to claim that John had actually ripped half a page from Mrs Bolshaw's personal diary. A fire canopy had been fitted at Mrs Bolshaw's home, and John had, in the past, fitted fire canopies. On the half page remaining in Mrs Bolshaw's diary was a diagram that the prosecution claimed was a fire canopy – the line of reasoning being that John had fitted Mrs Bolshaw's canopy, and had ripped out the part of the page that would have shown his name. The canopy was checked for forensics, and it was found that fingerprints on the back of it, left by whoever fitted it, did *not* belong to John. In spite of this, the prosecution repeatedly referred to the missing diary page and the fire canopy as "evidence." Remember, Barbara Taft had claimed John tore a page from a *work* diary – the switch to Mrs Bolshaw's diary almost slips by un-noticed. As it stands, even the reference to Mrs Bolshaw's diary proves nothing – as it wasn't John who fitted the canopy, he would have no reason to tear out the page in her diary!

The next two pieces of evidence are interlinked, and raise what are probably the most serious questions regarding this conviction.

Brown cotton fibres, thought to have come from corduroy cloth, were found on the bottom bed sheet of Mrs Bolshaw's bed, on her negligee, and on a stool in the bedroom. The same fibres were found on the seat of the car when it was found on the morning of October 9th

1983, and also on the stocking containing the jewellery. Initially, this appears to be pointless information, since no connection was ever made between these fibres and any clothing belonging to John Taft. *But,* the second, interlinked piece of information is the testimony given by the Taft's neighbours at the time, the Evans family. Mrs Evans claimed to have seen John digging a two foot hole in his garden at 11.30pm on the night of Saturday 8th October (apparently backing up the claim that John had buried clothing and footwear in the garden.) Her daughter claimed only to have seen a man – it was too dark for her to identify him, and to have heard scraping and digging sounds. Although I will come to this evidence in more detail in a moment, the significant point is this:

if John Taft was burying the clothes which would have incriminated him – ie, the clothes that shed the brown fibres – at 11.30pm, exactly the same time as Mrs Bolshaw's car was seen still on her drive, how did those fibres come to be found on the car seat the following morning? There was, quite clearly, no time for him to have taken the car, abandoned it and returned to his garden. Yet, if he had returned to move the car *after* burning and burying his clothing, he would have had to have been wearing different clothes from the ones claimed to have shed the brown fibres. This vital point would later be missed not only by the judge hearing the trial, but by later appeal judges as well.

There are several problems relating to the Evans testimony. Firstly, the pathologists' reports claimed that the time of death was between 3 and 6am. Therefore, if the Evans family were correct, John was burying his clothing whilst Mrs Bolshaw was still alive. Further, the Evans testimony, presented by the prosecution, gives John an alibi! This is important to another of the prosecution's claims – that John took Mrs Bolshaw's car, abandoned it around 5 miles away, at the entrance to a field just off the A540 High Road, walked more than a mile along this road, climbed down a 15 foot banking, and walked the eight miles home from there along an unused railway line *before* digging in the garden at 11.30pm. For this to be so, it has to be accepted that the pathologists, the general practitioner who was called to the house following the murder, and the first police officer at the scene have all been wildly inaccurate in their estimates of time of death, and that Mrs Bolshaw was, in fact, killed much earlier than 3 – 6am. It also precludes any possibility of John having returned to the scene to remove the car, since there is simply no time for this to have happened – Mrs Bolshaw's car was positively identified on her driveway at exactly the same time John is identified by his neighbours in his own back garden. Indeed, the more this case progresses, the more incredible John Taft's apparent abilities become – not only is he clever enough to dispose of the evidence *before* the crime is committed, we are also now asked to believe that he can be in two places at the same time. Looked at in this light, the prosecution's claims are patently ridiculous, and the Evans' family's testimony goes a long way to discrediting the entire case against John Taft.

During the initial investigation at the scene of crime, forty five sets of fingerprints were found. Thirty four sets were identified as belonging to people who had reason to be at the house, ten contained insufficient evidence for conclusive identification, and one, the one found on the open window, remains unidentified. None of John's fingerprints were found in the house, although he told police he had had a cup of coffee and a glass of brandy in the course of his visit earlier that evening. It was clear, given the existence of so many sets of fingerprints, that the scene had not been wiped clean yet the prosecuting barrister asked the jury to consider why John's fingerprints had not been found on the coffee cup or the brandy glass. Photographs of the scene show a coffee cup on the draining board, and a broken spirit glass in the waste bin. (Mrs Bolshaw had a small cut on her finger, covered by a sticking plaster, when her body was found). It does not take too much imagination to figure out that she had washed the cup and the glass, breaking the glass in the process – there was also bloodstained kitchen paper in the kitchen. Yet the implication underlying the prosecution's question is that the *absence* of fingerprints belonging to John suggests guilt.

The prosecution had further forensic tests carried out on a pillowcase from Mrs Bolshaw's bed. The results of these tests were actually returned during the trial. They showed the presence of DNA from two individuals, one being Mrs Bolshaw herself, and the other from someone who was *not* John. No explanation was offered as to how that other DNA got to be on the pillow, or to whom it may have belonged. Rather than supporting the prosecution's case, this evidence should have introduced further doubt, in that it proved that someone else was close enough to Mrs Bolshaw's bed to have left DNA on the pillowcase.

The prosecution also claimed that John deposited the jewellery in the telephone box some 50 miles away to throw investigators off the scent by making them think the killer was not a local man. The jewellery was found inside a piece of stocking cut from the lower end of a stocking or pair of tights on October 11th 1983, 2 days after the discovery of Mrs Bolshaw's body. The stocking did not match any stockings or tights belonging to Mrs Bolshaw, but it did contain a purple fibre from her bedspread, and the same brown fibres that had been found at the scene and on the seat of her car. It was believed that the stocking and jewellery had been placed in the telephone box no earlier than the previous day

(October 10th) on the basis that had it been left there earlier, it would have been found. Therefore, the conclusion is that John, having gone to the trouble of burning and burying clothes, removing identifying stripes from his car (more about this later), and wiping clean his fingerprints at the scene, held onto the stocking and the jewellery for at least two days, before driving 50 miles to leave them where they would definitely be found. This is not the behaviour of the "highly intelligent, calculating" person the prosecution had tried to portray John Taft to be. Why, for example, having taken the risk of burying clothing in his garden in full view of his neighbours, did he then drive 50 miles away with the jewellery? Rather than trying to lead investigators to the conclusion that the killer was not a local man (a risky strategy, to say the least), why did he not just dispose of the jewellery altogether – he could simply have thrown it into the nearby River Dee.

Innuendo and speculation

Much of the prosecution's case relied on testimony given by Barbara Taft, even though this evidence was shown to be flawed, and Mrs Taft conceded that, after such a long time "the mind can play funny tricks." The claim that John had removed distinctive stripes from his car to avoid identification is completely unsubstantiated. Further, as he was driving a company car at the time, it would, almost certainly have been a basic model, with no distinguishing features. However, John offered an explanation as to how this evidence may have come to be confused over the 16 year time lapse, explaining that he had earlier owned a car with distinctive markings. The car had been damaged on one side, and, following repair, the stripes could not be matched, so he had removed them from the remaining, undamaged side of the car. Whilst this is a perfectly feasible and plausible explanation, the implication of Barbara Taft's version adds weight to the prosecution's portrayal of John as calculating and scheming, even though there is no evidence to back it up.

Similarly, the Evans family's testimony appears to have sinister overtones – what on earth would anyone be doing digging a hole in their garden at 11.30pm on a Saturday night? It is odd behaviour, to say the least, and raises the suspicion that he must have been up to something. Yet several witnesses testified that John had a keen interest in wildlife, and would often go out into his garden at night to leave food for the local wildlife. The only person who saw John was Mrs Evans (her daughter said it was too dark to identify the man, even though she and her mother were looking from the same window), yet her testimony gives rise to more questions than it answers – she said she saw John holding a torch and digging a hole with a spade, or similar implement. (Her daughter saw no such implement). It is a very difficult feat indeed to wield a spade effectively enough to dig a two foot hole whilst hampered by having to hold a torch. Once again, the story of feeding wildlife, backed by the testimony of several witnesses, is an alternative, perfectly plausible, and, given the available evidence, more probable explanation. (Of course, once the timing of this back garden foray is established, any credibility for the claim that John was burying clothes, etc, is demolished.)

The fact that John had lied about certain matters in 1983 was used to suggest that he was "covering his tracks." Yet again, the alternative explanation is equally plausible and acceptable – John was committing adultery, and did not want to be found out. He was also very afraid that, having been with Mrs Bolshaw that evening before she died, he would be wrongly accused of her murder. He assumed the murderer would be caught, and, as time went on, it became more and more difficult to go to the police. The reason this is a perfectly plausible explanation is that there were many other men with whom Mrs Bolshaw was involved who *also* never came forward, presumably for the same reasons as John.

On the advice of the duty solicitor in 1999, John gave several "no comment" answers when interviewed by police. This was later used to suggest that John was buying time – finding out what approach the police were taking so that he could construct a fitting defence. Yet, on closer examination, the prosecution contention here makes absolutely no sense. The approach the police were taking was perfectly clear – John's DNA had been found at the scene, therefore, they suspected him of being the murderer. Yet he did not offer a "no comment" response to the question of whether or not he had had sexual intercourse with Mrs Bolshaw – he admitted that he had. Further, tests showed that the semen stain was "old" and "could not be dated" – if John wanted to construct a story, then surely he could have made very effective use of this information. The more innocent explanation – that John was acting on the instructions of the duty solicitor – is, of course, the most obvious conclusion to be drawn, yet once again, we find innuendo and supposition being used to actively support a much less credible or likely explanation.

The repetitive linking of the missing half page of Mrs Bolshaw's diary with the fitting of the fire canopy as "evidence" of John's involvement continued in spite of the fact that (a) Barbara Taft had claimed, quite specifically, that John had told her he ripped a page from a *works* diary, and (b) the fire canopy was proven to have been fitted by someone who was *not* John Taft, therefore, he would have had no reason to remove the half page. In terms of evidence, there was nothing, anywhere, to suggest that John had ripped a page from Mrs Bolshaw's diary. The subtle implication from the prosecution, however, was that if Barbara Taft had mixed up some other details over the years, perhaps this was an example of that – perhaps John had told her about Mrs Bolshaw's diary, but she had confused it with the works diary. In an extremely clever, but completely unfounded piece of semantic manoevering, that which had discredited a particular testimony was now being used to substantiate something which had not even been claimed in the original testimony. Brilliant intellectually perhaps, but devastating to the pursuit of truth and justice. Also, in spite of the clear fingerprint evidence that the person who fitted the fire canopy was *not* John, there appears to have been little attempt to find out who *did* fit that canopy. Perhaps this is because the link between the missing half page of the diary, and the diagram claimed by the prosecution to be one of a fire canopy, is so tenuous that it simply did not warrant further investigation.

Witnesses and Identification

Although the prosecution claimed that John had taken Mrs Bolshaw's car, then walked home after abandoning it, there were no sightings of anyone fitting John's description anywhere on the route he was claimed to have taken, in spite of the fact that anyone walking on certain parts of that route could easily have been seen.

For John to have taken Mrs Bolshaw's car, he would have to have left his own, yet there are no witnesses to say that this was the case. If he did *not* have his own car, how did he get there? Checks with taxi firms revealed that no-one had dropped a fare at or near Mrs Bolshaw's house, and there were no reported sightings of John walking in the area.

Other males, sighted in and around Buff's Lane, seen with Mrs Bolshaw, or seen walking on parts of the route claimed to have been taken by John that night have never been identified. These include the man seen with Mrs Bolshaw's car at 4.30am on October 9th. From the witness description, it is clear this man was *not* John Taft. Another man, seen with Mrs Bolshaw in an estate agents' three weeks before she was killed, has never come forward. A number of cars seen at the house have never been traced; likewise a bearded man walking in Buff's Lane carrying a bag at 11.00pm on October 8th, and a heavily built male with shoulder length hair running from the direction of Mrs Bolshaw's home in the early hours of October 8th/9th.

Therefore, between 11.00pm on October 8th, and 4.30am on October 9th, three men, who are clearly not John, are seen either in the vicinity of Mrs Bolshaw's home, or beside her car some 5 miles away, and John is witnessed, by his next door neighbour in his own garden at 11.30pm on October 8th, yet none of this has any impact on the prosecution claim that John murdered Mrs Bolshaw.

The police investigation and procedures

Two post mortems were carried out on the body of Mrs Bolshaw in 1983. At John's trial in 1999, one of the pathologists, Dr J Burns, gave evidence which first contradicted the findings in 1983, by saying that it had not been possible to estimate the time of death as the body had been in two mediums, air and water. However, he was reminded that, in 1983, he had been in full agreement with Dr Benstead, who had carried out the first post mortem examination, that the time of death had been between 3 and 6am. Dr Burns could not refer to any notes taken – in fact, there appeared to be no notes in existence for the second post mortem examination from either of the Home Office pathologists (Dr Benstead was, by that time, deceased).

A police sergeant who was the first police officer to enter the house stated that the bath water was "tepid" at 10.45 on the morning of Sunday 9th October, and local GP who had been called out by police concluded from the water temperature at 11.15am, that Mrs Bolshaw had been murdered within "the last few hours" rather than the previous night.

Therefore, by 17th October 1983, police had 4 separate accounts indicating that Mrs Bolshaw had been killed in the early hours of October 9th, rather than the night of Saturday October 8th. Yet sixteen years later, despite evidence placing John at home "burying clothing" at 11.30pm that night, charges were brought against John, based on a statement from his ex-wife, and new DNA evidence. That the statement from Barbara Taft was extremely flawed should have been obvious to the police from the beginning. That left them only the DNA match, and it is with this that a critical assumption was made. The semen stain on Mrs Bolshaw's negligee was proven to have originated from John. However, this proved only that sexual intercourse had taken place between the two. It did not, and of itself, could not, prove anything else. However, the police investigation appears to have proceeded on the basis that because John's DNA was found at the scene, he had to be the murderer.

Also, during the trial, two detective constables gave evidence regarding a visit they had made to Birkenhead Glass, where John had worked, in 1983. Neither of these officers was able to refer to their notebooks from the time, as they had been destroyed, apparently in line with police policy. Is it really the case that, in unsolved murder cases, such critical evidence is allowed to be destroyed? One officer could not recall even speaking to John. The other recalled that, after speaking to John, he had spoken to a manager within the company to confirm what John had told him (i.e. that no further records would have been kept after the quote had been passed to Mrs Bolshaw). However, none of the managers interviewed in 1999 mentioned having been spoken to by the police in 1983.

Mr Dawson, the witness who had seen the man with what appears to have been Mrs Bolshaw's car at 4.30am on Sunday 9th October 1983, said in 1999 that he was not sure he would recognise the man after such a long time. However, his description at the time was very definite and confident – the man had dark hair and was wearing distinctive glasses and a long Crombie style overcoat. This description, and the photofit derived from it, would have been available to police in 1999, along with a statement from Barbara Taft that her ex husband had never owned such a coat, did not wear glasses, and had fair hair which was graying.

The question has to be asked then, on what grounds did the police investigation leading up to John's arrest in 1999 proceed? The new evidence which they claimed led to John's arrest amounted to the statements from Barbara Taft and the Evans family, and the newly found DNA match. A rational, logical analysis of this new evidence, both in its own right, and against the backdrop of all the existing evidence would most certainly have raised doubts as to just how reliable it was in determining that John Taft was (or was not) the person who murdered Cynthia Bolshaw. Yet such a rational, logical approach does not appear to have taken place. Seizing on the scientifically 'irrefutable' DNA evidence, it appears that the rest of the evidence was shoe-horned to fit an extremely dubious theory, or was simply ignored. Clearly, the DNA match would be considered to be "scientifically irrefutable," insofar as it proves that the semen stain on Mrs Bolshaw's negligee came from John. This is *not* the same as claiming that it *proves*, irrefutably, that John murdered Mrs Bolshaw, although this appears to be the implication driving the police investigation. Indeed, the prosecution's suggestion was that, but for scientific advances in DNA testing, John would have "got away with murder," yet the new findings served only to prove that John had had sexual intercourse with Mrs Bolshaw, as had several other men. This is not intended as a slight in any way on Mrs Bolshaw, it is simply the fact of the matter. Using the prosecution's reasoning, anyone who could be proven to have had sexual intercourse with Mrs Bolshaw would also be proven to have murdered her!

One question which appears not to have been asked, though it appears to be quite an obvious one, is why Barbara Taft took 16 years to speak to the police. By her own admission, the divorce between her and John had been amicable some 11 years previously. What was it that prompted her, after such a long time, to come forward? It is interesting to note, also, that Barbara Taft does not claim that her husband confessed to any crime – her whole statement speaks of his fear of being *wrongly* accused, and explains the various behaviours to which she alludes in these terms. Why, also, when it became apparent that Barbara Taft's account of events was flawed, in that she claimed to have been told things by John weeks and months prior to these events having taken place, did the police push ahead with a prosecution which would rely on such a flawed testimony?

The prosecution and judges

The prosecution case contended that John had murdered Mrs Bolshaw, possibly in a "drunken rage" after having sexual intercourse with her. He had then stripped her, and placed her naked body in the bath, before stealing jewellery and taking her car. He had abandoned the car, returned to his own home, and burned and buried the shoes and clothing he had been wearing. Three days later, they claimed, John drove 50 miles to a telephone box and left the jewellery and the stocking mask, in order to make it look like Mrs Bolshaw had been murdered following a robbery, and also to make police think the murderer was not a local man.

The evidence, however, simply does not support the prosecution case.

No evidence was provided of John having a problem with drunkenness or violence in the past. Witnesses testified that John was not a heavy drinker, and he had no previous record of violence or drunken behaviour. This motive appears to have been plucked out of thin air, and is complete speculation.

Following the discovery of the body, investigation of the scene turned up the following evidence – a semen stain on Mrs Bolshaw's negligee, a damp patch on the bed, found to be urine, and the fibres. The most likely explanation for the urine on the bed is that Mrs Bolshaw's bladder emptied as she was strangled – both prosecution and defence did not contest this. However, it raises a problem with the prosecution claims, because, although there was urine on the bed, there was none on Mrs Bolshaw's negligee. This means, almost definitely, that she was *not* wearing the negligee when she was killed, contrary to the prosecution's assertion that John had stripped her *after* killing her.

The claims regarding the convoluted plot to plant the stolen jewellery in the telephone box, as already shown, simply make no sense. If John had been the evil, calculating man that the prosecution painted him to be, would anyone really believe that he would risk (a) walking for the best part of 8 – 10 miles, carrying jewellery stolen from a house where a murder had just been committed, (b) keeping the jewellery for three days, in spite of disposing of everything else that might link him to the crime, and (c) risking driving the fifty miles to the phone box, still in possession of the jewellery, and depositing it in a public telephone box? It is extremely unlikely that a "highly intelligent, calculating man" as the prosecution depicted John to be, would have taken such risks.

Also, the story about burying the clothing in the back garden is quite preposterous, when examined in detail. This would be a very clever killer, indeed, who buried the evidence *before* committing the crime! Incidentally, to the rear of the houses where John and Barbara Taft lived at the time was a large, overgrown area of rough ground – surely it would have made more sense to bury the evidence there, rather than in full view of the neighbours. Later testimony, from a Mr Round, who bought the house from the Tafts, stated that he had renovated the entire garden, and had never uncovered anything resembling clothing or footwear buried in the garden. A radar sweep of the garden in 1999 also came up with nothing.

Aside from these main planks in the prosecution's case, the dirty tricks approach is once again in evidence. When it became apparent that the claim by Barbara Taft (that John had ripped a page from the work's diary) was totally discredited by the evidence, the prosecution switched to claiming that it was, in fact, Mrs Bolshaw's diary that had the ripped out page – the implication being that Barbara Taft may have mixed up the details after so many years. Yet, Barbara Taft had mixed up other crucial details, claiming John had discussed certain things with her the weekend after the murder which, the evidence showed, it was completely impossible for him to have discussed at that point, because they had not yet happened! This switch enabled the prosecution to continually connect the diary page and the fire canopy, which had also been proven to have no connection whatsoever with John, in an insidious, but powerful innuendo.

The prosecution's own evidence both gave John an alibi, and destroyed their own case – if he had been burying clothes in the back garden at 11.30pm, after murdering Mrs Bolshaw, she would have to have been murdered *before* this time, yet both pathology reports, and the GP and police officer at the scene all put the time of death in the early hours of the morning of October 9th – the prosecution, with the jury absent, tried to persuade the judge that this evidence should be ruled as inadmissable on the grounds that John should have told them he had an alibi! Fortunately, they were not successful, but this is a clear example of the lengths to which prosecution teams are prepared to go to secure conviction, regardless of the facts.

The judge, in his summing up, added yet another factor which is likely to have prejudiced the jury, and worse, displays his failure to grasp the facts of the case.

He said

> "...Further, though the prosecution have suggested that the murderer took her car away after committing the offence, you may think this itself was speculation on the prosecution's part. There is no evidence whether this was done straight away or whether he may have taken his own car home first before coming back and removing hers..."

There are several points that must be made with regard to this particular statement. Firstly, this possibility had not been raised during the trial itself. The prosecution had, indeed, made no such claim, so why did the judge introduce this new possibility during his summing up? The defence had no opportunity to respond to it, so the jury were left with this new possibility, but no evidence with which to evaluate it. However, given that it came from the judge, who was supposedly impartial, then it seems fair to assume that the jury would give credence to it on that ground alone.

But, on examination of the evidence and facts, there are very clear indicators that John Taft could not have been the person who "came back later" to remove Mrs Bolshaw's car. The fibres found on the bed, the stool and on the car seat were believed to have come from the same source – i.e. the killer's clothing. If, as claimed, John had buried the clothing he had been wearing, how, then, did he come to leave those fibres in the car? The judge appears not to have understood this critical point when making his suggestion that the killer may have returned to remove the car. Further, the car was known to be still on Mrs Bolshaw's drive at 11.30pm – John could not possibly have taken the car, abandoned it, and made his way home on foot, to be seen in his garden at that time. Even if everyone else was wrong and the prosecution was right that Mrs Bolshaw had been killed much earlier in the evening of October 8th (a point, incidentally, that they never overtly claimed), and the killer had "gone back" to remove the car later, that person could not have been John Taft, for the reasons given here.

Prior to the paragraph printed here, the judge had outlined several scenarios, regarding timing, witness sightings, and so forth, in which he referred to John by name. It is only in the final paragraph that this changes to "the murderer," with no mention of John by name. However, it would seem reasonable, again, to imagine that the jury would link the "him" of the final paragraph with the "him" who was John Taft in the preceding paragraphs.

For one judge to misunderstand the nature of the evidence presented is bad enough - for five to make the same mistake is outrageous, yet that is exactly what happened. When John's legal team appealed, on the grounds that the judge's summing up was prejudicial to John's case by introducing a new possibility that had not been led in evidence, the first (single) judge responded thus:

> "The question of the precise time when the killer drove the car away was always going to be a matter of speculation. It is difficult to see in what material respect the trial would have taken a different course if the prosecution had suggested that the applicant had driven the car away some time after the murder."

Difficult to see? If John had, indeed, been the killer, the prosecution's own witnesses saw him burying his clothing and shoes in the back garden at 11.30pm. Therefore, no matter how much later he had returned to drive the car away, he would not – could not - have left the same fibres on the driving seat as those left at the scene of the crime. It is not at all difficult to see, it is blatantly obvious to anyone who examines the facts as presented to the court.

The panel of three judges concluded:

> "We find that our approach to this case is entirely the same as the single judge's. We have carefully considered the fairness of this conviction…. We, at the end of the day, having looked at the matter, can see nothing that suggests to us that the verdict was unsafe."

The findings of these later judges appears to rest on the basis that John's counsel was asked, at the time, if he had any objections to the judge including that particular passage in his summing up, and he had said that he did not. Whilst this was clearly an error on John's counsel's part, one which was realised too late, that the appeal judges should hold that as proof that the original judge's summing up was fair seems to miss the point completely. Clearly, they had not "carefully considered," because careful consideration brings one to the conclusion that the new possibility could not be applied to John Taft, based on the evidence led in court, yet the inference that it *may* apply to John was one the jury is likely to have drawn, particularly since the suggestion was raised by the judge himself. By stating that

> "The matter was fairly left to the jury in a way that they would readily have understood the issues that they had to decide,"

the appeal judges display a remarkable lack of understanding of the relationship between the "ordinary man" and authority figures. Because the judge had introduced a new possibility that had not been presented at any point in the trial, the jury may, quite reasonably, have concluded that the judge "knew something that they didn't" and was perhaps trying to hint at this in his summing up. To have suggested that this was a possibility that "inevitably any jury would consider for themselves" is pure guesswork – how could the appeal judges possibly know what the jury may or may not consider *if it had not been led in evidence*. Indeed, jurors are cautioned to base their decisions only on the evidence they hear in court – and this possibility was not one that had been given in evidence.

A further example of the failure of the appeal judges to evaluate *all* of the evidence is the claim that

> "...the inference...that the car had been driven away immediately after the murder was one that the jury had to decide whether it was proper to draw. They had to consider other possibilities......The Crown's case...was that ....he was then going to embark on a cover-up.....It required him to go back the short distance and remove the car...."

In John's case, based on the evidence, it was *not* another possibility. The judges at this point even refer to "hiding or burying clothing" as evidence of the "cover up," yet fail to realise that it is this very factor which precludes John returning to remove the car as "another possibility."

Summary

Once again, we have to consider, on what grounds was John Taft convicted of murder, and sentenced to life imprisonment?

He admits being with Mrs Bolshaw on the evening she died, but maintains that he left her, alive and well, at around 10.45 pm. The evidence, even as presented by the prosecution, backs up his statement.

The DNA found on Mrs Bolshaw's negligee, found to be a semen stain, was matched to John, but this proves only that sexual intercourse took place. It cannot even be used to prove *when* this happened. There was no evidence of a sexual assault, and the incidence of sexual intercourse in no way proves murder.

Several men were seen near Mrs Bolshaw's home, on the route John was claimed to have taken, and with Mrs Bolshaw prior to her death, but none of these men were John. Neither were any of these men traced or identified.

The so-called "fibre evidence," even by the Crown expert's own admission, proves nothing of relevance to the case – it cannot, for example, prove that fibres found on Mrs Bolshaw came from John Taft, or vice versa. In fact, to stretch the credibility of this theory even further, no garment belonging to John Taft was ever produced which could be shown to have produced similar fibres. As had been clearly demonstrated, neither scenario (either that John had burned the clothes, or that he had returned to the scene later to dispose of Mrs Bolshaw's car) supports the "fibre evidence" as presented in court.

In spite of a radar sweep of the garden, and the new owner completely over hauling the area, no evidence was ever found of clothing or footwear having been buried there.

The question remains, how could the jury have believed that there was no reasonable doubt? Surely the existence of one unidentified fingerprint at the scene of the crime must raise some reasonable doubt?

Both pathologists' reports placed the time of death at between 3 and 6am, and the first police officer and GP at the scene backed these findings independently, describing the bathwater as "cooling" and "tepid," yet the prosecution's case leads to the inevitable conclusion that Mrs Bolshaw was murdered, at the very latest, at around 8 – 9pm the previous evening. How can we reasonably explain such a large time discrepancy?

Further, this discrepancy encompasses one critical factor – the sighting of John Taft in his own garden at 11.30pm. This one sighting appears to completely demolish the prosecution case, leading to, one would imagine, a great deal more than *reasonable* doubt!

Once more, if we match this case of John Taft against the imaginary Twelve Points for a new justice system, the similarities with Derek Christian's circumstances are chilling:

- John Taft was convicted on purely circumstantial evidence.
- Reasonable doubt, as shown here, was glaringly obvious.
- What DNA evidence existed did not prove that John Taft murdered Mrs Bolshaw, or, indeed, harmed her in any way.
- John was not identified at or near the scene of the crime. Although he admitted to having been with Mrs Bolshaw earlier in the evening, the evidence supports the claim that he was not at or near the scene of the crime *at the time the crime was committed.*
- There were several suggestions of another person or persons being present at or near the scene, along the route claimed by the prosecution to have been taken by John, and in the company of Mrs

Bolshaw prior to the murder (against whom no charges were pursued).

- There was clear over-reliance on "expert" testimony to the detriment of John Taft (and, apparently, to the confusion of not only the judge hearing the case, but to subsequent appeal judges as well.)
- There were serious questions about the ability of John to have carried out the crime within the timescale suggested.
- Clothing constituted a strong part of the prosecution's case.
- Character assassination constituted a strong part of the prosecution's case.
- There was evidence of forensic experts selectively interpreting evidence to the prosecution's own ends.
- John Taft was a man of previously good character, with no psychological conditions or previous convictions.

Eleven of the Twelve Points raised apply to the case of John Taft, just as they did with Derek Christian.

Other similarities emerge between these two cases. Both men were convicted on the strength of highly dubious "fibre evidence" which, as has been shown, ultimately proves nothing of substance. In both cases, a clear description of a *different* man with a car was available to police, who appear to have ignored this evidence, or at least failed to properly follow it up. Both men were accused of behaviours which they had never previously displayed, and for which no evidence could be found. Police procedures were flawed, in that records were either poorly maintained, destroyed, or missing by the time the case came to trial.

The most worrying issues in John Taft's case are:

- Reasonable doubt is established, yet the conviction stands
- There is **no** concrete evidence
- The prosecuting counsel used extreme methods to convince the jury.
- "Expert testimony" was protracted and confusing
- The police acted on a statement which was clearly flawed and deeply inaccurate.
- Police failed to follow other leads.
- The judge introduced a "new possibility" which had not been led in evidence, and appeal judges tried to make this acceptable on the grounds that it was a possibility that the jury would have "inevitably" have considered themselves. Yet, the jury are clearly instructed that they must come to their decision based only on the evidence as presented in court!

Sandra Lean

References:

Exhibit, "Unidentified Fingerprint" 10/10/83
"Appendix"; Photograph of car, and position where it was found abandoned 9/10/83
Exhibit, Photofit of unidentified man January 2004
Transcript: Appeal Before Lord Justice Kay, Mr Justice Silber and His Honour Judge Mellor 02/10/2000
Excerpt: Written Application to Appeal, Oliver Blunt QC
When Science Opinion Outweighs Science Fact, Alex Wade, reproduced www.innocent.org.uk
Justice for All, JUSTICE response to the White Paper, October 2002, P38, Para112

Chapter Four

The case of Gordon Park

CAROL ANN PARK went missing from her family home in July 1976. Her body was found by divers in Coniston Water in the Lake District, in August 1997. Her husband, Gordon Park, was arrested and charged with murder, but the charges were dropped in January 1998, due to insufficient evidence. Six years later, Gordon Park was once again arrested in January 2004, and again charged with murder. This time, he was brought to trial at Manchester Crown Court in November of the same year. The trial was long and complicated, and culminated in Gordon Park being found guilty of his wife's murder. He was handed down a life sentence, with a recommendation that he serve at least 15 years, at the age of 61.

Once again, this case is based purely on circumstantial evidence, and there is no evidence to link Gordon Park with the murder of his first wife.

Carol Ann Park disappeared from her home in Leece, Barrow-in-Furness, on July 17th 1976. It was the beginning of the school holidays (Carol was a school teacher), and the family had planned to go to Blackpool for the day. Carol decided not to go, as she said she was feeling unwell, but Gordon went ahead with the trip, with the three children. When they returned, Carol was gone. She had left her wedding ring behind, and there was no sign of any kind of struggle or robbery.

However, it was not unusual for Carol to "disappear" for lengthy periods, often without warning. She had several affairs during her marriage, including with a police officer and a solicitor, but Gordon Park always took her back. On two separate occasions, Carol had left another lover completely without warning.

As a school teacher, Carol's disappearances often coincided with the school holidays, and Gordon assumed in July 1976 that Carol would return at the beginning of the new term in September. It was at that point, when Carol failed to return, that he reported her missing through his solicitor, and her family were informed.

Several of her friends and family who had seen Carol in the week prior to her disappearance had reported her as appearing to be down or depressed. She had spoken to some about tracing her real parents, as she was adopted.

A missing persons enquiry was launched, but no leads were produced. Police informed Gordon Park, however, that he would be their main suspect, should a body be found. It would not be until 21 years later, in August 1997, that Carol's body was found in Coniston Water, and Gordon was, indeed, charged with murder. The charge was dropped in January 1998 due to insufficient evidence, but a second charge was brought in 2004.

Because of the length of time Carol's body had been in the water, a full post mortem examination was not possible. However, the Home Office Pathologist, Dr Edmund Tapp, concluded that the probable cause of death was drowning and inhalation of blood due to severe facial injuries, which were probably caused by a heavy, blunt or sharp instrument.

Carol's body had been wrapped in packaging consisting of a pinafore dress, a canvas rucksack and some plastic bags, tied with several knots, and weighed down with lead piping, before being dumped in Coniston Water. According to the pathologist, Dr Tapp, the body was tied within 2 – 3 hours of death, before rigor mortis would have set in. What he failed to point out, however, is that rigor mortis passes within 24 – 48 hours, and the body *could* have been tied after that period. (This is important in that the prosecution would claim that Gordon had killed Carol in their own home, and trussed the body immediately – however, someone else could quite easily have killed Carol, and tied up the body at a later time, another factor of which the jury would not be aware.)

Identification and witnesses

The prosecution claimed that Gordon had not gone to Blackpool that day, but had used the story as a "cover." They claimed he had "drugged his wife, possibly on or around the 17th July, tied her up and stored her body in a chest freezer before dumping it in Coniston Water." There is no evidence whatsoever to support this theory – it is complete speculation.

Further, one of the children recalls seeing his mother that morning and going to Blackpool and, significantly, a neighbour reported seeing Carol at the bottom of the drive on the day of her disappearance. She (Carol) seemed to be "hanging around." Another neighbour reported a blue or grey VW Beetle going up the drive to the house, then driving back down some 20 minutes later. The neighbour was aware that the family had gone out for the day, and that it wasn't Gordon driving the car. She reported that it seemed "odd" that the car should stay for 20 minutes.

Another witness came forward to say that she had seen Carol that day at approximately 6pm, at the southbound Charnock Richard services on the M6. By the time of the trial, this witness was suffering from cognitive impairment, and her statement from 1997 was read out to the jury, as she was not able to give evidence. Two problems arise from this particular sequence of events – firstly, as it was not made entirely clear when this witness began to suffer cognitive impairment, the jury may have believed that the witness had been suffering that condition when the original statement was made, which she was not. Secondly, some evidence was led regarding possible confusion on the part of this witness at the time of her original statement – a particular line of questioning raised the possibility that she may have been mistaken about the date, and that she had seen Carol the day before, on the Friday, rather than the Saturday. (This confusion, it must be pointed out, had nothing whatsoever to the cognitive impairment later suffered by the witness – it was the "ordinary" confusion which can often be introduced during an investigation when several years have elapsed between events.) However, other, more concrete evidence casts serious doubt on this possibility – two other witness statements place Carol in Barrow at 6pm on the Friday evening, and there are some serious timescale issues for the original witness to have managed to get from Barrow to the Charnock Richard services within three hours, whilst towing a caravan! Once more, we are faced with the possibility of dubious prosecution procedures either pressurising witnesses or creating confusion in order to obtain only the "evidence" which best suits their required outcome.

Almost thirty years later, although the prosecution would shed doubt on the abilities of family and friends to recall events with accuracy, it would call witnesses, Mr and Mrs Young, who recalled seeing a man fitting Gordon's description dumping something over the side of a boat at around the time Carol went missing. Mrs Young claimed that the man kept "looking at the car" – if this were someone trying to dispose of a body, is it feasible to suggest he would do so in broad daylight, aware that he was being observed? Mrs Young did not report this incident at the time (in 1976), nor did she come forward during the 1997 investigation. She contacted the police *after* Gordon's arrest in 2004. In court, she was unsure as to whether the man wore glasses, whether she, herself, had used binoculars to look at the man (she and her husband were in a car parked a mile north of where the body was found), or what height the man was. Her description was of a man with dark brownish auburn hair, a moustache, and a thin face. By the time this witness came forward, there had been a huge amount of press coverage of the case – it would not be difficult for most members of the public to be able to give a description of Gordon Park! The Youngs were unable to give an exact date for these events. The best they could manage was that they had arrived in the district on holiday around July 25th and had stayed for five or six days. The sighting they reported was "towards the end of their holiday."

If family and friends' recollections are not to be given too much weight, given the passage of time, why was this vague, almost useless testimony given any credence whatsoever?

The timing and dates, however, are significant in *support* of Gordon's innocence, as will become apparent.

Evidence

The prosecution led several pieces of "evidence" which would later be completely discredited. The first was not evidence at all, but conjecture – that Gordon Park had murdered his wife in the family home. In spite of extensive forensic examination, not a single piece of evidence was ever recovered to suggest that this had been the case.

A rock recovered from the lakebed some 70 metres from where Carol's body was found was presented with the contention that it had come from the Park's garden wall. However, the diver who was supposed to have retrieved the rock said in court that he had no recollection of the rock, that if he had found a rock, he would have replaced it on the lakebed. He had no recollection of emptying the rock from his net bag after the dive. The rock only appears in police records several days later.

The judge criticised the recording of items removed from the lakebed, saying it was not to the standard that should be expected. Exhibits were handled by 5 or 6 different officers, and there were inconsistencies in signatures when recording exhibits at the police station. The expert for the prosecution could only state that it was "more probable" that the rock came from the family home than Coniston – the defence's expert witness testimony would raise the question of whether the rock had even been in the water at all, given the lack of diatoms or growths on its surface. A rock which had lain on the bottom of a lake for a considerable length of time (which the prosecution argued it had) would be expected to have these things, yet, when asked what evidence existed in support of the rock having been submersed in water for all that time, this witness's response was "None." Clothing beside which the rock was "found" was not proven to belong to Carol, although police appear not to have made any serious efforts to prove, categorically, that these clothes *did not* belong to Carol. This is important on several counts – firstly, without proof one way or the other, the suggestion that the clothing *did* belong to Carol can be left unsubstantiated, but hovering insidiously in the background. Secondly, it would obviously beg the question, if the clothing *was* Carol's, why would her husband want to dispose of it? Having reported his wife missing, there would be no need for Gordon Park to take such action as disposing of clothing – indeed, it would be an extremely risky move on his part to do so, if he had, in fact, murdered her. However, someone else, someone for whom it may be difficult to explain having clothing of Carol's in their possession, *would* have obvious reason for disposing of it. These issues were never raised in court, the whole smokescreen of suggestion and innuendo once again left to do its damage.

A piece of slate, also recovered from the lakebed at the same time as the body was claimed to be "very similar" to slate on the Park's house. This "evidence" also collapsed at trial, when the Judge, Mr Justice McCombe told the jury that even the prosecution accepted that "slate had been worked in the Coniston area for hundreds of years" and the piece produced in court "could have come from anywhere."

This first raft of evidence, concerning rocks, clothing and slate supposedly recovered from the lakebed where Carol's body was found, was clearly discredited.

Central to the prosecution's case, however, were the knots used in the trussing of Carol Park's body. It would be claimed that these knots were similar to those in Gordon Park's house, boat and garage. Further, the prosecution claimed that the knots had been tied by someone with "specialist knowledge." The original "knot evidence" produced by Roger Ide, for the prosecution, and Rob Chisnall, for the defence, essentially concluded that there were similarities *and* differences between the knots used for trussing the body and those in Gordon's house, garage and boat, but, significantly, that this proved nothing of any worth. However, one point was absolutely certain- the single most-used knot on the body was a granny knot, and, in fact, not a single granny knot was found amongst all of those on Gordon Park's property, because he did not use such a knot. A second expert for the prosecution, Mike Lucas, made several claims in the lead up to the 2004 trial (indeed, it was, in part, this expert's "findings" which led to the second trial), then retracted his evidence *after* it had been reviewed by Rob Chisnall, and, more importantly, *after* the 2004 trial was certain to go ahead. The jury was never informed that the "new evidence" about the knots had been discredited. It would later transpire that the knots to which the protracted and confusing testimony referred indicated only a level of "ability," which would have been common to a number of people, and not "specialist knowledge" of knots, as the prosecution had claimed.

Regardless of knot similarity or dis-similarity, however, the rope fibres used to truss Carol Park's body did not match any rope fibres belonging to Gordon Park.

Similarly, lead piping which had been used to weigh down the body had what the prosecution claimed were "hammer marks" matching a hammer in Gordon Park's possession. Expert evidence, however, concluded that there was nothing to suggest, far less prove, that Gordon's hammers could have made the marks on the lead piping, and to further distance Gordon from this particular line of reasoning, the hammer belonging to him, which was exhibited in court, actually had a bevelled, not a sharp edge! The lead piping could, quite simply, have been hammered by anybody with a sharp edged and flat surfaced hammer. Tests comparing the lead piping with lead at the Park's family home found no match – the lead at Bluestones was from a different manufacturer. Likewise, paint marks on the lead piping were compared to paint marks found on the toilet bowl in the garage of the Park's garage, and again, these tests came back with no match.

Finally, there were "witnesses" who claimed Mr Park had confessed to them, whilst on remand in 1997, that he had murdered his wife. It was claimed that neither of these witnesses stood to gain by giving evidence against Mr Park, even though there was still a 5000 GBP reward for information on offer from 1998, which had been highlighted at the end of a Channel Four documentary in 2000.

The statement from Michael Wainwright, a heavy drug user who admitted to the court that he suffered from memory loss and claimed he heard voices, stated that Gordon had told him he had gone home, gone upstairs and found his wife in bed with another man, and killed her in a fit of rage. There is a glaring inconsistency in this account – the Parks' home a bungalow, so there is no "upstairs." Also, extensive forensic testing had failed to turn up a single shred of evidence to suggest that the murder had taken place anywhere in the family home.

Glen Banks, the second prisoner to claim Gordon had confessed to him whilst on remand, was to change his story several times. First, he claimed that Gordon told him he had given his wife some "white powder" and she had then fallen overboard. Later, he would claim that Gordon had killed his wife on the boat, then placed her body in some bags with weights, before throwing her into the lake. Glen Banks had serious learning difficulties and was therefore considered by some psychologists to be "suggestible."

He was shown to have been suggested several key words during a video interview with one police officer in 2001/2002. He was also shown to have changed his story after the first break in the tape, to have had access to media coverage of the case, and to prison gossip, and to have been spoken to by Michael Wainwright before coming forward with his allegation of Gordon's "confession." He was also shown to have been encouraged on certain points by his social worker. Indeed, legal arguments over the admissibility of Glen Banks' evidence were to involve several psychology experts, yet it was Glen Banks' statement which would, in part, lead to the re-instatement of the murder charge. Further, in spite of police denials that Banks evidence had been in any way manipulated, because he was suggestible, the following comment from a DCI Churchman, in a recent ITV *Real Crime* programme, appears to suggest quite the opposite:

> ...this "actually strengthened his evidence.....because the way his learning difficulties were, it meant he couldn't make things up. *You could give him a story to remember, and he could remember it*, so the medical experts were saying 'anything he tends to say is the truth.'"

Following the Channel Four documentary, Wainwright made mention of an ice axe as a possible weapon. He had seen a climbers' axe during a drug rehab day out to the lakes previously, and appears to have attempted to tie this to the 1997 pathologist report that Carol had been beaten about the face by a "heavy" object, as reported in the documentary. Wainwright claimed that Gordon's "confession" had included reference to an ice axe, even though the description he gave was completely different to the axe owned by Gordon. When we consider that Wainwright and Banks did not come forward until after this programme was aired, the implications are obvious, yet the prosecution actually encouraged the jury to consider that Gordon had used an ice axe with which to beat his wife! Note, too, that neither the police investigation nor the prosecution approach had made any connection whatsoever with an "ice axe" until after Wainwright mentioned it, after which, it was adopted as "evidence."

The Police and the Investigation.

As has already been stated, the police were criticised by the judge for their handling of the exhibits retrieved from the lakebed. Inconsistencies in signatures and recording created confusion, leading the judge to state that this part of the operation was "not to the standard that should be expected." The fact that the diver involved had absolutely no recollection of the rock, and claimed he would not have brought it up, but replaced it on the lakebed, coupled with the fact that reference to it did not appear in police logs until several days later, leads to the uncomfortable suggestion that the rock may not, after all, have been retrieved by the diver. A defence expert would later compound this doubt by agreeing that there was no evidence to support the suggestion that the rock had been submersed in water for such an extensive period of time.

The police claimed that Gordon owned a boat at the time Carol disappeared, and it was from this boat that he dumped her body in Coniston Water. During the 1997 investigation, the commodore at Coniston Sailing Club mistakenly told police that Gordon had a boat at the sailing club during the 1970s. This information was later proved to be incorrect by the sailing club records. Gordon's own sailing log indicates that he sold his dinghy in July that year, although he maintains that it was sold in June, to an instructor on a course he had taken – the course had finished in June. However, this timing need not be too significant – if the Youngs version of events is correct, then Gordon must have sold the dinghy literally within a day or two of him "disposing of the body." This does not make sense – after holding onto the body for almost 2 weeks, he disposes of it and gets rid of the boat within a couple of days?

Records from the original missing persons enquiry were lost.

It was claimed by the prosecution that Gordon had killed his wife in a fit of jealous rage after discovering that she was having an affair. Yet there had been previous affairs, and Gordon had always taken his wife back. There was no previous history of violence – medical records revealed that Carol had told a doctor in 1975 that Gordon had never used violence or threats towards her. It would seem that the police enquiry from 1997 did not focus sufficiently on other men who may have had reason to become violent or jealous towards Carol Park.

Alistair Webster QC, prosecuting, told the court:

"Whoever killed and disposed of Carol Park would have the following characteristics; a person who knew her sufficiently well to come across her in her short nightdress; a person who had reason to strongly dislike her or to lose his temper with her; a person who was thoroughly familiar with knots, both as a sailor and a climber; a meticulous person; a person with access to a boat and familiarity with Coniston Water. One man fits this description: Gordon Park."

The knots which Mr Webster appeared to claim would be known mostly to sailors and climbers were shown to be commonplace, and widely practiced by a number of different people engaged in work in the local shipyards, as well as hobbies such as scouting, climbing and sailing

In actual fact, there could have been several people who could have fitted the description presented in court by Mr Webster. Any of the men with whom Carol had affairs would, during the course of such an affair, presumably "know her sufficiently well to come across her in a short nightdress." The police had told Gordon in 1976 that if a body was discovered, he would be their "main suspect." That being the case, it seems the police "investigation" then proceeded on the basis that they had their man, they only had to get the facts to prove it. In spite of Carol's many affairs, the police do not seem to have considered other lovers to have had the same "reason" (ie, jealousy) to have attacked her in a "fit of rage." Yet, according to those who knew her, Carol had left one lover on two occasions without warning, just as she had previously left Gordon without warning. If these factors were reason enough for Gordon to "lose his temper with her" as the prosecution contended, then surely they would also have been reason enough for anyone else with whom Carol had had a relationship?

The so-called "cell confessions" raise serious doubts as to the thoroughness and professionalism of the investigation into this case. Firstly, Michael Wainwright did not come forward until after seeing a Channel Four documentary about the case. This was broadcast in 2000, and included the information that Gordon had been held on remand in 1997 at Preston. Wainwright was to claim that it was then (Preston 1997) that Gordon had "confessed." In spite of the fact that Gordon was adamant that he had never met Wainwright, and the fact that Wainwright's account included details of Gordon going "upstairs" to a bedroom, when Bluestones was a bungalow, this statement was accepted and used as evidence. There are other factors regarding this confession that should be examined – if, as claimed, Gordon had "lost it" on finding his wife in bed with another man, what happened to the other man? There were three children in the house – would they not have witnessed such a disturbance? Ironically, Wainwright's claim that Gordon had "come home" to find his wife in bed with another man is in direct contradiction to the prosecution's claim that he had never gone out that day, but had used the Blackpool story as a "cover" for his actions.

Similarly, Glen Banks changed his story as to what it was, exactly, that Gordon had confessed – on one occasion, he claimed Gordon had given his wife some "white powder" and she had fallen overboard, before changing his account to claim that Gordon had "killed his wife on the boat" before throwing her overboard. Taken together, these statements suggest that Gordon told three different stories about what had happened to his wife, including one in which he mounts a non-existent staircase to find her, and *all three* are presented to the court as "evidence" of his confession. At no point does anyone appear to ask the obvious question – if Gordon had maintained his silence for 21 years, never confiding in anyone, and continued to consistently protest his innocence from the run up to the 1998 charge being dropped to the present day, what on earth would have possessed him to confess to two complete strangers?

The VW Beetle, seen by a neighbour at the family home that day, *after* the family had gone out, has never been traced. The neighbour was adamant that the driver was not Gordon. That driver has also never been traced. Carol was seen alive at around 6pm that evening, yet no explanation of what she was doing in a service station on the M6, or where she was going, has ever been offered. These two elements of the case appear to simply have been shelved.

There was one other factor in this case which appears not to have been as thoroughly investigated as it might have been. Carol Park's sister, Christine, was murdered on April 10th 1969. Their mother was also attacked in the incident. Christine had a one year old child, Vanessa. Gordon and Carol Park adopted Vanessa after her mother's murder. The murderer was a man named John Rapson. Although sentenced to life, Rapson was released after about 7 years, on 3rd September 1976. Prior to his release, Rapson had been allowed weekend liberty from March 1976 onwards. Sometimes he stayed in Barrow, others he stayed in Liverpool. According to the judge, Justice McCombe

"it cannot be said with certainty where he was {that} weekend."

This man had murdered the sister of Carol Park, and attacked her mother, he was allowed weekend release in the area where relatives of his victims still resided, but no-one knew where he was on that particular weekend?

Further, Ivor Price, Carol's brother, worked at Vickers, the shipbuilders at the time. Rapson had been a fitter (or perhaps apprentice fitter) at Vickers when he attacked Christine and her mother. He had applied for re-appointment after his release, and stayed in hostel accommodation prior to his release. So Rapson would also, presumably, know his way around boats, and admitted that he could tie most of the knots found in the trussing of Carol's body.

The Media and the Trail

Press coverage of the "Lady in the Lake" in 1997 and 1998 was intense, sensationalist, and extremely prejudiced. The negative connotations, and thinly veiled hints in 1998 that Gordon had "got away with it" purely because of the passage of time, and the portrayal of him as cold, calculating, controlling, and violent were without substance, but there was little Gordon could do to stem the seemingly endless tide of media "interest" which was, essentially, harassment.

After charges were dropped in 1998, the press maintained their interest, printing ever more inaccurate and sensationalist articles. Gordon agreed to co-operate with the Daily Mail, in the hope that an "official" interview would put an end to the speculation and harassment. This decision was taken on advice from his solicitor at the time. When the case came to court again in 2004, a protocol was agreed between the prosecution and the defence not to raise this matter before the jury, since it was of no relevance to the case. In spite of this, the prosecution raised the matter of payment for the article, to support an argument that Gordon was prepared to "profit" from the death of his wife. Ironically, the fact that the two men claiming Gordon had "confessed" did stand to profit from giving evidence *against* Gordon, was a factor quietly passed over by the prosecution.

This was not the only example of "dirty tricks" in the trial, but it is one of significance, since it was, in reality, nothing more than an attempt by the prosecution to blacken Gordon's character. The article, and payment for it, had nothing whatsoever to do with the case, a fact which had previously been agreed by both prosecution and defence, therefore, the fact that it was raised in court at all demands investigation.

In spite of the many testimonies to Gordon's good character, and to the fact that no-one had ever witnessed him behaving in a violent manner, the prosecution continued to portray him as cold and violent, almost caricaturing him as a strict disciplinarian who beat his children. (This was in spite of the fact that his children *and* step children described him as "very loving" and "patient.")

In the 1970s, whilst Gordon and Carol were separated, Gordon was awarded custody of his children, a highly unusual move at the time. Given that the state would normally have done everything in its power to keep the children with their mother in such cases, this decision alone surely casts serious doubts on the portrayal of Gordon as violent, or in any way "unsuitable" as a parent, yet the prosecution chose to ignore this.

By the time of the 2004 trial, there was a great deal of "information" (much of it non-factual and inaccurate, or downright dishonest) in the public domain. Following the collapse of the 1998 charges, the media continued to turn out articles, postulating various theories and possibilities. What effect this might have had in terms of creating prejudice within the jury is impossible to say. But there is a clear connection between the Channel Four documentary in 2000, and the subsequent statements from Wainright and Banks.

Even prior to the 2004 trial, press coverage regarding Gordon's arrest in the January carried heavy hints and implications as to what had been done, how it had been done, and who was responsible. The Times, for example, on January 14th 2004 printed the following:

> "Cumbria police said that the arrest had come after a further six years of state-of-the-art forensic science analysis and wider enquiries. Though the suspect has not been named officially, sources close to the investigation confirmed that it was Mr Park."

In other words, they always knew it was him, they just had to get enough evidence against him. This is surely prejudicial, and bound to have an effect on the perceptions of potential jury members – rather than entering the court on the premise that the defendant must be "presumed innocent until proven guilty," they have been exposed to information that says, 'this man has been guilty for a very long time, and now we have the evidence to prove it.'

In November 2004, as the trial began, the Times printed:

> "The jury was told that the police investigation had never closed and fresh evidence had emerged."

Just what that "fresh evidence" was, is not stated clearly, although the article makes reference to Joan Young's testimony, and then, later, to the "cell confessions." From other documentation, it is clear that the prosecution *thought* it had new evidence concerning the knots, but that this was discredited, and, as a result, not brought before the jury.

Although the case against him was that Gordon Park killed his wife in the family home, trussed her body, and dumped it in Coniston Water, no explanation is offered as to exactly how this sequence of events was achieved. Aside from the trip to Blackpool, there has never been any suggestion that the children were away from the family home. Therefore, Gordon Park would have had to have beaten his wife to death with the three children in the house, but without alerting any of them to the event. He would also have had to truss the body, and clean up all traces of evidence from wherever he had beaten her, and from himself. The body would then have to be secreted into the some sort of vehicle, in order to transport it to the boat. It would then have to be taken from the vehicle onto the boat, without raising any suspicion. If, as Gordon maintains, he did, in fact, sell his own boat in June that year, then he would have had to risk borrowing a boat for the sole purpose of disposing of his wife's body. If it was his own boat, then he left himself only a very short time to ensure all traces of evidence were removed from the boat, after having "stored" the body, apparently in his own garage, for almost a fortnight.

Throughout the trial, with the focus on the brutality of Carol's murder, and the character assassination of Gordon Park, a hugely disproportionate amount of attention was given to the insignificant, the irrelevant, and the speculative, with the resultant lack of attention given to the logical and factual difficulties.

Following Gordon's conviction, a national newspaper alleged that Gordon and a police commander had been freemasons. The implication was that the missing files from the 1976 enquiry had been deliberately removed or destroyed. Whilst portraying yet another negative possibility regarding Gordon (i.e., that he somehow used his "contacts" to help cover up what he had "done") this article unwittingly raises the suggestion that police corruption "helped" Gordon evade justice for many years! Gordon is not, and has never been, a freemason, yet this is another piece of misinformation which will be absorbed into the general public's perceptions. Given the nature of the case, and the possibility of future appeal, the role of the press continues to damage and undermine the course of proper justice.

<u>Summary</u>

In this third example, close examination of the case, and of the evidence, leads us to some disturbing conclusions. Gordon Park was not proven guilty "beyond reasonable doubt," since a great deal of reasonable doubt remains. There were several factors which could have had "perfectly plausible, alternative explanations", and there were several "facts" which were clearly in dispute.

There was never any confirmed sighting of Gordon Park which related him to the murder of his wife. He was not seen with her on the day of her disappearance, he was never identified as having removed or transported a large, heavy package, either into his car, from his car, or onto a boat. The one "sighting" presented to the court was from someone who had not come forward in 1976, or in 1998, but had come forward *after* Gordon's arrest in 2004. This lady's testimony was sketchy, to say the least, and the description of the man could have fitted many, many people. At the same time, Carol Park was seen that day, on the driveway of her home. Another witness confirms that the family had gone out that day, and reported the "odd" circumstance of a VW Beetle at the house for 20 minutes, whose driver was not Gordon Park. As a result, we are led to conclude that the family had gone out, but Mrs Park had not.

Gordon was not, therefore, convicted on the strength of eyewitness testimony. Indeed, the eyewitness testimonies appear to be supportive of Gordon's story.

There was no DNA or forensic evidence linking Gordon to the crime. In spite of extensive tests, no evidence was ever found in the family home that Mrs Park had died there. The rock and the piece of slate, allegedly recovered by divers close to the body, could not be conclusively linked, forensically, with the family home. The prosecution expert could state only that it was "more probable" that the rock had come from Bluestones than Coniston. The defence expert appeared to support this finding, but in a way which supported Gordon Park, and implicated the police – he claimed that the rock did not have any evidence to support the contention that it had been submersed in water for such a long time, raising the obvious question of whether the rock had ever been in the water at all, and leaving an unspoken, but obvious implication. The clothes found on the lakebed were not found to have belonged to Carol Park. No forensic or DNA evidence was ever recovered from any car or boat. An ice axe belonging to Gordon Park produced no trace evidence whatsoever.

He was not, therefore, convicted on the strength of physical, forensic or DNA evidence.

The prosecution portrayed Gordon as a cold, calculating man with a temper, and the tendency to resort to violence. He was accused of losing his temper in a fit of jealousy, and strangling his wife before battering her about the face with various implements.

There was absolutely *no* evidence to support these accusations. Several witnesses reported quite the opposite. Not a single witness could be produced who would testify to ever having seen Gordon Park behave in a violent manner. Records from a doctor in 1975, the year before Carol Park went missing, report that she told that doctor that Gordon had never used violence or threats against her – in this instance, the victim herself speaks *for* the defendant from beyond the grave.

Carol Park had had several affairs with other men – this was not disputed in court. Gordon Park always took her back.

He was not, therefore, convicted on the basis of previous behaviour proving him to be likely to resort the type of behaviour involved in the accusations against him.

The VW Beetle and its driver have never been traced and identified. Mrs Park's appearance at a service station on the M6 has never been explained. There had been other men in Carol Park's life – as late as 1975, she had been living with another man, and Gordon Park had been awarded custody of the children. There is the unanswered question of where John Rapson was that weekend.

Gordon was not, therefore, convicted because of the absence or elimination of other possible suspects.

The knots used to truss Carol's body were not "specialist" as the prosecution had claimed, but were, in fact, quite common. Also, the fact that there were significant similarities *and* significant differences between the knots on the body and the knots on Gordon's property meant that no conclusion of any worth could be drawn from this evidence.

Therefore, the link between Gordon and knots was not established. He was not, then, convicted on the grounds of association with specialist knowledge.

The lead piping used to weigh down the body did not come from the family home. Paint marks on the lead piping did not match paint from the family home. Hammer marks on the lead piping "could have come from any sharp edged, flat surfaced hammer," and Gordon's hammer had a bevelled edge, even when it was new!

Therefore, Gordon was not convicted by association with the lead piping found with the body.

The rock, alleged to have been found with some clothing (which was not proven to belong to Carol), some 70 metres from the body, may have come from Bluestones. However, the diver accredited with bringing the rock to the surface has no recollection of doing so, and claims he would *not* have done so. Reference to the rock does not appear in police records until several days later, amidst inconsistent and shoddy recording procedures, and at least one expert cast serious doubt as to whether this rock had ever even been in the water at all, given the absence of markings on its surface.

The most that can be concluded is that the rock may have come from Bluestones. How it came to be included with the "lakebed evidence" is not clear - that it was claimed to have been found with clothing *not* found to have belonged to Carol makes its significance to the case minimal. It certainly does not 'prove' anything of note.

Therefore, Gordon was not convicted by association with the rock.

The so-called "cell confessions" relied on extremely dubious testimony from two men who stood to gain financially by giving evidence against Gordon. Regardless of the basis for their testimony (which in itself should have raised reasonable doubt – Wainwright had seen a documentary giving details of the case, Banks was proven to be highly "suggestible" and to have been encouraged by a social worker and police officer on certain points), their testimonies did not support the allegations against Gordon Park.

Wainwright claimed Gordon "confessed" he had gone upstairs to find his wife in bed with another man. This is impossible, since the Parks lived in a bungalow.

Also, Gordon had the three children with him that day – if Wainwright's claim that Gordon had "lost it" on finding his wife in bed with another man had any truth in it, the children would have witnessed such a disturbance.

Banks first claimed Gordon had "confessed" to giving his wife some "white powder" after which she fell overboard, then changed his story to claim the confession had been that Gordon killed his wife on the boat. Until that point, there had never been any suggestion that Carol Park was murdered on a boat, Gordon's or anyone else's.

Therefore, he was not convicted on the grounds of confessions he is claimed to have made.

The question remains, then, on what basis *was* Gordon Park convicted? Reasonable doubt exists as to the reliability of the "cell confessions" as reported by Wainwright and Banks. Reasonable doubt exists regarding the rock, and the entire police operation involved in recording evidence recovered from the lakebed. Reasonable doubt exists even regarding the prosecution's main contention, namely that Gordon had not gone to Blackpool that day, but had, instead stayed at home and murdered his wife in the family home.

From the evidence presented, Gordon Park has not been proven guilty of anything, far less proven guilty "beyond reasonable doubt."

- As we have done with each case highlighted so far, we will examine the case of Gordon Park against the imaginary Twelve Points for a new justice system raised in the introduction to this book:
- Gordon Park was convicted on purely circumstantial evidence
- Reasonable doubt was glaringly obvious on several fronts
- There was no DNA or forensic evidence linking Gordon Park to the crime
- Gordon was not identified at or near the scene of the crime (partly because no "scene of crime" or, indeed, time of crime, was ever ascertained.)
- There were suggestions of at least one other person within the area who may be considered a suspect (although we cannot say that this person was "at or near the scene of the crime" for the reasons given above).
- There was clear over-reliance on expert testimony, to the detriment of Gordon Park.
- There were serious questions about the suggested timescale of the murder and disposal of the body, for Gordon Park to have been the perpetrator.

- Character assassination constituted a strong part of the prosecution's case.
- There was very definite evidence of forensic experts selectively interpreting evidence to the prosecution's own ends.
- Persons with a vested interest in seeing Gordon Park convicted (ie, reward money) gave crucial evidence against him.
- Gordon Park was a man of previously good character with no psychological conditions or previous convictions.
- In this case, therefore, all twelve points are present.

Other similarities which emerge between the cases of Gordon Park, Derek Christian and John Taft are as follows:

Like the others, Gordon was accused of behaviour which he had never previously displayed, and for which no evidence could be found – indeed, all of the witnesses produced testified *to the contrary*. As with John Taft, the passage of time was used to imply that both men would have "got away with murder," but for the tenacity of police or new scientific developments. Also, in both of these cases, the claim that prosecutors had uncovered "new evidence" proved to be inaccurate, yet the cases were allowed to proceed anyway. The police investigation in all three cases is flawed – all three feature missing police documents or records, and confusion over who was responsible for particular police procedures. The impact of these failures in police investigatory procedures cannot be over emphasised – in every case, they relate to critical pieces of evidence – unidentified fibres in the body bag with Mrs Wilson, *original* statements from John Taft, taken some 16 years earlier, and documents pertaining to the time of death, which is so crucial to ascertaining John's innocence, and the exact source of the rock used to attempt to create a link between Gordon Park's home, and the place where his wife's body was found.

With each new case, the number of similarities increases. How can it be that so many cases have so many similar factors going wrong?

- The issues which cause most concern in the case of Gordon Park are:
- Reasonable doubt is established
- There was no evidence linking Gordon Park to the murder of Carol Park
- "Expert testimony" was flawed, incorrect, extremely detailed and confusing.
- The judge misled the jury (by suggesting in his summing up that a wooden implement handle had been found, when in fact it was a naturally growing twig)

- Police files were inconsistent and poorly recorded.
- Police files from 1976 were lost.
- The police investigation was flawed, in that other possible suspects were not pursued in the same manner as Gordon Park
- The existence of the rock, and how it came to be amongst exhibits from the lakebed have not been properly explained.
- Police handling of the "confessions" testimonies is questionable.
- Certain evidence was not made available to the jury
- Massive media coverage may have prejudiced the jury
- The prosecution relied on character assassination, (portraying Gordon as violent, controlling etc) without producing a shred of evidence to back their claims.

An important Development

Just as this book goes to press, news has been released that the Independent Police Complaints Commission (IPCC) has upheld an appeal by Gordon Park regarding the non-recording of a complaint against Cumbria Constabulary.

The complaint consisted of the following:
1. Police coaching of vulnerable witnesses
2. The manner in which evidence was processed, lost, and fabricated
3. A decision to mislead the jury by taking them on a circuitous route (in order to make them think that only someone with extensive local knowledge of the area could have been the murderer, and
4. Then lying under oath with regard to this decision.

Cumbria Police had a duty to record this complaint (an action which would have automatically resulted in the police being investigated), but did not do so.

The IPCC upheld the complaint about non recording, then allowed the police to *dispense* with an investigation on the basis of a twelve month time limit.

Remember, this was a 21 year old crime, and thereafter, it took police seven years to convict Gordon Park, yet investigation into clearly flawed police procedures is waived on the grounds that more than twelve months have elapsed!

Gordon Park was given just *seven days* to respond to the police's application for dispensation.

References:

"*Rocks and a hard place,*" *Private Eye, 2006*
BBC News, Cumbria, Friday January 28th 2005
BBC News, Cumbria, Thursday January 13th and Monday January17[th] 2005
Times Online, January 14th 2004
Times Online, November 26th 2004
Transcript: Summing Up. Before; The Honourable Mr Justice McCombe, Regina – V- Gordon Park, 26/01/05.
Transcript: Jury Deliberation. Before; The Honourable Mr Justice McCombe, Regina –V- Gordon Park, 28/01/05.

Chapter Five

The Case of Simon Hall

ON THE morning of December 16th 2001, Joan Albert, 79, was found dead in her home. She had suffered multiple stab wounds, and a small window to the rear of her house had been broken. All other windows and doors to the house were locked, indicating that her attacker had entered and left through the broken window. Neighbours reported hearing loud noises at approximately 2am, some describing these as "crashing" noises. Although the police investigation proceeded on the basis that this was a burglary gone wrong, nothing was ever found to be missing from Mrs Albert's home. In recent months prior to the murder, Mrs Albert had been troubled by youths knocking on her door and creating a nuisance.

Two footprints were found in the mud outside the broken window, and two fingerprints were found inside the house – one on the kitchen door at shoulder height, another on the push plate of a door upstairs. Further forensic investigation uncovered a pubic hair found in Mrs Albert's upstairs bathroom, and some clothing fibres. The pubic hair, however, was eliminated when it emerged that it had come from one of the police officers investigating the case.

The investigation into the fingerprints, footprints and fibres, therefore, would appear to be the grounds on which the investigation would continue.

However, this is not quite as straightforward as it first appears. The Home Office pathologist (whose role in other cases would later be severely criticised by his own peers) failed to attend the scene of crime, leaving the post mortem to take place more than 10 hours *after* the discovery of the body – as a result, the chances of essential details being recovered were severely diminished, and it was not possible to estimate the time of death. Because of this one factor (the failure of the pathologist to attend), from the very beginning, any subsequent trial could not be held on the basis of "all the evidence," since some of it had already, unnecessarily, been lost.

What *was* ascertained was that the victim had not only been stabbed to death, her attacker had inflicted other wounds, after the point of death, over a period estimated to be up to 30 minutes.

Simon Hall was convicted of her murder in 2003, and jailed for life.

Identification and witnesses

There were no witnesses whatsoever placing Simon Hall at or near the scene. Several witnesses claimed to have heard loud "crashing" noises at approximately 2am, although the prosecution would later claim that Mrs Albert was murdered at around 6am. Simon Hall had substantiated alibi for the whole of the evening of December 15th, and into the early hours of December 16th. He was with a friend, Gareth Hampson in a public house (the Old Rep) from around 8pm. From there, they drove to the Woolpack, leaving at around 10.30pm, this verified by a witness, Scott Doughty, with whom Simon left his car keys to be kept behind the bar. He and Gareth headed back into town on foot, arriving back at the Old Rep at around 10.55pm. He then left with a group of people for the Liquid Nightclub. Several other witnesses confirm Simon's whereabouts up to some time between 5 and 6am, when Simon and Jamie Barker, another friend, returned to the Woolpack to retrieve Simon's car, waking Scott Doughty by throwing pebbles at his window.

Simon's car had been developing some problems – a noisy exhaust and trouble with headlights. Angela Barker, Jamie Barker's mother, was woken by a "throaty exhaust" at around 5.30am – Jamie was being dropped off. Jamie, himself, thought he had been dropped off between 5.45am and 6am. Simon then drove himself home to his parents' house. His mother Lynne, recalled the time as being about 6.15am. Simon would tell police later that the time was 6.28am – apparently a very precise memory, but he said he had glanced at the clock on the microwave and registered that time. The discrepancy between the times given by Jamie Barker and his mother, and Simon and his mother mean that there is one hour during which he does not have a solid alibi – namely 5.30am – 6.30am.

Timing

It is this hour which the prosecution presented to the court as the "window of opportunity" for Simon to have committed the murder. This flies in the face of much of the other evidence. Firstly, no time of death was established by the pathologist, therefore, the "window of opportunity" was, in fact, any time from when Mrs Albert was last known to be alive (the previous evening around 7pm) and the finding of her body. Even assuming the time of death could be pinpointed to "around 6am," as the prosecution claimed, it now has to be accepted that Simon dropped his friend at 5.30am, drove (drunkenly) 7 miles to Mrs

Albert's home, parked his car somewhere (no theory has ever been presented as to where he left the car, and the car has never been identified within the vicinity of the crime scene), made his way through two fenced gardens, broke the window, climbed in, murdered Mrs Albert, then hung around for 30 minutes to inflict further injuries after death, climbed back out of the window, back through the two fenced gardens, made his way back to the car, and drove to his parents home, behaving perfectly normally, and continuing to do so throughout the remainder of the day. If Mrs Albert died at 6am, it follows that Simon was still inflicting the after death injuries at 6.30am, if he was the killer. Therefore, he could not have been at home.

The judge, in summing up, was to direct the jury that they should consider the loud, crashing noises reported by neighbours as possibly coming from "clumsy cats," even though this suggestion was not raised during the trial.

Yet a further piece of evidence, with regard to timing, was initially found by Simon's solicitors in an unused evidence file - the police had simply never mentioned it to the defence team. It was the Gastroenterologist report, and it showed that the content in the stomach of the victim was still recognisable. This is crucial to the timing theory on several counts. According to the gastroenterologist, the following are accepted as fact:

1. Food digestion for an average adult, having a normal digestive system (which Mrs Albert was described as having) is usually 2 – 5 hours for a full meal.
2. Food digestion for an average adult, having a normal digestive system (which Mrs Albert was described as having) is usually 3 hours or less for a snack.

It was known that Mrs Albert had eaten a meal between 6pm and 7pm, as she had spoken to others about it – saying in particular that she had not liked it. This meal, therefore, would have been fully digested by midnight, at the latest. However, Mrs Albert was in the habit of consuming a "midnight snack" – her dog was old and sick, and she regularly had to let the dog out at around midnight, when she would have this snack. Again, this snack would have been fully digested by 3am, at the latest. This leaves a gaping hole in the 5.30 – 6.30 "window of opportunity" theory.

Quite simply, for the stomach content to have been recognisable at post mortem examination, either Mrs Albert was murdered prior to midnight (using the known fact that she had eaten by 7pm) or prior to 3am (using the suggestion that she had consumed a "midnight snack").

Photographs of Mrs Albert's kitchen showed dirty plates and implements which appear to indicate that a snack had, indeed, been prepared sometime during the evening of the murder. Note, also, that this timescale, between midnight and 3am, covers the time neighbours reported the "loud crashing noises" at around 2am.

Forensic and other physical evidence

The two footprints found in the mud outside the broken window did not match Simon's footwear. These footprints have never been matched to any other person, and it is unclear as to how much effort was made to find the owner of the shoes which created these prints.

The break in the window was, it its widest point, just 14 inches wide. Simon is 6'1" tall. There were never any traces of glass found on Simon, or in his car, nor were there any traces of blood or other forensic data from Simon found on the window. Further, no glass or paint fragments from the window were ever found either at the site of the "fibres," upon which the prosecution would so heavily rely, or, indeed, *amongst* those fibres. It bears further scrutiny that someone of Simon's size and build, having consumed a large amount of alcohol, would be able to get through such a small opening (twice), without cutting or scratching himself, without catching any of his clothing, and without further damaging the window. The broken window was never reconstructed in an effort to ascertain whether it was even possible for Simon to have fitted through the gap in the first place.

The two sets of fingerprints found inside Mrs Albert's home did not belong to Simon Hall. Again, it is unclear just how much effort was expended in attempts to find out to whom those fingerprints belonged.

In spite of police claims that they were trying to eliminate every possible suspect, they never took fingerprints from Simon's brother Shaun (raising the question, where else might they have had opportunity to take fingerprints, but failed to do so?) Also, whilst proclaiming a "foolproof" system regarding forensic evidence, the police left four bags of forensic evidence at Shaun's flat. These omissions and mistakes raise serious questions as to the thoroughness and professionalism of the investigation, and the safety of any findings as a result of that investigation.

Lynne Hall, Simon's mother, was taken to the victim's house by two officers on January 8th to check whether anything was missing. (Mrs Hall was a friend of Mrs Albert, and often helped the older lady out). Neither Mrs Hall nor the police officers were wearing protective clothing (although full forensic examination of the house had not yet been carried out), but things were touched, and broken glass trodden in. Therefore, the house and its contents are likely to have been contaminated by Mrs Hall, and the officers.

No DNA linking Simon to the crime scene or the victim has ever been produced.

The Fibre evidence

A quantity of black flock fibres, commonly used in the production of velvet or velour clothing, along with a smaller quantity of green polyester fibres were found on Joan Albert's body, along the route the killer took through the gardens, and on a fence post at the bottom of the garden.

"Microscopically indistinguishable" fibres were found on the floor of Simon's bedroom wardrobe at his parent's house, some at his house in Ipswich, and some in the two cars to which he had access.

Simon stated that he had not been wearing anything black velvet or green that evening (in fact, that he had never owned black velvet or velour trousers, as alleged by the prosecution). Not one witness could be produced to testify that Simon had worn such trousers.

Although fibres were recovered that were "indistinguishable" from places common to Joan Albert and Simon Hall, no source garment was ever found. Further, Lynne Hall had access to Joan Albert's home, Simon's cars, and her own home (obviously). According to Robert Falconer, a widely acknowledged fibres expert, giving evidence in another case,

> "The domestic environment is likely to account for the majority of fibres found on clothing. In an ideal world, we need to check that fibres did not come from a domestic source."

In other words, the fibres found at the scene of Mrs Albert's murder could have a perfectly innocent explanation, in that Lynne Hall may have transferred fibres between the various locations.

Further, indistinguishable fibres from those found at the murder scene were found in two other houses, but never followed up.

Mr Falconer, and another fibres expert, Alison Duberry, have both pointed out in other cases, that "microscopically indistinguishable" does not mean "the same." Mr Falconer is on record as saying

> "No single fibre, or group of fibres, can be attributed to a garment to the exclusion of all others. Garments are not unique,"

and

> "Fibre testing is not an exact science, it is not comparable, in this regard, to DNA testing or blood samples. The findings cannot

produce an unequivocal link between Mr C's clothing and those fibres found on the victim's clothing."

This is the third case in which this highly dubious "fibre evidence" has been used to great effect in the prosecution case, and yet, by the admission of the experts themselves, it proves *nothing*, other than that hundreds and thousands of garments shed similar fibres. In the case of Simon Hall, for example, the prosecution focused on just one chain of supply for the black flock fabric, in spite of the fact that there were undoubtedly many more. Yet that single chain alone produced some 30,000 garments.

Simon was accused of buying a garment used at the scene of the murder from a local Tesco store on the morning of the murder. This raises two separate issues – firstly, there is no CCTV footage that shows Simon even entered the store that day. He is on film withdrawing money from the cash dispenser, but there is simply no evidence that he bought anything, clothing or otherwise. Secondly, if "microscopically indistinguishable" fibres found at the scene are adjudged to have come from an article readily available in a local Tesco store, does it not follow that those fibres could have come from *any* such garment sold from that store? Were any questions ever asked as to how many of the alleged garments were sold from that store, or others in the vicinity? It seems there is no effort to make it clear to juries that "microscopically indistinguishable" can, and does, sit quite comfortably alongside "extremely common." As was proven in the Derek Christian case, microscopically indistinguishable fibres (from those found on the victim) were found from clothing belonging to two officers involved in the case, and from garments bought, brand new, for the purposes of the enquiry.

The Judge, Prosecution and Police

The police had kept quiet about the gastroenterologist report, and had also suppressed statements from neighbours testifying to loud noises in the direction of Mrs Albert's home at 2am. This left the way clear for the prosecution to place heavy emphasis on the "window of opportunity" being that time in which Simon Hall had no alibi. Of course, the facts simply do not back up this assertion, so we have some sort of circular reasoning taking effect – in order to fit the window of opportunity to the time where Simon has no alibi, we need to remove or play down anything which points away from this timeframe. Even the judge attempted to play down the significance of witness statements of "loud, crashing noises" (which police had previously tried to "lose" in an unused evidence file) by suggesting that the noise may have been made by "clumsy cats." Whilst this may, indeed have been the case *in the absence of other evidence,* to attempt to dismiss it as such in these circumstances could be seen as an attempt either to mislead, or to sway the jury.

The alleged murder weapon had nothing whatsoever to link it with the crime, or with Simon Hall, in spite of the fact that the victim had been stabbed "repeatedly." Police officers also allegedly advised a member of the public to dispose of a knife found in the vicinity of the crime scene because detectives were too busy following up other leads.

Also, there is the factor of the pubic hair, found in Mrs Albert's bathroom. After a great deal of investigation, it was to emerge that this belonged to one of the investigating officers. Not only was the crime scene contaminated by officers failing to ensure protective clothing was worn by themselves, and by those they took to the scene, it was clearly contaminated in other ways as well. How sure can anyone be, given the nature of "fibre evidence," that any or all of those fibres did not come from investigating officers, or those whom they allowed to enter the crime scene? Indeed, was any clothing belonging to members of the investigating team ever tested for such an eventuality?

It is interesting to note the comments of forensics expert, Peter Bull, of Oxford University on May 19th 2005. He told BBC news that he was "very surprised" that the fibres did not appear to include any glass particles from the broken window.

> "I am very surprised that the very distinctive type of glass (from the broken window) was not found anywhere else. If there was no attempt to clean up the fibres, there would have been glass there as well" and

> "Glass should have been associated with (the fibres)", he said.

This raises yet another question. If, as is most probable, the person who came through that broken window would have had glass particles on them, and there was no trace of glass in the fibres, is it not reasonable to conclude that the fibres may have come from someone who was *not* the murderer? Given the poor management of the scene of crime, it is entirely possible those fibres came from a member of the investigating team, especially in view of the absence of glass fibres which would have been associated with the murderer.

DS Roy Lambert, in court, was forced to admit that a bag containing forensic evidence was "wrongly labeled," and that this never should have happened - just one more flaw in the police investigation.

On January 16th 2002, a month after the murder, Suffolk Police released CCTV footage of Mrs Albert shopping the day before she died. DS Roy Lambert is quoted as saying;

– "We have decided to release this footage in the hope....{that it} may jog the memory of those people who saw something unusual that night, but have yet to contact us..."

– Note the wording – "that night." Not "in the early hours of the morning," – not even "that morning." At this stage, at least, police seem quite certain Mrs Albert was murdered *the night before*, and not, as will later be claimed, around 6am the following morning.

– Questions were raised as to the methods used by police when questioning potential witnesses, and dealing with persons involved in the enquiry. Some potential witnesses claim that confidential information regarding Simon Hall and details of the case were disclosed to them which could have influenced their statements and opinions. When police tried to contact Mrs Hall's brother at his place of work, on being told he was not available, information was passed to his colleagues regarding the case. This was *prior* to Simon's arrest, and must surely shed considerable doubt as to the fairness of his treatment and subsequent trial? Further, there appears to be no suggestion of the officer involved being disciplined in any way.

Mrs Hall was, of course, a critical witness in Simon's defence. It would be her testimony which placed Simon back in his own house by 6.30am at the latest. Yet the prosecution, in a common move, attempted to discredit Mrs Hall, calling her honesty into question over circumstances which had perfectly innocent explanations. In an attempt to help the investigation, Mrs Hall recollected a jacket which had been borrowed by a work colleague which may have been made from the same fibre as those "central" to the prosecution case. When this garment was produced in court, it emerged that it was made from the "wrong" fabric; the prosecution used this to accuse her of lying, and trying to mislead the court. Also, the prosecution accused Mrs Hall of being dishonest about the fact that she had once run a clothing business, because she "did not tell the police about it earlier," completely missing the point that she had not, in fact, been asked about it earlier! It is a well used ploy in these circumstances to introduce doubt as to a key witness's honesty – the implication being, if this person has lied about one thing, they must be lying about everything else.

–The failure of the Home Office Pathologist to attend the scene of crime is surely a major dereliction of duty? This pathologist (Michael Heath) would later come to public attention when the conviction of Steven Puaca was overturned on the grounds that there were serious flaws in Mr Heath's evidence. Quashing the conviction against Mr Puaca, on November 10th 2005, Lord Justice Hooper said:

"We confess to a certain surprise that the deceased could have been suffocated in this way, but that was the evidence which Dr Heath gave."

This surely goes some way to highlighting just how strong dependence on "expert" testimony is. If it is so for the judge himself, then how much moreso for members of the jury?

Three of his own colleagues criticised Dr Heath for his role in the Simon Hall case, for apparently forgetting his role as an "objective expert." It was, they said, "wholly wrong" of him to carry out a post-mortem examination for the police or coroner, but to then leave it to the defence to carry out a post mortem to set out the contrary arguments. This statement appears to be suggesting that Dr Heath's evidence in the Simon Hall case was biased towards the police investigation, with no attention given to other possibilities.

Can this case, given this information, honestly be seen to have been fair, just, or impartial?

During the summing up, the judge, Judge Rafferty, said:

"What is Simon Hall's defence? It is alibi; he says he was not at the scene of the crime when it was committed."

There are several points to be raised regarding this statement. Simon Hall's defence was *not* only alibi. Simon Hall's defence was that the footprints found outside the window did not belong to him, the fingerprints inside Mrs Albert's home did not belong to him, Mrs Albert was almost definitely killed sometime prior to 3am, when Simon *did* have an alibi, the fibres found at the scene could have implicated hundreds, and perhaps thousands of other people, and, importantly, the Crown had failed to establish a time of death, so how could the judge feasibly claim that Simon's defence was that he was not at the scene of the crime "when it was committed."

The judge also questioned the honesty of Lynne Hall. It is an accepted fact that both acceptance of information from "authority figures" and "primacy and recency affects" means that non-experts, or laymen and women (i.e. the jury) are likely to give greater weight to the judge's words, and especially those used during the summing up, since they will be the last words the jury will hear prior to retiring to consider their verdict. The judge, in this case, appears, quite blatantly, to have ignored much of the factual evidence and, as a result, to have misled the jury.

Motive, speculation, and character assassination

The prosecution alleged that Simon was in debt. Because of his mother's association with Mrs Albert, they alleged that Simon had formed the opinion that Mrs Albert was wealthy, and had decided to burgle her home to alleviate his financial position, but, realising Mrs Albert would recognise him, he had to murder her.

There was nothing in Simon's history to suggest such actions. His debt situation was not pressing – he had just been accepted for a loan to buy a car.

The motivation proposed by the prosecution suggests a pre-meditated series of events. This being the case, it would seem more than a little strange that this pre-meditated plan should then be carried out after a night out during which large quantities of alcohol had been consumed, at a time when people were beginning to wake up and go about their day's business (increasing the chances of being seen, identified, or caught). It is stranger still when one realises that Lynne Hall had a spare key to Mrs Albert's house. Why risk climbing over fences, traveling through gardens, breaking windows and the like, all of which are likely to attract attention, when he could simply have let himself in at a convenient time, and carried out the burglary? Rather bizarrely, nothing was taken from the house, so the suggestion of murdering Mrs Albert "because she would recognise him" becomes a "burglary gone wrong." If it had always been his intention to murder Mrs Albert, why did he not complete his primary motive for being in the house, i.e. to carry out a burglary?

Not only was the prosecution's case built almost entirely around a "window of opportunity" which the evidence proved was highly unlikely to have been the case, during the summing up, the jury were effectively directed to infer that the murder took place during this "window of opportunity," simply because Simon could not account for his whereabouts at that time, and despite the evidence which pointed to the murder having taken place much earlier.

The correct definition of "indistinguishable" as meaning "similar to" was not given. In summing up, the judge surmised that it meant "identical." The possible ramifications of this error are clear to see – "similar" fibres prove not a great deal, but "identical" fibres can mean only one thing – that they came from the garment(s) to which the prosecution referred. (This, even though no source garments were ever produced in court.)

Summary

On what grounds, then, was Simon Hall found guilty, beyond reasonable doubt? What are the facts, and where is the evidence?

Two footprints found outside the broken window were proven not to be his. Yet this window was the only means of entry and exit. If someone else left prints there, it would appear to follow that Simon, had he been there, would have done so too.

Two sets of fingerprints inside the house did not belong to Simon, and have never been identified. The existence of unidentified fingerprints *must* imply reasonable doubt, as an unidentified someone has been in the house.

There is no DNA or other forensic evidence linking Simon to the scene of crime or to the victim, or vice versa.

Neither Simon nor his car were ever identified by any person as having been at, or near the scene of crime, and there were no reports of a "noisy exhaust" in the area, in spite of the prosecution's contention that he drove to the area, parked his car in some unspecified place, then climbed over fences and through gardens to Mrs Albert's house.

The police investigation has been proven to have been flawed – a pubic hair belonging to an officer was found at the scene, persons not wearing protective clothing were allowed into the crime scene, and allowed to touch things, and forensic evidence was left unattended and wrongly labeled.

No attempt was ever made to reconstruct the scene, in order to ascertain whether it was even possible for someone of Simon's size and build to get through the window.

The police attempted to "hide" evidence which appeared to point to a time of death much earlier than that claimed by the prosecution, and other evidence which supported this earlier time. The judge would later encourage the jury to disregard this evidence in favour of the "window of opportunity" between 5.30 and 6.30. There is *no* evidence whatsoever to support the notion that Mrs Albert was killed at around 6am.

The fibre evidence proves only that fibres similar to some found in Simon's parents' house, some found in his Ipswich house, both cars belonging to him, two other houses, and garments from a local Tesco store, were found on Mrs Albert's body. There is no evidence which proves that these fibres could have come only from garments worn by Simon. No garments belonging to Simon exhibited similar fibres.

Further, no glass or paint fragments from the broken window were ever found on Simon's clothing, in his car, or, importantly, at the site of, or amongst, the clothing fibres found on Mrs Albert's body. This could further suggest that the fibres did not come from the murderer at all.

The timescale, as suggested by the prosecution, makes it impossible for Simon to have been the attacker. The prosecution states that Mrs Albert was murdered at about 6am, and the pathologist report states further injuries were inflicted after death, up to thirty minutes later, but Simon was already in his parents' home by 6.30am at the latest (his mother's testimony puts him there at 6.15am). He could not have still been inflicting further injuries to Mrs Albert, and have been in his mother's house at the same time. There has never been any suggestion of more than one attacker.

Although the jury is required to decide upon a defendant's innocence or guilt, this decision is bound by specific parameters. Firstly, the decision is to be made based only on evidence as presented in court, during the course of the trial. It is for this reason that juries are often directed, by the judge, to put out of their minds anything they may have seen, heard or read outwith the court. Secondly, the judge is duty bound to warn jurors that if any one of them feels that there is any dispute concerning the facts, or that an alternative, perfectly plausible explanation exists, they must find for the defendant.

Analysis of these factors in the case of Simon Hall reveals some interesting possibilities:

The evidence, as presented in court, shows that the footprints and fingerprints at the murder scene do not belong to Simon, and there is no evidence, physical, forensic or eyewitness, to connect him with the crime. Simon cannot account for his whereabouts between 5.30 and 6.30am that morning. The murder most probably occurred sometime prior to 3am. Fibres common to several sources, and incapable of identifying any single, unique garment, were found at the scene of the crime. Glass fragments from the broken window were not found amongst, or in the vicinity of, these fibres.

As such, there is *no* evidence presented in court which connects Simon Hall with the murder, the murder scene, or the victim.

Dispute concerning the "facts" (as opposed to assertion, supposition, innuendo and conjecture) can only arise with regard to the timing of the murder, since the pathologist, through his own neglect, was unable to establish time of death. The gastroenterologist, however, was somewhat more thorough, and provides a plausible theory for time of death, based on accepted data regarding digestion times. This time of death is in direct opposition to the prosecution's presumed time of death, for which no evidence is offered.

Examination of the Simon Hall case against the imaginary Twelve Points for a new justice system reveals a depressingly familiar story:

- Simon Hall was convicted on purely circumstantial evidence.
- Reasonable doubt is more than glaringly obvious.
- There was no DNA or forensic evidence linking Simon Hall to the crime, or to the victim.
- Simon was not identified at or near the scene of the crime.
- Witnesses testified to "loud crashing noises" coming from the vicinity of the victim's home at a time when Simon had a substantiated alibi.
- There was clear over-reliance on "expert testimony" to the detriment of Simon Hall.
- There were serious questions about the ability of Simon to have carried out the crime within the timescale suggested.
- Clothing constituted a strong part of the prosecution's case.
- Character assassination constituted a strong part of the prosecution's case.
- There was evidence of forensic experts selectively interpreting evidence to the prosecution's own ends.

In this case, therefore, ten of the twelve points apply. Simon Hall did have one minor conviction in his early teens, but had otherwise been of good character, with no psychological conditions or other convictions.

Comparison with the other cases highlighted so far reveals an increasing number of similarities:

Unidentified footprints at the scene, similar to the Derek Christian case, and unidentified fingerprints, similar to the John Taft case. The devastating use of the, by now, completely discredited "fibre evidence" common to both John Taft and Derek Christian, and, like John Taft, Simon is required to be in two places at once.

Flaws in the police investigation are alarmingly similar – wrongly labeled evidence (Gordon Park), evidence contaminated (Gordon Park,) crime scene contaminated (Derek Christian), evidence lost, manipulated, or altered (Derek Christian, John Taft, Gordon Park).

The judge in this case, similar to John Taft's case, appears to lead the jury towards a particular possibility, even though that possibility had not been raised during the course of the trial.

As with all three previous cases, Simon is accused of suddenly behaving in a manner which is completely out of character, and for which no evidence can be produced of previous, similar behaviour. As with Derek Christian, we are also asked to believe that within literally moments of such completely uncharacteristic behaviour, Simon returned immediately to his "normal self."

By this stage, it is clear that this is not a case of random, chance mistakes and errors – the emerging pattern is becoming both clear and strong.

The most worrying issues raised by the Simon Hall Case:

- Reasonable doubt is established
- There is no concrete evidence
- The prosecution relies on conjecture and innuendo
- "Expert testimony" is misleading and contradictory
- Definition of the term "facts" which the jury may find to be in dispute is not made clearly.
- The judge fails to properly direct the jury, and at times appears to lead them in the direction of the prosecution argument
- The judge fails to comprehend vital technical data
- Police files were suppressed or hidden
- The police investigation was severely flawed to the point of negligence
- Police interview techniques included releasing confidential information to potential witnesses, and to persons unrelated to the case
- Police failed to follow up other leads
- The jury appears to have ignored "the facts"
- Certain evidence was not made available to the jury
- Character assassination of vital defence witnesses forms a central role of not only the prosecution case, but also the judge's direction and summing up
- The judge and the Crown Pathologist did not adopt the required "impartial" role.

Given the purely circumstantial nature of the Simon Hall case, it would seem pertinent to introduce other circumstantial events which may require further examination:

At 12.30pm, Sunday 25th November 2005 (exactly 3 weeks prior to the discovery of Mrs Albert's body), Mabel Leyshon (90) was found dead in her home in Lon Pant, Llanfairpwll, on Anglesey. She had been stabbed repeatedly, following a break-in.

The similarities are striking; both were elderly women living alone, both were subjected to brutal and frenzied knife attacks, both had their houses broken into, and both were killed on a Saturday night, and discovered on a Sunday. Both were also extremely security conscious. Both were confirmed alive and well on the Saturday.

References:

"The role of Juries in the British System," Dr Zakaria Erzinclioglu at *www.innocent.org*

"Science and the Law," Dr Zakaria Erzinclioglu at *www.innocent.org*

The Guardian, Clare Dyer, Legal Editor, Friday November 25th, 2005

BBC News, England, "CCTV of Murdered Widow", January 16th 2002

BBC News, Wales, "OAP Murder," November 27th 2001

BBC News England, August 18th 2005

"Justice Without Science Isn't Justice," Frank Ward, 17/09/03, reproduced at www.portia.org

Chapter Six

The case of Luke Mitchell

ON THE night of June 30th, 2003, the body of 14 year old schoolgirl Jodi Jones was found in woodland just yards from her home. She had been beaten about the head and face, her throat had been cut between 12 and 20 times, and her body mutilated after death. Police described the attack as "brutal" and "frenzied," and issued requests through the media for anyone who had been in the vicinity between 5pm and 10pm that evening to come forward. They also called for anyone who had noticed someone they knew behaving oddly – perhaps changing their appearance, or becoming anxious or agitated – to contact police.

Jodi, it was claimed, had left her home in Easthouses in the early evening of June 30th, to meet her boyfriend Luke Mitchell, who lived in Newbattle, a neighbouring village. A path, running in front of a stone wall which bordered the woodland where Jodi's body was found, was a shortcut between the two homes, and popular with walkers and dog-walkers. However, Jodi's mother insisted that Jodi was not allowed to use the path alone, because of its secluded nature, and insisted that Luke always met Jodi at the Easthouses end of the path, just a few minutes from her home, to walk with her down the path to his home in Newbattle. The path is not quite a mile long.

The alarm was raised when Jodi failed to return home at her curfew time of 10pm. Jodi's mother Judy contacted Luke (because Jodi's mobile was broken) to be told that he had not seen Jodi that evening. Arrangements were made for Luke to meet members of Jodi's family at the Easthouses end of the path to search for the missing girl. Luke was also 14 years old. He met the others as arranged, taking with him his German Shepherd dog and a torch. The rest of the search party comprised Jodi's 17 year old sister Janine, Janine's 19 year old fiancé Stephen Kelly, and the girls' grandmother, Alice Walker, 67. The finding of Jodi's body would later become central to the prosecution case. Luke would claim that he instructed the dog, which had had some training as a tracker dog to "Seek Jodi, Find Jodi," after asking family members if they had anything of Jodi's from which the dog could get a scent. (This part of the story has never been contested by the prosecution.) Some way down the path, the dog, he says, began sniffing the air and pawing at the wall, as if she had picked up a scent. Luke and Alice Walker returned a little way back in the direction they had just come, to a V shaped break in the top of the wall, through which Luke climbed, and discovered the body. The prosecution would later claim that the dog did not lead him to the body, but that he went straight to the V, proving that he knew where the body was, and only the person who had murdered Jodi could have had that information. In spite of the fact that there was not a single scrap of evidence to link Luke Mitchell to the murder of Jodi Jones, and, in fact, there was a great deal of evidence pointing to other persons, Luke Mitchell was convicted of murder in January 2005, and handed down the longest sentence ever imposed on a person under 18 years old – a minimum of 20 years.

Witnesses and Identification

Initial press reports stated that Jodi had left home at around 5.30pm that afternoon. She was not positively identified at any point until her body was found at approximately 11.15 that night. Police distributed posters to be displayed in local shops, businesses, bus shelters and bill boards, all depicting Jodi as a young child, rather than a teenager – it would not be until late afternoon on Friday 4th July that up-to-date pictures were released. Yet on July 1st or 2nd, certainly well before these up-to-date pictures appeared, a witness, Andrina Bryson came forward to say she had seen a girl "matching Jodi's description" with a youth in his late teens or early twenties at the Easthouses end of the path at approximately 5pm. Checking till receipts from her shopping trip, the police reconstructed this witness's journey, and concluded that she must have been at the bend in the road between 4.49pm and 4.54pm in order to see these two people. She described the youth with "Jodi" as having long, curly or wavy, brown or ginger hair. This witness was later shown twelve photographs. One photograph was of Luke Mitchell – he was the only one of the 12 with long hair (although it was blond and poker straight), and his was the only photograph with a light background. The following day, this same witness "recognised" Luke (as the youth she had seen) from a photograph in the newspapers. Interestingly, although this witness claimed to have recognised Jodi from the description in the newspapers, in the ensuing court case, she was unable to describe the clothing worn by the girl she saw. Jodi was wearing a sweatshirt with a large, very distinctive logo that evening. Ms Bryson also told the court that she had only seen the back of the girl's head, and had not been able to view her face.

Other witnesses identified a youth "very like" Luke at the Newbattle end of the path at around 6pm, yet others still described a "mystery man" following Jodi towards the Easthouses entrance to the path.

Luke *was* positively identified, by some schoolboys who knew him, sitting on a wall at the end of his street in Newbattle, at approximately 5.45pm, and again some 10 minutes later.

What becomes critical here is the prosecution's claim as to the sequence and timing of events. They would claim that Jodi left home at approximately 4.50pm, and was murdered around 5.15pm, her body being stripped and mutilated thereafter. In an attempt to pin down these timings, police video footage timed the walk from the point where Luke was identified at the end of his street to the Newbattle entrance to the path where Jodi was killed, at just over 5 minutes at a brisk walking pace. Walking the full length of the path, from end to end, at a similar pace would take an absolute minimum of 10 minutes. If, as the prosecution claimed, Luke left to meet Jodi in response to texts they'd exchanged earlier (the last one being at 4.38pm), we have to accept that Luke was at the end of his street when these texts were exchanged, he left immediately, took a very brisk walk up the path, covering the distance in the minimum possible time, and arrived to meet Jodi with just one minute to spare within the "identification" window produced by Andrina Bryson's sighting. Had Luke been at home when he received these texts, it would have been impossible for him to have reached the Easthouses end of the path in time to have been "identified" by Andrina Bryson – yet by Jodi's own mother's admission, up until the exchange of those texts, Luke Mitchell would still have believed Jodi to be "grounded" that evening – the decision to "unground" her had been taken, completely by chance, by Judy at around 4.30pm. Luke, therefore, would have had no reason whatsoever to have been anywhere near the path.

All initial reports claimed that Jodi left home at around 5.30pm, yet if she had not left home until 5.30pm, then she could not have been the person seen by Ms Bryson between 4.49pm and 4.54pm. However, it is interesting to note that the 5.30pm timing, taken with the positive identification of Luke in Newbattle at 5.45pm would have clearly and categorically excluded Luke as a suspect. Following Andrina Bryson's statement, however, the time of Jodi's leaving changed to 4.50pm, opening a "window of opportunity" during which Luke Mitchell, according to the prosecution, did not have a solid alibi.

Some days after Andrina Bryson's statement, some other witnesses came forward to say they had seen two youths "mucking around" with a noisy motorbike at the Newbattle end of the path at 5pm, and had later seen the bike propped against the wall, close to the V shaped break, at approximately 5.15pm. Neither of these youths matched Luke's description.

No-one positively identified Luke or Jodi between 4.50pm and 5.45pm. Luke's alibi, that he was at home preparing dinner, was completely discredited by prosecution claims that his mother and brother had "lied" to give him an alibi. There was nothing to suggest, far less prove, that Mrs Mitchell had lied, aside from the prosecution's claim that this was so – charges of attempting to pervert the course of justice against her and Luke's brother Shane, were dropped. Also, although it would be suggested over and over in court, and reported widely in the press, that Mrs Mitchell had lied in court, she was never charged with perjury.

In an attempt to ensure he had given as accurate a statement as possible, Luke's brother gave a second statement to police following discussion with his mother – in the event, this was used against the Mitchell family, the prosecution claiming it as "evidence" that Mrs Mitchell had persuaded Shane also to lie to cover for Luke, even though it is clear from the two statements that Shane is simply trying to further clarify a slight ambiguity in his earlier statement. Other witnesses who admitted discussing their statements before talking to police were *not* accused of any wrongdoing – indeed, the statements produced as a result of their discussions were later used against Luke Mitchell in evidence!

The Police Investigation

On the night Jodi's body was found, police officers arrived without tracker dogs, although they had access to such dogs. Luke was taken directly from the scene to Dalkeith Police Station, but the remaining three members of the search party were not. In spite of the fact that he was just 14 years old, he was stripped and questioned without the presence of a responsible adult, being told his clothing was needed for forensic examination as "routine procedure." Later, it would become apparent that none of the other members of the search party had had their clothes taken in this manner, a point which would be of great significance.

A forensics officer who arrived at the scene was unable to climb over the wall to get to the body because she had a "bad back." As a result, the body was left, uncovered, in the rain, for a further 7 – 8 hours, until another forensics officer, a Mr Scrimger, attended the following morning. By the time he arrived, the body had been moved, and items around it gathered up.

That same morning, although the location of the body itself had been cordoned off, local schoolchildren were walking through a field and playing fields directly adjacent to the scene, council gardeners were cutting hedgerows in the immediate vicinity, and the refuse collection went ahead as normal. Later, in court, Mr Scrimger would be forced to admit that the crime scene had not been "ideally managed" - it would later emerge that the body had been rolled onto plastic sheeting *prior* to forensic examination.

On Friday 4th July, Luke was taken for further questioning, and his house searched amidst a blaze of media coverage. (Later that day, the first up-to-date photographs of Jodi were released.) On Saturday July 5th, police appealed for the two youths on the moped to come forward (this was the first mention of these youths), and by Monday July 7th, reported that those youths had come forward, and been eliminated from the enquiry. This was in spite of the fact that, on Friday 4th July, a police source had reported that the results of DNA and other forensic tests were expected to take approximately another week to be returned. This begs the question, of course, on what grounds were these two youths eliminated from the enquiry?

On August 14th, some six weeks later, the police arrived at the Mitchell household at 7.25am. A huge contingent of reporters and photographers was already waiting, and Luke was photographed being led away in handcuffs. Luke Mitchell had just turned 15 years old, yet the police did nothing to shield his identity. The question has never been answered as to how such a large group of press knew to congregate outside the Mitchell home at that time of the morning on that particular day. Luke was again released without charge, but the tone of press reports claiming to be from police sources had, by that stage, begun to carry the clear and obvious implication that Luke was the only suspect, and that police were just gathering enough information to prove the point.

On September 7th 2003, for example, the Sunday Herald printed the following:

> *"Meanwhile, detectives say they are focusing on only one suspect in the hunt for Jodi's killer. A police source added: "Although we are centering the investigation on one suspect, we are not doing this to the exclusion of all other possibilities – to do that would be to court disaster. There are other lines of inquiry – such as vagrants who had been in the area – but as time goes by these are being eliminated.*
> *Police say they were "still interested" in Luke, particularly in relation to the last meeting he had with Jodi and the fact that he was involved in finding her body."*

The implication is obvious, but the police did nothing to refute or discourage these reports, although they did "break their silence" to quash rumours that the murder had been ritualistic, or had had black magic or satanic connotations (as reported in a few newspapers.) How ironic, then, that this satanic connection would ultimately provide one of the main planks in the prosecution's case!

On November 25th 2003, the Edinburgh Evening News reported that a dossier had been submitted by Lothian and Borders Police to the Procurator Fiscal, *naming* Luke Mitchell as the only suspect. The police did not deny this report, re-iterating only that a report had been submitted. He was still, at that time, only 15 years old.

In spite of a massive police investigation, the murder weapon was never recovered.

Although the report was sent to the procurator fiscal in November 2003, Luke was not arrested until April 2004. He was, at that point, charged with attacking Jodi, striking her about the head and face, compressing her neck until she fell to the ground, and repeatedly striking her with a knife. He was also charged with possession of a knife or knives, and "in relation to the supply of cannabis." He was held under the 110 day rule, meaning that he had to be brought to trial or released by the end of that period. Two weeks and two days before the end of that period, Luke Mitchell turned 16. This had two important effects – firstly, he would be tried as an adult. Secondly, the press, who had freely named and photographed him (even though he was a minor) until his arrest, had been prohibited from doing so after his arrest. However, following his 16th birthday, in that critical two week period prior to the trial, they were once again free to name him and print his photograph. At this stage, they were also free to report that his mother and brother had been charged with "attempting to pervert the course of justice."

The trial and the evidence

The evidence presented in court was purely circumstantial, and based on speculation and innuendo. The prosecution claimed that Luke had known where the body lay, and had carried out an extremely cold and calculating plan. He had escaped without detection, and his mother had burned his clothes in the back garden. His fascination with the satanic was presented as evidence of his preoccupation with evil. School jotters scribbled with so-called satanic slogans, along with essays questioning Christianity and the existence of God were produced to back up these claims, yet two of the slogans, which were widely reported, were actually lines from the popular computer game, Max Payne.

DNA found on Jodi's underwear and trainer belonged to two people, neither of which was Luke. The DNA on her underwear, shown to be from semen, belonged to Stephen Kelly, her sister's fiancé. This was explained away thus: Jodi had borrowed her sister's T shirt, and the DNA had transferred from the T shirt to her bra. The only proof that this was the case is the word of Janine Jones and Stephen Kelly himself. Further, Jodi lived with her mother, and Janine lived with her Grandmother. Judy Jones claimed Jodi had "gone upstairs to get ready to meet Luke" that evening. Therefore, she had changed into a semen stained t-shirt, borrowed from her sister at an earlier date, but not washed? The DNA on her trainer remains unidentified, in spite of later police claims that "no DNA at the scene was unaccounted for" – this statement would later come back to haunt the investigating team.

John Ferris, Jodi's cousin, and Gordon Dickie, a second cousin, were the two youths on the moped that evening. However, it emerged that when they had finally come forward after almost a week of pleas from the police for *anyone* who had been in the vicinity, they both lied to police about the time they had been on the path. John Ferris, who had long, curly, reddish brown hair had hacked it off himself after reports emerged that police were looking for someone fitting that description. He could not explain why he had done so, but agreed that he had done so before contacting police. He was reported as having been shaking whilst watching a television appeal for the youths on the moped to come forward. These two did not even come to the attention of police for almost a week after Jodi's death, yet investigators eliminated them from the enquiry within 48 hours, before the results of DNA tests were returned. The moped, and the clothes they were wearing that evening were never tested for forensics. John Ferris would go on to give damning (but uncorroborated) testimony against Luke – that he (Luke) had left a knife at a friend's house which Ferris had handed to police, that Ferris had witnessed Luke jabbing Jodi in the leg with a knife, telling her to shut up, and so forth. John Ferris was a drug dealer, who admitted supplying Luke and others with cannabis. John Ferris was never charged "in relation to the supply of cannabis."

A great deal was made of the "fact" that a parka jacket that Luke had been wearing that night had disappeared, "burned," the prosecution claimed, in a log burner in the back garden by Luke's mother Corrine. No evidence was ever provided as to how this was achieved – Luke would have had to travel up a wide street, in broad day light to his front door, without being seen, (at a time when people would be beginning to arrive home from work), get into the house, and stripped out of the incriminating clothing without leaving a single trace of forensic evidence.

Nothing was found in the contents of the log burner to suggest that any articles of clothing had been burned there, far less a bulky, eyelet studded jacket. Furthermore, witnesses who claimed to have noticed "burning smells" coming from the garden that evening reported these as being "between 6.30pm and 7.30pm" and later, "some time around 10pm." Since Luke had been positively identified at the end of his street at 5.45pm, is it really conceivable that his mother was still trying to burn the evidence, in her own garden, some 4 hours later? It was light until around 10pm, Jodi had been murdered in an area popular with walkers; her body could have been discovered at any moment. Also, to return momentarily to the timing aspect of the prosecution's claims, Jodi, it is alleged, was murdered at 5.15pm. Just 30 minutes remain, therefore, for Luke, had he been the killer, to strip and mutilate the body, get back to his own house, strip out of all of his clothing and get cleaned up and changed, and organise for his mother to dispose of the evidence, then return to the wall at the end of his street.

Several witnesses were produced in court to say they had seen Luke Mitchell wearing such a parka jacket. Indeed, several hundred people could honestly have made the same claim, since he had been pictured in newspapers wearing one. The ludicrous (and completely unsubstantiated) claim by the prosecution was that Corinne Mitchell had burned the parka jacket her son had been wearing that night, then gone out and bought him an identical one to cover up for the "missing" one. The necessary proof that Luke owned a parka jacket *prior* to Jodi's death was never produced. Receipts proving that the parka jacket had been bought after Jodi's death *were* produced, but the prosecution dismissed these as irrelevant, continuing to claim that this was a replacement jacket.

If Luke Mitchell *had* committed such a brutal murder, wearing such a recognisable garment, is it feasible to believe that his mother would provide him with an identical (and therefore readily identifiable) one? It simply makes no sense – having disposed of the jacket, the obvious move would have been to buy something completely different.

It was also claimed that Corrine Mitchell had lied to give her son an alibi, as had his brother Shane. The prosecution did not back up these claims with evidence – rather, it opted for character assassination instead, introducing, for example, the completely unrelated suggestion that Shane had been "viewing pornography" on the internet, in an attempt to both discredit and humiliate him.

Again, these events raise the question of timing. For Corinne Mitchell to have received the clothes to be burned in the back garden, it has to be accepted that Luke must have returned home prior to his appearance on the wall at the end of the road at 5.45pm. The prosecution contention that he was not "at home" between 5pm and 5.45pm begins to unravel at this point – how did the clothing, alleged to have been burned in the garden, get to his home without him? There is not, and has never been, any suggestion that Corinne Mitchell collected clothing from anywhere else that evening – indeed, other, concrete evidence, such as cctv footage in a local store, rules out any such eventuality.

Jodi was brutally murdered. Her throat was cut several times, and her body mutilated, some of the injuries being very precisely inflicted after death. She had been stripped, her arms tied behind her back with her own jeans, after her throat had been cut, the prosecution claimed. The police had stated repeatedly that her killer would have been "heavily bloodstained" and that she had "fought to the end" (a fact later confirmed by the pathologist), so they were looking for someone with fresh scratches or other injuries. When Luke Mitchell was examined by police that night, he did not have a single mark on him. No traces of Jodi's DNA were ever found on him, nor his on her.

According to William Clegg QC, in a completely separate case,

> " this lack of forensic evidence {is} extremely unusual." Clegg quoted Lockhart's Theory - the accepted foundation of forensic science - which states that 'every contact leaves a trace'. "That being so," said Clegg, 'the murderer would have left a trace of himself at the scene.'"

If this theory is "the accepted foundation of forensic science," then the weight of forensic science would appear to be stating, quite categorically, that Luke Mitchell was not present at the scene, given the amount of contact between Jodi and the person who murdered her.

On two occasions, expert witnesses made statements which fly in the face of all the evidence, in their attempt to support the prosecution case. Susan Ure, who had been involved with examining DNA found on Jodi's clothing and body, stated that a stain had been found which was "similar in parts to parts of DNA belonging to Luke" – in other words, No Match! This is a clear example of wording a statement in a specific way so as to mislead – what this woman was clearly saying was that there were not enough similarities between the two pieces of DNA to conclude a match with Luke's, yet it is stated in such a way that is sounds like she is suggesting exactly the opposite! The fact of the matter is that *all* of us have parts of our DNA which are similar to parts of other people's DNA.

Mr Scrimger, the forensics officer who was first to examine the scene of the crime, stated that the killer would "not necessarily" be heavily bloodstained. To back this up, he agreed with the prosecution suggestion that Jodi may have been sitting or kneeling when her throat was cut from behind, explaining a blood spray stain on the wall being the result of the blood spraying *forwards* – i.e., *away* from the killer. However, there are a few problems with this explanation – firstly, the case against Luke was that he had compressed her neck until she fell, unconscious, to the ground. Since we know that unconscious people tend not to sit or kneel, Mr Scrimger's explanation requires us to now believe that the killer was *holding* Jodi in a sitting or kneeling position. In this case, he is far more likely to have become bloodstained. Further, the case against Luke claims that he stripped her, tied her hands behind her back with her trousers and mutilated the body, all *after* he cut her throat. Mr Scrimger had to concede that, whilst the killer would "not necessarily" have been heavily bloodstained, it was "highly likely" that he would have been.

Once again, we are faced with serious anomalies in the prosecution case. Several witnesses were identified as having been on the path at the critical time that evening. In total there were a minimum of five – John Ferris, Gordon Dickie, his father, David Dickie, Stephen Kelly, a witness who claimed to have heard a disturbance behind the wall, and the "mystery man" seen following Jodi onto the path. Yet of the four who have spoken to police, none makes any mention of having seen either Luke or Jodi, or indeed, any of the others, on the path. At this point, the murderer is highly likely to have been heavily bloodstained, probably scratched or having other injuries consistent with having been in a fight, almost certainly behaving in an agitated manner, and attempting to flee the scene. It is possible, once these factors are taken into consideration, that Jodi Jones was *not* murdered at the time all of these other people were known to be on the path, and we are required, once more, to consider the original time of Jodi leaving home as reported at 5.30pm.

Due to the scarcity of definitive evidence (and perhaps because of the mounting evidence pointing away from Luke Mitchell as the murderer), in a highly dubious move, the prosecution introduced "evidence" pertaining to the gothic rocker Marilyn Manson, in an attempt to prove that this person's art had influenced Luke Mitchell. It was shown that a few days after Jodi's murder, Luke had purchased a music magazine at the local Sainsbury store which contained a free cd and bonus dvd of some of Manson's work. The audio cd was called Golden Age of the Grotesque, and the dvd showed images of apparent violence towards two young women. The police had investigated the "Manson connection," one officer accessing a website which showed paintings by Manson depicting the "Black Dahlia" murder of Elizabeth Short in the 1950s. The prosecution claimed that there were startling similarities between the injuries inflicted on Elizabeth Short, and those on Jodi Jones. Under cross examination, those "startling similarities" were reduced to "some similarities," and "superficial similarities" but even that is irrelevant – Luke Mitchell was proven to have come into contact with Marilyn Manson "influences" (which did not contain any images of the Black Dahlia paintings) *after* Jodi's death. There was never any evidence whatsoever that he had come into contact with the Black Dahlia images at any time – the police officer who found the images admitted that it was highly unlikely that anyone who had not visited the website would have seen those images. There were no connections to that website on the computer taken from the Mitchell home.

Still, the prosecution repeated its contention that Luke had "copied" the Black Dahlia murder because, in part, he was so heavily influenced by Manson. Even the Judge, after the jury returned their verdict, would show his complete lack of understanding on this point – i.e., that something which happens *after* an event cannot possibly have influenced that event.

Although it was clear that Luke indulged in cannabis, the same was true of Jodi – the prosecution tried to imply that Luke had somehow corrupted her, even though he received his cannabis from Jodi's cousin! Indeed, several school-friend witnesses were also shown to indulge in cannabis, as was Jodi's brother, Joseph, who was also supplied by cousin John Ferris. Amidst this particular group, cannabis was hardly an indicator of anything odd or peculiar, yet the claims that it was cannabis which fuelled the 'frenzied' attack on Jodi were repeatedly reported. Unfortunately, no expert witnesses on the effects of cannabis, or its likelihood of fuelling such an attack were called, either by the prosecution or the defence; however, there is a general understanding that the effects of cannabis are quite the opposite to those claimed by the prosecution.

Another complete red herring was the finding of bottles of urine found in Luke's bedroom. Just what, exactly, these had to do with Luke's likelihood of having been Jodi's murderer is still unclear, yet the finding of these bottles was given great significance by both the prosecution and the press, in a blatant attempt to encourage suspicion and revulsion towards Luke Mitchell. The perfectly innocent explanation – that the trauma of events had triggered a form of Obsessive Compulsive Disorder (OCD), compelling him to "hold on" to literally everything, never made it to the public domain.

Similarly, proof that Luke had other girlfriends was not only used to blacken his character, it would later be used by the detective in charge of the case to provide a motive for Luke murdering Jodi, even though all of the evidence actually proved that this officer's explanation simply could not be the case. Unfortunately, this motive theory was not presented to the jury – it was offered to the press *after* the trial. However, it does beg the question, if teenage boys two-timing their girlfriends is an indicator of their likelihood to commit murder, then surely none of us can sleep safe in our beds!

In another attempt to show the Mitchell family as unreliable, the prosecution called witnesses who had not, previously, been made known to the defence team. Staff from a tattoo parlour were called to show that Corrine Mitchell had "lied" for her son, by providing him with fake id, so that he could have a tattoo. The fake id was not produced in court – only the word of the staff that it had been produced was available. It was, they claimed, a birth certificate, and Corrine Mitchell had claimed her son was the person named on that certificate. With prior warning, the defence would have been able to prove that either (a) Corrine Mitchell produced no such document, or (b) the staff at the tattoo parlour had broken the law by tattooing someone with an obviously fake id - the person they named on the birth certificate which Corrine Mitchell is supposed to have provided is a 58 year old man!

In summary of the trial and evidence presented so far, therefore, there were several pieces of "evidence" led which should not have been allowed to be led, on various grounds – the eyewitness testimony of Andrina Bryson, who failed to identify Luke Mitchell in court, was flawed from the start – the mug shots highlighting Luke as the only one of 12 with long hair, pictured against the only light background, shown to her by police, were, the judge agreed, misleading. In what the defence called a deliberate tactical decision to treat Luke Mitchell unfairly, no identity parade was held. Andrina Bryson also admitted making a statement some weeks later that she recognised Luke from his picture in the newspaper, even though the judge had expressly instructed jurors that they should "put out of their minds anything they had seen, heard or read outside of the court proceedings."

All that was ever proven with regard to the parka jacket was that Luke owned one after Jodi's death. There was no evidence whatsoever that he had owned one *prior* to the murder of Jodi, nor that clothing of any description had been burned in the garden. Much confusion was encouraged between reports of both Luke and his mother *denying* the existence of the parka jacket, and pictures of him wearing such a jacket – the deliberate omission of the fact that they claimed he did not own the jacket prior to Jodi's death making it appear self evident that they were lying. Further, the prosecution repeatedly referred to the "missing" jacket, although there had never been a single shred of evidence to suggest that there had been any "missing" jacket.

The tattoo evidence, led to prove the dishonesty of Corrine Mitchell, was not revealed to the defence prior to being led in court. Further, this evidence raised serious questions as to the honesty of the people testifying – they had no corroborating evidence (such as the birth certificate and photographic id they claimed to have been shown), and the name they claimed to have been given was that of a 58 year old man.

All of the Marilyn Manson evidence should not have been allowed on the grounds that it proved nothing – the cd and dvd were purchased *after* Jodi died, and the Black Dahlia connection had nothing to support it whatsoever.

The urine bottles found in Luke's bedroom were in no way connected with the case – they could not be used to prove anything related to the crime.

But what is most interesting is the weight given to uncorroborated testimony from Jodi's family members.

According to Alan Turnbull QC, there were three things that proved that Luke was the killer:

> The "identification" of him at the Easthouses end of the path with Jodi at around 5pm.
>
> The "fact" that Shane said Luke was not at home between 5pm and 5.45pm.

The testimony of the other three members of the search party.

These three things were "central" to the prosecution's case, he claimed. Yet Andrina Bryson's identification was nothing of the sort, as has already been shown.

Shane did not claim that Luke "had not been at home between 5pm and 5.45pm." He said that he did not know if Luke had been at home, and that he had thought he (Shane) was alone "in the house," a subtle, but very important difference.

Finally, the testimony of the other members of the search party, and the evidence of Jodi's family in general, raises many more questions than it answered.

Firstly, the timing of Jodi leaving her mother's home on the evening of June 30th: Judy Jones claimed that Jodi had been grounded, and that she had decided that evening to end the punishment. Texts were exchanged between Judy's phone (Jodi's phone was broken) and Luke's between 4.34 and 4.38pm – this obviously being the time Judy told Jodi her punishment had been lifted. The description of what occurred between then and the claimed time of Jodi leaving is very detailed, involving cooking lasagna and playing a Rod Stewart track. These events left Jodi less than 7 minutes to "go upstairs and get ready to meet Mitchell," then come back downstairs, give her mother a kiss and leave. Texts on both Judy's and Luke's phones had been erased, so there is nothing to prove what was said in those texts. However, if this was the first point at which Luke became aware that he would be seeing Jodi that night (since she was still "grounded") an important issue arises. There are only 11 – 16 minutes between those texts being exchanged, and the "sighting" by Andrina Bryson at the Easthouses end of the path. It is not possible for Luke to have made the journey, on foot, from his home to the Easthouses end of the path in that time. Yet, what reason would he have, prior to that time, to be anywhere near the path? He believed he was not meeting Jodi because she had been grounded.

Alan Ovens, Judy Jones' partner, took a call, on the home phone, from Luke at 5.40pm, apparently asking where Jodi was. He said he told Luke Jodi had already left to meet him. A great deal of emphasis was put on the fact that Luke did not call back later, when Jodi failed to show up. But by 5.40pm, Jodi had been gone from her home for 50 minutes. She was expected to have met Luke at the Easthouses end of the path within "a couple of minutes" of leaving her house, yet Luke's call did not raise alarm with either Mr Ovens, or Mrs Jones? It was portrayed in court that 14 year old Luke had somehow failed in his responsibility to his girlfriend, by not calling back when Jodi failed to show, the implication being that he was covering up what he had done by trying to appear normal. Yet basic logic suggests that the last thing he would do at that time, had he been the killer, would be to alert her parents to the fact that she was not where she should be. What if they had launched an immediate search following his 5.40pm call? Jodi's body would have been found much more quickly – surely the murderer would want to buy as much time as possible? If, as the prosecution claims, Jodi died at around 5.15pm, and the murderer needed time to strip her after death, and mutilate her body in a calm, deliberate fashion, then the timing of this call suggests that he was calling almost immediately after carrying out these actions. Yet nothing in his voice or manner raised even the slightest alarm in Mr Ovens. It would later be shown from telephone records that Luke had actually tried to phone Jodi's home 8 minutes earlier, at 5.32pm, just 17 minutes after the claimed time of death, but had been unable to connect. This makes the timescale even less believable.

Given that there were *no* positive sightings of Jodi that evening, there is no proof of what time she left the house. When police later claimed that they were interested in Luke because he had been "the last person to see her alive, and the first to find her dead," they appear to have missed this critical factor! In an interesting display of double standards, the police accept, without corroboration, the word of one mother, but not another! Similarly, there is *nothing* to prove that Mr Ovens told Luke that Jodi had "left to meet him," except Mr Ovens own contention that this is so. Had he said, "Jodi's gone out," or "Jodi's not here," the whole insinuation surrounding the reasons for Luke not calling back collapses.

When it emerged that DNA belonging to Stephen Kelly had been found on Jodi's t shirt and underwear, the explanation given was that Jodi had been wearing her sister Janine's T-shirt. Yet we have only Stephen Kelly (who is implicated by the presence of his DNA) and Janine (his fiancé)'s word that this was, in fact, the case. The significance of the fact that none of the other members of the search party's clothes were taken for forensic testing that night becomes immediately apparent – no-one can ever know what evidence such testing may have yielded.

Similarly, the elimination of John Ferris and Gordon Dickie from the enquiry *before* forensic testing had been completed, the failure to test the bike or their clothing, and the fact that Ferris had dramatically changed his appearance and stalled for five days before contacting police leaves a raft of possible evidence that could never be recovered. In fact, these two were supposed to go to Jodi's house that evening, to smoke cannabis with her brother Joseph. They did not go, and could not explain why, nor could John Ferris or Judy Jones explain, by the time of the court case, why John Ferris had been ostracised by the Jones family.

But the central, critical evidence is that of the members of the search party. All three of Jodi's family members, by the time the case came to court, some 17 months after the event, told exactly the same story; one which differed in fundamental respects from that told by Luke Mitchell. Janine Jones, Stephen Kelly and Alice Walker all reported that the dog had not alerted Luke, but that Luke had gone straight to the V in the wall, climbed through, and immediately knew to turn left, rather than going straight ahead or turning right. All three claimed that he remained calm and emotionless throughout.

Careful examination of these statements, however, reveals that crucial aspects of them *cannot possibly be true.*

Luke's version of events is that the search party had passed the V in the wall when his dog began pawing at the wall and sniffing the air. He went back to the V, because it was slightly easier to get over the wall at that point, then made his way to where the dog had reacted on the other side of the wall (i.e. he turned left.) Both Janine and Stephen said that they were "shouted back" by Luke. But back from where, exactly? By their own contention, Luke had gone straight to the V. This being "shouted back" suggests that, after Luke had gone over the wall, they had carried on down the path. If that is the case, then they were not at the V to see what Luke did when he got to the other side of the wall. Or, Luke was telling the truth , and they had all gone past the V before he and Mrs Walker had gone back, hence Janine and Stephen having to be "shouted *back.*" Moreover, even if they had been at the V itself, the lowest point of the V is around 6 feet high. The wall is stone built, around 12" thick, and has no other breaks – it would not have been possible for them to have "seen" what Luke was doing. A reconstruction of the wall and the V shaped gap was built for the trial. Stephen Kelly was unable to state where the various members of the search party were at the crucial times. Janine Jones said she *ran back* to the V and saw Luke standing at the other side. Ms Jones is quite short – around 5'3" – unless she had climbed onto the top of the wall (and it was never suggested that this happened), it would have been physically impossible for her to see anyone standing on the other side of the wall. Prompted by Alan Turnbull as to whether Luke was shaking, or what the expression on his face was like, she provided the expected negative responses, yet these were things she could not had have seen. She was also the only member of the search party *not* to have gone over the wall, so she is the one least likely to have noted Luke's behaviour.

From the accounts of all three family members, Luke stayed at the other side of the wall whilst Stephen Kelly went over, then returned to the path, then Alice Walker went over the wall. At the point where Stephen has returned to the path, and Alice Walker has been helped over the wall and started screaming, Janine claimed that Luke "looked fine." At the same time, she claimed that she, herself, had also started screaming. Cross examined by Donald Findlay, quoting from a statement given to police by Janine a month after the murder, it was put to her that she had told police that when they had been "shouted back" by Luke, her "heart sank" because it was clear from the "concern in his voice" that he had found "something bad." She had also stated that "everyone was in hysterics."

Alice Walker, Jodi's grandmother, who was reported as shaking, screaming, and "a mess" following the discovery of the body, made the same claims as the others regarding Luke's reaction. Yet, just after the murder, when police had called "some days later" to collect the clothing they should have collected on the night the body was found, Mrs Walker could not remember what she had been wearing.

(The police operator who took Luke's call asking police to come quickly noted, "The laddie's in a right state.")

The prosecution case rested almost entirely on the evidence given by these three people. The prosecution claimed that only the killer would have been able to find her body in woodland, in the dark, with such ease. There was, they claimed, no other explanation as to how he knew to turn left after climbing through the V in the wall. Yet there were, clearly, other equally reasonable explanations – that he had turned to where the dog had reacted, or, alternatively, that the others had continued down the path, he was a 14 year old boy, alone on the other side of the wall in woodland, so he was likely to travel in the same direction as the others for safety and security.

The testimonies given by these three people, which were so crucial to the prosecution's claims, are dangerously flawed, in that what was claimed to have been "seen" could not possibly have been seen.

Repeated references to being "shouted back" or "running back" to the V are not adequately explained. If, as the prosecution claimed, Luke did not pass the V, but went straight to it, how did Janine and Stephen get to be so much further down the path as to have to be "shouted back." If they *were* that much further down the path, how can they have seen what they claimed to have seen at the V, since they were clearly not there.

Finally, there is the problem of "time of death" – no official time of death appears to have been recorded – all of the reports state that Jodi's death is "presumed" to have occurred between 5pm and 5.45pm –the only point in the evening that Luke does not have an alibi other than the word of his own family.

The Media

From the outset, this was a high profile media case. Initially, newspapers and tv reports carried images of a very young Jodi, aged ten or eleven. By the end of the first week, the link with the satanic, and claims of a ritualistic murder began to emerge. Coverage of Luke Mitchell first being taken for questioning, and his house being searched on July 4th blazed from every paper, and was reported on national television, despite the fact that Luke was just 14 years old, and had not been charged with anything. This would set the tone for the remainder of the press coverage of the case. Everything Luke Mitchell did made the news. He was excluded from returning to school at the beginning of the new term for his own safety, even though he had not been charged with any wrong doing. Newspaper photographs of him being driven away from the school by his mother claimed he was making "obscene hand gestures" to reporters, yet the photograph in question clearly shows him reaching back for his seat belt. Any right he my have had to be presumed innocent until proven guilty evaporated following two very highly publicised events. Both happened on the day of Jodi's funeral. Police told Luke that Jodi's family did not want him to attend. In what, retrospectively, was probably a misguided move, he gave an interview to Sky News that day, in an attempt to stem the barrage of negative publicity, and to proclaim his innocence of any involvement in Jodi's death. Later that evening, after the funeral was over, and he felt sure all the mourners would have left, he visited the grave and laid some flowers. The headlines the next day could not have been more damaging. Bordering on hysteria, headlines such as "How Could You?" portrayed him as completely uncaring, insensitive, and downright cruel. Completely untrue reports claiming that he had been smoking at the graveside, discarding cigarette butts on the grave ran alongside others insinuating a less than normal relationship between mother and son. That the press must have hung around the graveside for hours in the hope of Luke turning up at some point slips by almost un-noticed. A female friend who also visited the grave was reported as his new girlfriend, the negative implication being obvious. (Interestingly, although she and Luke were the same age, her face was blanked out from photographs, and she was not named). Reports that Mrs Jones had dumped the flowers back on the Mitchell doorstep all fed a growing tide of hatred, prejudice and suspicion.

By the time of the trial, the press had been reporting, for the best part of 14 months, that Luke was the only suspect. During the trial, the majority of the reporting was biased and prejudicial – much of the prosecution evidence was reported in detail, whilst the defence information was kept to an absolute minimum. The insinuation regarding the abnormal relationship between mother and son emerged again with reports that, when police had gone to arrest Luke, he was sharing a bedroom with his mother, although this was completely untrue.

After the verdict, stories were run about other girls who had apparently been threatened and frightened by Luke in the past, yet these were not presented in court.

The Judge and the Chief Investigating Officer.

Questions as to why the judge allowed certain evidence to be presented need to be answered. Holding the trial so close to Luke's home meant that the danger of jurors having been influenced by gossip, media, and so forth, was very great. The first trial had to be abandoned because one jury member had expressed her 'delight' at being selected for the case. The second trial was halted, and when it resumed, the judge told the jury that "following an incident with one of {their} number" they should be aware that if anyone tried to approach them, they should tell the court!

As has already been shown, Andrina Bryson was allowed to give evidence, even though the identification she had made was discredited.

The tattoo evidence was sprung on the defence, in spite of the requirement for all evidence to be made known to both prosecution and defence, yet the judge allowed this evidence to be led. Indeed, the judge, in his charge to the jury before they retired to consider their verdict stated,

> "…the Advocate Depute's purpose in leading that evidence was to seek to discredit Mrs Mitchell…"

– knowing that to be the case, surely it becomes even more critical that the rules are seen to be obeyed?

But it is Lord Nimmo Smith's comments *after* the verdict which give rise to the most serious questions.

On 11th February 2005, he said,

> "Jodi regarded you with affection and trust, she went out joyfully to meet you"

– yet this is in complete opposition to what Craig Dobbie (the Chief Investigating Officer in the case) claimed to be the very motive for the murder – i.e. that Jodi had found out about another girlfriend and had set out that evening to confront Luke, leading to the fight which culminated in her death.

The judge continued,

> "You found evil attractive and you thought that there might be a kind of perverted glamour in doing something wicked,"

but then says,

> "Looking back over the evidence, I still cannot fathom what led you to do what you did."

This suggests that the statement regarding finding evil attractive etc, has not been taken from the evidence. On what, then does the judge base his claim?

Regarding the Black Dahlia murder, the judge says,

> "I think you carried an image of these paintings in your memory when you killed Jodi,"

yet, having looked back over the evidence, he should have realised that it was not possible for Luke to have carried these images in his memory, because there was no evidence to say that he had ever even seen these images, and what evidence there was of Luke coming into contact with Marilyn Manson material shows that this occurred *after* Jodi's death.

The judge said that nothing in the reports prepared on Luke would have suggested that he was liable to commit such a serious crime, and then goes on to say about cannabis,

> "I believe that in some instances, at least, it can seriously damage the mental processes of those who habitually consume drugs"

– it appears now that the judge is questioning the abilities of the experts who prepared the reports which showed "nothing to suggest he was liable to commit such a serious crime." If habitual consumption of drugs had so damaged Luke's mental processes, one would have expected the psychology and psychiatry reports to have picked this up.

The judge then makes an outrageous suggestion:

> "In your case, I think that it {cannabis} may well have contributed to your being *unable to make the distinction between fantasy and reality which is essential for normal moral judgements*, and that this, along with other factors I have mentioned, may have meant that when you killed Jodi *you were unable to recognise what a truly wicked deed this was.*"

If the judge truly believed that, then surely he should have deemed Luke Mitchell mentally unfit to stand trial?

In fact, when clarifying the definition of "murder" to the jury, the very same judge states:

> "someone who brings about the death of his victim by carrying out an assault with the necessary degree of wicked recklessness...commits murder."

How could Luke have been deemed to have carried out an assault with the "necessary degree of wicked recklessness" and at the same time have been "unable to recognise what a truly wicked deed this was?"

Whatever the judge based these comments on when sentencing Luke Mitchell, it was not the evidence which had been presented in court during the trial, and suggests that the judge, himself, may have been influenced by "other factors."

Craig Dobbie, who led the police investigation, gave a press interview following the verdict on January 23rd 2005. He claims that by July 3rd 2003, his suspicions regarding Luke as the murderer led him to have Luke re-questioned, and his house searched. These suspicions were caused by alleged inconsistencies in Luke's statement, given in the early hours of July 1st, immediately after Jodi's body had been found. Mr Dobbie claims that the other members of the search party's statements were consistent, in both how he had gone over the wall, and in his lack of emotional response. Yet Janine Jones, a month later, was saying that she had known because of the concern in Luke's voice that something was wrong. Also, this was prior to the appeal for Ferris and Dickie to come forward, yet, when they did, Mr Dobbie's suspicions appear not to be raised by the obvious inconsistencies in the statements given by these two people. It also fails to address the most glaring inconsistency of all – that Janine Jones could not possibly have seen what she claimed to have seen.

Mr Dobbie also claims that Luke came under suspicion because he was the last person to have seen Jodi alive, and the first to have found her dead. Yet there is no evidence, anywhere, which places Luke Mitchell with Jodi Jones that evening. Indeed, what evidence exists proves that the last person to see Jodi alive was her mother.

Although Shane and Corrine Mitchell's discussion about their statements raised enough suspicion to have them charged with attempting to pervert the course of justice (although these charges were later dropped, having served the purpose of creating suspicion of wrongdoing, without actually having to prove it), the admitted discussions between Ferris and Dickie, before speaking to the police, raise no such suspicions or charges. Indeed the composite story from these two is used as evidence *against* Luke in court. It is worth noting that these two people had almost five days to discuss their story – the amendment to Shane's statement was made within 48 hours.

Mr Dobbie then offers his theory of motive for why Luke killed Jodi. He claims that Jodi had found out about Luke's "other girlfriend" during the day at school, and had set out to challenge him about it that night. An argument had ensued, leading to Luke attacking her. There are several problems with this theory. Firstly, Jodi did not know she would be *un*grounded that evening. There is no evidence to suggest that, even at the point that she was ungrounded, Jodi was setting out to challenge Luke about anything. The girl who had written in her diary "I think I would die if he finished with me" would, presumably, have been devastated to find out he was two-timing her. Yet according to her mother, she was "chuffed" at being allowed out, and left the house perfectly happy. According to the judge, Lord Nimmo Smith, "She went out joyfully to meet {Luke}." The two just do not fit together.

The judge claimed that there had been at least some pre-meditation on Luke's part, but Mr Dobbie seems to be suggesting that it was an argument that got out of hand.

Mr Dobbie's suspicion of Luke also seems based more on Luke's personality than on any evidence. Regarding the questioning of July 4th, Mr Dobbie says,

> "..all he did was make me more suspicious. In the interview he was confident and very controlling. He displayed a high level of intelligence,"

and in the questioning of August 14th, he says,

> "…He was challenging. He was totally in control of himself and challenged the abilities and authority of the police. It was like taunts. He had the mental ability to sit and take control of the interview, and that's incredible from someone who has not previously been part of the criminal process…."

Luke raises suspicion because he is intelligent and unafraid? Confident enough to "challenge the authority and abilities of the police?" Could this not just as easily be evidence of his innocence? Knowing 100% that he has done nothing wrong, he is most likely going to challenge, in the strongest terms, any suggestion to the contrary. Mr Dobbie seems to be suggesting that Luke should have been intimidated by police procedures if he was innocent! Also, Mr Dobbie's perception "it was almost like taunts" must surely have influenced the manner in which the interview proceeded. Was this negative opinion a result of Luke's responses themselves, or did it arise from Mr Dobbie's unshakeable conviction regarding his suspicion of Luke?

Another point which requires examination is that by Craig Dobbie's own admission, Luke Mitchell had become a suspect (rather than just a witness) by July 3rd. The Police and Criminal Evidence Act does not apply under Scottish Law, so Luke was classed at this point as a "voluntary attender." The general understanding of this term is that it applies to *witnesses*, not suspects. Although Luke was informed that he did not have to answer any questions, he was encouraged the whole time to believe that he was no more than a witness. The caution itself is completely misleading – still believing he is a witness, Luke is told that he doesn't have to answer any questions, but any information he gives may be recorded and used in evidence at a later date. This wording is critical – of course it may be used in evidence at a later date – there would be no point in police obtaining information if they did not intend to use it as evidence later. What is *not* stated is that it may be used as evidence *against him*. On that occasion (ie, July 4th 2003), Luke was questioned for six hours with no solicitor present. Similarly, no solicitor was present during the questioning of August 14th either – having arrived at the Mitchell home at 7.25am, police took Luke to the station and began questioning him immediately, despite several requests from Luke to speak to either his mother or his solicitor. At just fifteen years old, he was held and questioned for six hours, having been told that he had no right to speak to anyone!

Further, the Mitchell family were assigned a "liaison officer" on July 1st. What they were not told was that this officer was a member of the investigating team, even after Luke had been confirmed a suspect, by Craig Dobbie's own admission.

The reasons for Mr Dobbie's newspaper interview remain unclear. Having claimed that his force carried out a "first rate investigation," and knowing that the jury had returned a guilty verdict, why did he feel compelled to give an interview explaining why police had been suspicious of Luke from such an early point, and what the "motive" had been?

In an unprecedented move, Alan Turnbull, the prosecuting QC also gave a press interview at the same time, explaining why *he* was convinced the right person had been prosecuted. Surely the verdict vindicates both of these people, without any need for further explanation?

More than a year after the guilty verdict, as the defence team were preparing to appeal, the existence of unidentified DNA was once again raised. Eventually, documents were released which clarified the situation – in spite of police claims during the initial investigation that there had been no DNA at the scene which had been unaccounted for, it now emerged that there had always been one DNA sample that remained unidentified.

Just prior to this book going to press, further witness statements, pointing to another, far more credible suspect were passed to the defence. The police claimed that these statements had not been followed up because the case was "closed."

So where is the evidence which convicted Luke Mitchell?

He was not convicted on the basis of eyewitness testimony placing him at, or near, the scene of the crime, nor with Jodi at any point during that evening.

He was not convicted in the absence of other suspects.

He was not convicted because of DNA or forensic evidence linking him to the body or the scene of the crime (although there was DNA linking others to the scene)

He was not convicted through association or identification with any weapon.

He was not convicted on forensic proof of any clothing having been destroyed or disposed of by his mother.

He was not convicted on the basis of wounds or marks associated with having been in a fight of any description.

He was not convicted on the basis of what he was seen to do once over the wall, as this testimony cannot, physically, be true.

Evidence concerning restricting Jodi's throat until she fell to the ground unconscious, then slashing her repeatedly with a knife shows that this series of events is inconsistent with the evidence.

He was not convicted on the basis of his mother or brother lying either to the police or to the court – neither of these individuals was charged with any such behaviour

He was not convicted on the basis of the Black Dahlia connection, since there was no evidence to even suggest that such a connection existed.

He was not convicted on the basis of a history of similar behaviour or psychological likelihood to offend in this manner.

He was not convicted on the basis that this was a "drug fuelled" attack, since his voluntary blood sample that evening showed this not to be the case.

He was not convicted on plausibility of timescale to have carried out such an attack.

In the case of Luke Mitchell, of the imaginary Twelve Points raised in the introduction, the following apply:
- He was convicted on purely circumstantial evidence
- Reasonable doubt was glaringly obvious
- There was no DNA or forensic evidence linking Luke Mitchell to the scene of the crime, or to the victim
- He was not identified at, or near, the scene of the crime, or with the victim at any point that evening
- There were other, more credible suspects
- There was clear over-reliance on expert testimony to the detriment of Luke Mitchell
- There were serious questions about both timescale and physical ability for Luke Mitchell to have been the killer
- Character assassination constituted a large part of the prosecution case
- There was definite evidence of forensic experts selectively interpreting evidence to the prosecution's own ends
- Persons with a vested interest in seeing Luke Mitchell convicted gave crucial evidence against him
- Luke Mitchell was a child of previous good character, with no psychological conditions or previous convictions.

In this case, therefore, all twelve points are present.

The similarities with the others by this stage hardly need to be highlighted: poor police procedures leading to evidence being contaminated or lost, heavy emphasis on innuendo and speculation, and accusations of behaviours which have never been previously displayed. Like Simon Hall and John Taft, a central aspect to the case involves a piece of clothing *claimed* to have belonged to the defendant, but that claim is never, at any point, backed up by proof. Also, as with Simon Hall, the lack of a definitive time of death allows a presumption to be presented almost as fact – neither Luke nor Simon had a cast iron alibi at a specific time, therefore the prosecution *presumes* that to be the time of death. Failure of forensic experts to attend the scene in a timely manner allowed evidence to be lost in both of these cases. Similar to the case of Gordon Park, a series of events is claimed for which no explanation is offered – the "how" is not made clear and, on further examination, appears to be at the very least implausible, if not impossible. Police officers, after the cases have been concluded, make public remarks which appear to demonstrate prejudice in both this case and the case of Derek Christian.

Finally, as with Derek Christian and Simon Hall, we are asked to believe that Luke Mitchell suddenly and inexplicably "flipped," behaving in a manner which is completely uncharacteristic, then almost instantly returns to normal. In fact, in the case of Luke Mitchell, he first loses control completely, then he regains so much control as to become coldly ruthless in his task, and finally, returns to his completely normal self, all within twenty five minutes, and at the ripe old age of fourteen years!

Even before the final two cases are highlighted, it is apparent that something is fundamentally wrong with our judicial system. It cannot possibly be pure coincidence that so many cases throw up so many similar mistakes or discrepancies. Indeed, what appears to be emerging is an alternative system, one which runs by a completely different set of rules to the official system, and one which has somehow managed to become both embedded and hidden within that official system.

The most worrying issues raised by the Luke Mitchell case:

Reasonable doubt is established, but the conviction still stands.
The police investigation is flawed to the point of negligence.
- Although a child, in the eyes of the law, Luke Mitchell's identity was not protected

- He was not advised he had become a suspect, and was questioned without clear caution or a solicitor present.
- He was stripped and questioned on the night of the murder without an adult present
- Police failed to follow up other leads – in fact, police appeared to *dismiss* other leads without first checking evidence
- The press were fed a constant stream of negative information leading to extremely negative publicity regarding Luke Mitchell
- Critical aspects of the prosecution case were allowed to be led as evidence without proof to back them up
- The definition of circumstantial evidence as being corroborated by two independent sources was not met on several counts
- Discredited, non-legal and unfair evidence was allowed to be led.
- The judge drew conclusions from sources which had not been presented in court

---

References:
Transcript, Interview, ADS Fulton, DC Steven Quinn, Luke M Mitchell, July 4th 2003
Transcript, Interview, DC George Thomson, DC Russell Tennant, Luke M Mitchell, August 14th 2003
Transcript, Interview, DC George Thomson, DC Russell Tennant, DS David Gordon, Luke M Mitchell, August 14th 2003
Report; Copy Psychiatric Report on Luke Mitchell, October 29th 2004
Transcript: "Charge to the Jury", Lord Nimmo Smith, January 20th & 21st 2005
Transcript: Note of Appeal, August 1st 2005
Transcript; Report by Lord Nimmo Smith, Note of Appeal, February 7th 2006
Transcript: Opinion of the Court, November 14th 2006
Scotland on Sunday, "Mitchell Holiday Plan led to Murder," January 23rd 2005
Daily Record: "My Luke Torment," Feb 14th 2005

Chapter Seven

The Case of Susan May

SUSAN MAY cared for her elderly aunt, Hilda Marchbank, and her mother Dorothy Shelton. Mrs Marchbank lived in her own home, and Mrs Shelton lived with Susan, as she had done since having both hips replaced. Every weekend, however, Susan would take her mother to her aunt's house to stay. On the morning of March 12th 1992, Susan went, as she did every day, to her aunt's house, to check that Mrs Marchbank was out of bed, and to take in some lunch. She found her aunt dead on her bed, beaten about the head and face, with the lower parts of her body uncovered. The room had been ransacked, with drawers and cupboards tipped out.

Susan ran out of the house and went to a neighbour for help. The police were called, and for some seven or eight days, their investigation appeared to proceed on the basis of searching for a burglar, but without success. Eighteen days after the murder of her aunt, Susan May was arrested in connection with the murder. Immediately, 80 local people volunteered character references as to Susan's kind and caring nature.

The case against Susan May, it emerged, rested upon the discovery of three stains on a wall in the downstairs dining room which her aunt used as a bedroom. One of these contained a partial hand print which was found to be Susan's, and which the prosecution claimed was made in blood. The motive, according to this theory, was that Susan was running short of money, and needed to inherit her half share of her aunt's house (her sister would have inherited the other half share) to spend on her boyfriend.

Critical to the police decision to treat Susan May as the main suspect in her aunt's murder was a claim that Susan had referred to scratches on her aunt's face – only the killer, they asserted, could have known about those scratches.

Susan was found guilty of murder in May 1993, and sentenced to life imprisonment.

The Evidence

The last person to have seen Mrs Marchbank alive was Susan May herself. The previous evening, Mrs Marchbank had called Susan, worried that she had misplaced some door keys. This was not unusual – the elderly lady was known to call Susan several times a day, and those who knew her said that Susan was very patient and loving with her aunt, responding to her calls and reassuring her. On this occasion, Susan went to her aunt's house some time around 9pm, found the keys, and left her aunt to lock up after she had left. She then picked up two friends and dropped them off at a local pub before returning home. Her daughter, Katy, stated that her mother had returned at around quarter to ten, after she had dropped off the two friends at the pub. One of the friends, however, recalls that it was, to the best of his recollection, around ten or five to ten when Susan dropped them off at the pub and drove off. In between times, Susan had spoken to another friend on the telephone at "some time after 9.30pm." Therefore, the timescale for Susan May to have murdered her aunt, cleaned herself up so as to raise no suspicions, and to be acting perfectly normal is, at most, 50 minutes. The two friends, it must be stated, were picked up separately – the one who recalls being picked up at ten or five to ten was Susan's *second* lift, so the timescale is further reduced to allow for the time spent picking up the first friend and driving to the house of the second friend.

The time of death, according to pathologist reports, was most probably between 9pm and midnight. This timing was used to establish opportunity for Susan May to have been the murderer.

The court was told that three sets of stains on the wall had been extensively tested for various possibilities, the findings appearing to conclude that all three marks had been made in blood. One, it was claimed, was made by a right hand, in a second, the blood had run too much to gain any positive identification, and the third, by the light switch, was "just a smear." No tests were carried out to ascertain whether the "blood" was human or animal. The judge, in his summing up, was to remark,

> "….as I listened to all the talk about animal blood I did wonder where one could imagine that hand prints with animal blood in them could have got on this wall, but there it is…",

effectively dismissing the possibility of the marks having been made in animal blood. This is critical to later facts which emerged from unused evidence.

Also, it is important to realise at this stage that the jury was only shown the stains *after* they had been chemically enhanced. The power of suggestion here is immediately apparent – having been offered the possibility that the stains were "bloodstains," jurors are then shown stains which had been turned a brown colour by the chemical enhancement process (and, of course, the very colour one would automatically connect with dried blood).

The suggestion was that these prints had been made by the murderer "feeling her way" out of the room after the murder. As Susan May had run for help to a neighbour on the discovery of her aunt's body, and there had been no evidence of blood on her hands at that point (and expert witnesses would claim that the blood at the scene, by that time, was dry), the prosecution concluded that the "bloody handprint" trail must have been made the night before, at the time of the murder.

Yet, there was no evidence ever produced to show that all three marks had been made at the same time, and tests to identify the source of the "blood" were unsuccessful. One would assume, therefore, that what evidence existed relating to these stains was of very little worth or relevance to the case, yet, once again, we see extremely weak evidence ending up as a pivotal part of the prosecution's case, and this being allowed by the judge.

The police would claim that early in the investigation, they suspected that what had happened in Mrs Marchbank's house was "not a real burglary," as nothing had been taken, but had, in fact, been made to look like a burglary. The only way the police could know that nothing had been taken was because Susan May told them so! If Susan had carried out some elaborate plot to make her aunt's murder look like a burglary gone wrong, can we honestly believe that she would then alert the police by pointing out that nothing was missing?

Worse still, evidence which was never heard by the jury points compellingly to this being an attempted burglary which had gone terribly wrong, but one which Susan May had nothing whatsoever to do with – more about this later.

The crux of the whole case, however, rests on an allegation that Susan had said to an investigating officer, Sgt Rimmer, "Do you know the scratches on my aunt's face, can they get stuff from down your fingernails at forensics." It is this statement, the police claim, that put Susan May in the position of prime suspect, since only the killer could have known about the scratches on Mrs Marchbank's face. Sgt Rimmer contends that she went to the Senior Investigating Officer on the case, a Mr Kerr, and was told to write in her notebook what had been said. Another officer, D C Ogden, present at the time of this alleged question, made no note in his own notebook, but apparently signed the entry in Sgt Rimmer's. At this stage, since Susan May was now clearly considered a suspect, a note should have been made on the HOLMES computer database, and a note made in the crime log records, but neither of these actions were taken. Sgt Rimmer's notebook was not available as evidence, as it had been lost in the run up to the trial, but an alleged photocopy of the page in question was produced. This circumstance alone raises some very interesting questions. A critical piece of evidence, which shifts Susan into the prime focus of suspect, fails to be recorded in several locations – HOLMES database, crime log, another officer's notebook – yet the *only* document in which the information is claimed to definitely have been logged is lost, and an apparent photocopy of that page *only* is produced as evidence! It does somewhat stretch the definition of "circumstantial evidence," (ie, that such evidence be corroborated by two *independent* sources), that this photocopy is "verified" as correct only by the officers whose logs have either been lost, or were not properly kept in the first place!

To add insult to injury, Susan was told that Sgt Rimmer had been appointed as a liaison officer. Like Luke Mitchell's family, she had no understanding, and was not made aware, that this officer was, in fact, part of the *investigating* team.

Susan denied ever having asked this question regarding scratches on her aunt's face. According to rules within the Police and Criminal Evidence Act (PACE), she should have been approached at the earliest opportunity, shown the entry in Sgt Rimmer's notebook, and asked to either sign her agreement as to the accuracy of what had been reported, or to make any alterations to what had been recorded. Any refusal to sign should also have been recorded. None of these actions was taken, and Susan was not informed that she was now a suspect – had this happened, she would have been formally cautioned, and would have been advised of her right to legal representation. In the event, the next interview with the police was conducted with Susan still believing she was only a witness. Further, the main thrust of this third interview, which should have been conducted under caution, was to get Susan to state, categorically, that she had not touched her aunt on the morning the body was discovered. (This would be critical to evidence pointing to the "bloody handprint" having been deposited on the wall at the time of the murder, and not the more innocent explanation that she may have touched her aunt, and the wall, the following morning, after discovering the body.) Yet even in this interview, Susan continues to state that she cannot be sure, that she doesn't think she touched anything, but she can't say for certain. The police approach begins to lead Susan, by phrasing questions in specific ways: "So you didn't touch anything…" and "…so you wouldn't have had any blood on you then…." so as to elicit the required response. This line of questioning continues "When you found her you wouldn't have any blood on you...." "...you wouldn't have any on your hands....", and on and on, Susan answering "No" each time, and ending with, "I didn't touch her. I'm only surmising her face had blood on." It is only after repeatedly putting questions to Susan in this manner that she is asked "Then tell me why we've found your bloodstained fingerprints on the wall." In spite of Susan's earlier confusion as to exactly what she did in those first moments, and in spite of her statements that she could not be "certain" or was "not absolutely sure," the police were now in a position to put to her that she had been "very, very sure that you had not touched your aunty or anything in that room."

This line of questioning effectively removed any possibility of Susan May providing an innocent explanation as to how her fingerprint may have come to be on the wall – she had no idea of the significance of questions relating to whether or not she touched anything, and was essentially bulldozed into agreeing that she had not done so, yet at this stage, she was not even aware that she was suspected of murdering her aunt. Furthermore, and perhaps more importantly, the question put to Susan related to "bloodstained fingerprints." Susan's fingerprints anywhere in the house could not be considered suspicious, given the amount of time she spent there. Even "bloodstained fingerprints" of Susan's would not necessarily have been suspicious – there had been an incident, for example, some days earlier, where Susan had cut her hand with a screwdriver, causing her finger to bleed. It is at this point that the police appear to make two inter-related decisions which will later prove critical to the prosecution case – firstly that the fingerprints to which they refer *are* made in human blood, and secondly, that they are the *only* fingerprints to form part of the investigation. Both of these contentions will later be categorically disproved, but, as we have seen so often, by that stage, it is already too late.

Other "evidence" led by the prosecution, as we have seen in so many other cases, was not, in fact, of any real relevance to the case, but was led more to discredit the suspect than to prove or support other contentions.

At the time of her aunt's death, Susan was involved in a sexual relationship with a married man. When questioned about her relationship with this man, Susan had initially maintained that the relationship was purely platonic. She had maintained this stance for some time, reasoning that, on the one hand, it had nothing whatsoever to do with her aunt's murder, and on the other, that his family would be damaged should such information become public. The prosecution would use this to "prove" that Susan was perfectly capable of lying if it suited her purposes, and to blacken her character. It also allowed them to provide motive, and to lead another, compelling, but ultimately unsubstantiated theory regarding misappropriation of her aunt's, her mother's, and her children's money. The prosecution contended that Susan had showered her younger lover with expensive gifts, funded by taking money from accounts belonging to her relatives, over which she had power of attorney, in order to prevent him leaving her for a younger woman.

A great deal of attention was afforded financial matters during the trial. For example, In August 1986, Hilda Marchbank had around 46,000 GBP in various accounts, Dorothy Shelton had 12,000 GBP, Susan May's children had 16,000 GBP between them and Susan herself had 11,000 GBP Within the year to August 1987, Susan's personal account declined to the point whereby she was "marginally in the red." The remaining 74,000 GBP in the combined other accounts "steadily declined" until, by the date of Hilda Marchbank's death there was "virtually nothing left." *But*, on closer examination, these figures show that, on average, 15,000 GBP per year was used up. Susan May did not have paid employment, nor (obviously) did Hilda Marchbank or Dorothy Shelton. Susan's sister Ann had also had health difficulties. In reality, 15,000 GBP to run at least two households, and to support at least three adults is not a "substantial" sum of money by any stretch of the imagination.

The prosecution also placed a great deal of emphasis on the fact that Susan's sister Ann had stopped signing "twinned" cheques, leaving Susan as the sole signatory on her aunt's account, yet there was ample evidence to support the suggestion that Ann was simply not well enough during that period to be actively involved in her aunt's affairs. Ann was, in fact, mentally ill, suffering from advanced alcoholism- under normal circumstances, persons suffering mental illness or instability are *not* called to give evidence, for obvious reasons. Serious ethical and legal questions are raised in this case, by the prosecution's insistence on using Ann's evidence, and requiring her to testify.

The suggestion that Susan had killed her aunt in order to inherit half of her estate is further undermined when it becomes clear that Susan had full power of attorney over her aunt's affairs – there were shares worth 11,000 that she could have sold, jewellery worth more than 5,000, and, if she had been really desperate, Susan could have moved her aunt in with her own mother, all three of them then living in the same house, and sold her aunt's house, keeping all of the proceeds for herself.

Clearly, the suggestion that Susan had misappropriated funds has no basis whatsoever in fact, nor does it support the prosecution's motive theory, since there were other means by which Susan could have raised funds, should she have needed to, without resorting to murder. But the implications brought into play by leading these details in court could only have impacted negatively on Susan's credibility. This is, by now, one of the most commonly used dirty tricks in so many of the cases both highlighted in this book, and elsewhere in the pubic domain – evidence, which is actually evidence of nothing at all relevant to the case, being used to completely discredit either the suspect, or crucial defence witnesses.

The Police and the Investigation

As already stated, the manner in which the police set about constructing the case against Susan May raises many questions. Rather than advise Susan that she was a suspect, and interview her under caution, using proper procedures, a tactical decision was taken to try to elicit information, prior to such caution, which would not only support the police theory, but could also be used to extremely detrimental effect at a later date. Even something so simple as stating "but you said then that you *didn't* touch your aunty, and now you're saying you might have" would have been sufficient to cast doubt on the accuracy of Susan's testimony. Again, as has been seen in so many cases, the mere implication that a suspect *may* have lied about one thing being used to infer that they must therefore be lying about everything else is used to devastating effect. Yet the neighbour to whom Susan had run that morning for help stated that she had to tell Susan to *stop* touching things.

The central plank of the case against Susan May was that of the three stains on the wall, allegedly made in "human blood."

On later investigation, it emerged that Peter Fitton, the force photographer, shot video footage of the scene on the afternoon of March 12th. He arrived at 1.29pm and left at 1.58pm. There are no images of **any** of the marks on the wall recorded in his footage. Mr Fitton was asked;

> "A significant feature of this case were marks on the wall to the right of the bed when facing the body. These marks were noted on the day the body was discovered. The marks were described as giving the appearance of blood. Is it reasonable to assume that had these marks been noticed prior to your video recording you would have been asked to record them?" Answer: "Yes"

Greater Manchester Police were required to produce all negatives of still photography relating to the case. These turned up two photographs, taken in succession, of two of the marks on the wall, but there was no photograph of the third. There was also no way of telling when the photographs of the first two marks had been taken.

There was also no record of when, how, or by whom Mrs Marchbank's body was removed from the bed and taken into the kitchen. The body was later removed from the kitchen, in a body bag, by the funeral company. There was no evidence to show whether the body was placed in the body bag in the bedroom or in the kitchen. This is significant because further testing of the mark near the light switch has shown it to be Mrs Marchbank's own blood. There was some suggestion that a small quantity of wet blood had drained from the body when it was moved during examination. This could have accounted for the mark on the wall, in a variety of other, perfectly feasible explanations, but, of course, none of these were examined because of the chosen direction of the police investigation.

Mark Naylor, a civilian scenes of crime officer "lifted" a footwear mark from the entrance porch. This footwear mark remains unidentified, as do other fingerprints, of which the jury was not made aware.

The role of Detective Superintendent Kerr, who was Senior Investigating Officer in the case merits close examination. It was Mr Kerr who apparently told Sgt Rimmer to record Susan May's alleged question relating to scratches on her aunt's face in her notebook. He did not point out that Susan should now be treated as a suspect, and appears to have endorsed the decision to continue to interview her as a "witness." In court, Mr Kerr had given the impression that failure to record Susan's alleged question in the HOLMES database was not particularly important, when, in fact, it was a significant breach of procedures. He claimed that he had been suspicious that the crime scene had not appeared to him to be a "real" burglary, indicating that he had been suspicious of Susan for a substantial period of time prior to her *actually* being treated as a suspect. It is also important to note that this officer had access to information regarding another possible (and some would say far more credible) suspect who was directly related to the theory of a burglary gone wrong, information which he had clearly chosen to dismiss in order to encourage his suspicion of Susan. D. Supt Kerr implied at trial that he was the first to notice the stains on the wall, saying that he noted the marks after opening the curtains when he first entered the room. He could not remember if the lights had been on in the room, or if he had turned them on. Prior to his arrival, the two ambulance men had been first on the scene, followed by Detective Inspector David Taylor and PC Roy Kelly. Both ambulance men stated that they had switched on the light in the room, but left the curtains closed. After establishing that Mrs Marchbank was dead, they left the room and radioed for the police, stating that there was a suspicious death. Although Mr Smith said in his statement at this point that they had left the light on, in evidence, he could no longer remember whether or not the light had been left on or switched off. DI Taylor, the next person to arrive, stated that the lights in the room were off when he arrived, but were turned on by someone behind him. He, too, agreed that the curtains were closed. He confirmed that a photograph shown to him showed the room exactly as it was when he entered, at 10.05am, with the curtains "very effectively blocking out the light." This photograph was taken by Mark Naylor, who did not commence his photography until sometime after midday, and the video footage also shows the curtains being closed as late as 1.58pm.

In other words, the curtains do not appear to have been disturbed at any time between 10.05am and 1.58pm, despite D. Supt Kerr's claims to have opened them shortly after entering the room at 10.32am.

Mr Kerr also stated, in evidence, that he had touched Mrs Marchbank's injured cheek in order to check whether she was still alive. The ambulancemen had already ascertained that she was dead, and had radioed police to report a "suspicious *death*"- Mr Kerr's explanation for his action was that

> "no medical officer had been in attendance and {he} considered {he} had a responsibility to check whether there was anything that could be done for the victim, should she still be alive."

He did not explain why he had touched her cheek, rather than trying to find a pulse, but what is most significant is that wet blood, which later appeared on the pillow, may have come from a blood blister on Mrs Marchbank's cheek.

The implications regarding contamination of the crime scene, particularly with reference to the marks on the wall, are obvious, especially if Mr Kerr had also turned on the light. (The stain made in Mrs Marchbank's blood was near the light switch.) By the time he came to give evidence, this officer "could not remember" if he had switched the light on or not.

Although Mr Kerr claimed in court to have noticed three separate areas of staining in the wall, and this happened *after* he opened the curtains, there is no evidence to support his claims. He did not direct the videographer to record them, the photographer recorded only two stains, at an unspecified time, and there is nothing anywhere to show that the curtains were, in fact opened.

Very briefly, by this stage, the role of D Supt Kerr involves instructions to officers which, at the very least, do not follow codes of practice, attempts to minimise extensive failures to follow procedures, possible contamination of a crime scene, failure to properly direct forensics experts, unsubstantiated claims regarding forensic evidence, and, at this, as well as later stages, this officer justifies changes in evidence he gives by explaining, "…what I meant by that was……." No other witness or suspect would be allowed to alter testimony by suggesting that they had actually meant something quite different to what they previously said, yet for reasons known only to themselves, the judges not only allow, but positively endorse this behaviour in a Senior Investigating Officer.

Similar discrepancies arise in the statements of Michael Davie, the Forensic Scientist. He and his assistant, Joanne Ashworth, entered the house at 1.10pm. They left the house at 2.07pm, returned at 2.25pm, and left again at 4.20pm. During these two periods of time, also present in the house were Mr Kerr, the photographer, and the videographer. Had Mr Davie noticed the marks on the wall, one would imagine he would have pointed them out to the others. (Indeed, since D Supt Kerr claims to have noticed the stains shortly after 10.30am, it is surprising that he did not instruct Mr Davie to note them for further investigation.)

He (Michael Davie) claims to have examined the body at 13.30, and noted three small areas of wet blood on the pillow under Mrs Marchbank's head. Photographic evidence shows that this cannot be so – there are no wet blood marks when the body is still on the bed, they appear only after the body has been moved. Further, Mr Davie indicated in his notes that Dr Lawlor, the Home Office Pathologist, was present when he (Mr Davie) carried out his examination of the body, but Mr Lawlor did not arrive until 2.45pm, fully one and a quarter hours later.

Mr Davie's first specific reference to the stain on the wall near the light switch does not appear in his notes until March 17th, five days after the murder. Why would such critical evidence have been left, unexamined, for such a length of time, especially as the SIO claimed to have noted it almost immediately upon his arrival at the scene?

Different additions to Mr Davie's notes raise serious questions as to their accuracy or reliability. For example, one document has an addition regarding a test result, claimed to have been secured at the time (ie, March 1992), but which was actually added in June 1995. The original document, without the additional note, was "lost" at the appeal stage, but subsequently re-appeared amongst CPS papers.

Two of the stains removed from the wall for testing, including the one in which Susan May's handprint was identified, were tested by Mr Davie. The form on which he recorded his findings was dated 29th April 1994, not 29th April 1992, which was the date on which they had been removed from the wall. Although Mr Davie was quite certain that this 2 year discrepancy was a clerical error, it emerged that the form on which the results had been recorded did not come into use until November 1993.

The care of these stains, so crucial to the case against Susan May, leaves some serious unanswered questions. Firstly, they are left on the wall of the house for some seven weeks before being removed for testing. After testing in the Chorley lab in 1992, the stains were stored in the secure property store at Oldham Police station until October 1994, *when they were removed by D. Supt Kerr.* He kept them in a locked filing cabinet until he passed them to Timothy Clayton, a FSS scientist on January 5th 1995.

Mr Davie found another stain in the kitchen behind a radiator, which tested positive for blood, although the distinction between human or animal blood could not be made. He concluded that this bloodstain was not linked to the murder because towels on the radiator prior to the murder had not been disturbed. However, the jury was told that, aside from the three "bloodstains" in the dining room, there had been no other bloodstains anywhere in the house, a claim which is quite clearly untrue.

A paper bag found in the kitchen contained tea bags and scraps of meat. On March 24th 1992, Javaid Hussain advised the Senior Investigating Officer (ie, D Supt Kerr) to consider submitting the bag to the lab for further tests. The bag was submitted to the lab on 26th March, then brought back from Oldham by **Michael Davie**. Although the instructions on the form with the bag included "Establish whether marks on outside of bag are blood and what are contents of bag," no record of such examination was ever found.

Michael Davie confirmed that no further tests have been carried out. The significance of this particular sequence of events is of critical importance. Had the bag been tested, and the marks on the outside proven to be animal blood, then the existence of this evidence, plus the fingerprint behind the radiator in the kitchen, effectively destroys the prosecution case. Why did Michael Davie bring the bag back from Oldham, and on whose instructions were those critical tests never carried out?

Even though the judge had confessed to some confusion as to how animal blood could have been found on the wall leading to the kitchen, the contents of this bag may have provided a perfectly innocent explanation, had the correct tests been carried out. To further compound the issue, the bag had been listed on the unused exhibits list as

"Craftsman Baker Paper Bag" with no reference to its contents, or the fact that it was bloodstained. A mark on a dress belonging to Susan May had also tested positive for bovine blood, providing further proof that bloodstains resulting from food preparation can and do exist in the home, but this item was again listed on the unused exhibits list as "dress," its significance lost.

The claim that Susan's question regarding scratches to her aunt's face could only have been made by someone who *knew* of such scratches also requires further examination. DC Ogden's notebook contains the note

> "..speak to Ann{e} Mellor and Susan May informed re cause of death bruising on head hand over mouth…"

Far from the claim that Susan could not possibly have known the details of her aunt's injuries, here is a clear indication that at least some of her injuries were discussed by police officers with Susan and her sister. DC Ogden's notebook, however, was not made available to the defence, presumably on the grounds that the "incriminating" question had only been logged in Sgt Rimmer's notebook, which was then subsequently "lost." Further, Susan originally claimed that she thought there had been blood on her aunt's face when she found her. The police claim was that, because of the way her aunt was lying, Susan could not have seen the scratches from the position she (Susan) claimed to have been in when she discovered the body. ***But***, this completely misses a crucial point with regard to the behaviour of D Supt Kerr. He admitted touching Hilda Marchbank's cheek. How can anyone ever be sure that this action did not move the old lady's face slightly, from a position where her injuries may have been apparent to someone entering the room, to one where such observation might be less likely?

Other evidence not led in court

Just after midnight on the night Hilda Marchbank was murdered, two separate witnesses reported cars in the area. A "Mr W" saw a red car with three occupants, and a "Mr O," Hilda's next door neighbour, looked out of his bedroom window to see a red car without occupants, but with its engine running, both witnesses claiming these sightings as being "shortly after midnight." Given the time of death adduced by the pathologist to be between 9pm and midnight, the presence of this car, or these cars, would appear to be of significance.

Although a great deal of attention was given to the marks on the wall in the downstairs room in which Mrs Marchbanks slept, the jury was not told about the fingerprint behind the kitchen radiator. There are three significant factors to this omission – firstly, the jury were led to believe that the three prints led in evidence were the *only* prints found in the house, secondly, the three prints were claimed to have been made at the same time, although there was no evidence to back up this claim, and thirdly, the marks were claimed to be bloodstains in human blood. The existence of a print which *had* existed prior to the murder would surely have cast more serious doubt on the claims made about the other three prints? Also, the jury was not made aware of the unidentified footprint found in a wardrobe.

Clothing fibres were found on Hilda's hand which did not match any of Susan's or her aunt's clothing. As with the "Craftsman Baker Paper Bag" and "dress" referred to earlier, this evidence was filed under the label "hairs." The existence of these fibres could be seen as supportive of any question Susan may have had regarding "forensics" from her aunt's nails.

Ironically, in so many of the other cases highlighted in this book, "fibre evidence" has been used, wrongly, to extremely detrimental effect. In this case, its existence could actually have been used in support of the suspect's innocence, but is, in reality, completely dismissed.

A woman, referred to as "KB", told police that her brother "B," a known, violent burglar, had spoken to her about the murder, even before Susan had found her aunt. This statement was made on the morning of the murder, although "KB" later retracted her statement. This statement also referred to a car which matched the description of the car seen by Hilda Marchbank's neighbours that night, although the jury were never made aware of this. In fact, the police filed her statement in the wrong file, and as a result, it was lost to the defence.

Much was made of the fact that there was no sign of forced entry, and that nothing was taken, indicating that the scene had been "faked" to resemble a burglary. However, Mrs Marchbank did not always lock her door, and the question must be addressed; if burglars had entered the premises through an unlocked door, how might they have reacted to confronting someone in a downstairs room?

Perhaps most critical of all of the evidence in the case against Susan May was that discovered by later, independent tests of the stains on the wall which had been so central to the prosecution case. Tests carried out by FSS Wetherby police scientists of the stain which contained the imprint of Susan May's handprint obtained "negative for blood" results. A German Scientist, Professor Brinkman, also obtained "negative for blood" results, yet it was presented to the jury that all three stains were bloodstains, deposited from Susan May's hands, after they had become contaminated with her aunt's blood as she killed her. If so-called "bloodstains" tested *negative* for blood, then we are surely led to the conclusion that they are not, in fact, blood stains after all.

As if all of this is not bad enough, we then find another example of appeal judges appearing to be unwilling or unable to understand the information before them, or to interpret that information in biased and selective ways.

For example, the conclusion of the 2001 appeal contained the following:

> "We found Detective Superintendent Kerr and Mrs Ashworth to be impressive witnesses and we see no reason to doubt their evidence that separately they observed all three marks on the wall at an early stage, well before the body was moved from the bed. We reject as fanciful, and in conflict with their evidence, any suggestion that the third mark may have got there as a result of transfer by Detective Superintendent Kerr, Mr Davie, Dr Lawler or whoever assisted Dr Lawler with the removal of the body. In reality there was no liquid blood available to transfer until Dr Lawler examined the body and, quite apart from the observation evidence which we accept, for the reasons explained by Dr Lawler we cannot see how the third mark could have got onto the wall thereafter........"

As has already been shown, the evidence of D Supt Kerr was conflicting, contradictory and unreliable. There are, of course, several possibilities as to how the "third stain" (in Mrs Marchbank's own blood) may have been transferred to the wall, including that D Supt Kerr touched the victim's cheek, where a blood blister had been observed.

The report continues:

> "........ we accept that there were no grounds to suspect the appellant of having committed an offence such as to require that she be cautioned in the earlier stages of the inquiry. In {that} sequence of events we are unable to detect any breach of any provision of any code which was then in force, and we see no reason to treat later changes in the Code as though they were in force at the relevant time."

Unbelievably, this finding came *after* a Police Complaints Authority investigation in 1999, looking into whether the questioning of Susan May without caution amounted to a breach of rules under PACE. Following that investigation, PCA member, Mr Ian Bynoe concluded:

> "My analysis of the evidence leads me to the conclusion that the statement taken from you on 23 March 1992 should only have

been taken from you after you had been formally cautioned. Mr Kerr should bear the main responsibility for the fact that this was not done. To this extent, your complaint is upheld."

Remember, too, that D Supt Kerr claimed to have suspected from "early in the investigation" that the burglary had been faked, suggesting strongly that his suspicions regarding Susan had begun to crystallise by then.

The 2001 Appeal document concludes:

".......With the benefit of hindsight it is unfortunate that Detective Superintendent Kerr and Mrs Ashworth did not record the time at which they separately observed the three marks, and that Detective Superintendent Kerr did not cause Mr Naylor to photograph all three marks. The reason is obvious. At the time the third mark did not appear to be of great significance, and it is unrealistic to expect every step at an inquiry to be time-recorded, whatever its significance. It is also unfortunate that the evidence of the reporting officer assigned to this case by the FSS was such that counsel appearing for the Crown before us felt obliged to invite us to set it aside, and the shortcomings of that witness may explain why there seems to have been no further examination of the Craftsman Baker paper bag. But the significance of that item was overtaken by events, and, for the reasons which we have explained, we do not think that the conviction is unsafe. We must therefore dismiss this appeal."

How can Appeal judges, with the enormous power they wield, appear to display such unbelievable naivety – it is not "unfortunate" that two separate officers failed to properly carry out their duties, it is serious error which requires much more extensive explanation. The "reason" to which they refer is only "obvious" when following the appeal judges' own line of reasoning. Other, more feasible interpretation of the available information provides a much more "obvious" reason – at the time, the third mark did not exist, because it was deposited later. While it may be unrealistic to expect every step at an inquiry to be time recorded, it is both realistic and essential that what must appear to be *significant* steps, such as the discovery of apparent bloodstains in a murder inquiry, *are* recorded in this manner.

Susan May served 12 years before being released on license on 26/04/05. Yet the case against her was never proven – indeed, all of the available evidence points to Susan's innocence, and Susan continues the fight to clear her name.

The decision by police, from so early in the case, to pursue Susan rather than other, more plausible options, and the requirement for evidence to be shoe-horned to fit the police theory is not, by now, unusual. What *is* unusual is the statement by "K.B." Other witnesses had come forward describing a car at the scene of the murder that night, at a time which fitted with the pathologist's time of death. It seems almost unbelievable, then, that when a witness came forward to say her brother had told her about the murder before the body had even been found, and that he drove a car similar to the one described by other witnesses at the scene, the police failed to follow it up.

The flimsiness of the case against Susan May is shocking. The whole bloodstains on the wall issue is mired in confusion and neglect – procedures were either shoddily carried out or ignored completely, documents were amended literally *years* after the event, and the various expert testimonies contradict each other. The judge, during the trial, dismisses any possibility of the stains being animal blood, going so far as to say he can't see how it would even be possible to imagine how handprints in animal blood could come to be on the wall. Yet there is evidence, although it has been "lost" by the police, that there were meat scraps in a paper bag on the kitchen table, and that a stain on one of Susan's dresses had tested positive as bovine blood – in other words, there was always a perfectly reasonable possibility of fingerprints in animal blood being deposited as a result of food preparation. The judge's outright dismissal of this possibility can be seen to have misled the jury, particularly in view of the later "negative for blood" test results.

Summary

On what grounds, then, was Susan May found guilty, beyond reasonable doubt?

The "prints in blood," claimed by the prosecution to have been made by Susan "feeling her way" out of the room in darkness emerge, after later, independent testing, as "*negative* for blood."

The bag containing meat scraps could have provided a perfectly innocent explanation for any "marks in blood" found anywhere in the house, yet, not only were the required tests never carried out, the judge actively *dismissed* the possibility of any marks in animal blood being deposited.

Police statements were altered, lost, or incomplete. Several significant breaches of procedure cast the whole police case in an extremely unreliable light – the loss of critical notebooks, failure to register important details in the HOLMES computerised system, failure to advise

Susan that she had become a suspect, and to caution her formally before interview, alongside later altered details all highlight a flawed operation.

No adequate explanation was ever given for Mr Kerr touching the body, and thereby contaminating the crime scene.

The entire forensic operation was shoddy, inaccurate and unreliable, with documents being completed or amended literally years after events.

Other possible suspects were never followed up, yet police did not follow recognised protocol in order to ensure that Susan, as a suspect (a fact she was not even made aware of) was treated fairly.

Evidence regarding the moving of Mrs Marchbank's body, and placing it in the body bag is lost – given the reliance of the prosecution of the "marks on the wall," this evidence could have been crucial. In the event, we will simply never know whether Mrs Marchbank's blood may have been deposited on the wall as a result of her body being moved (or of Mr Kerr transferring blood from the body to the wall after touching Mrs Marchbank), because any evidence regarding these events is not available.

The contention that only the killer could have known about the scratches on Mrs Marchbank's face is ridiculous, on examination of the facts. From early statements, in spite of her obvious shock and confusion, Susan mentions blood on her aunt's face. Later records show that police discussed some of her aunt's injuries with Susan and her sister. Most ordinary people would assume that, in a murder case, some sort of forensic examination would take place – even if Susan *did* ask the question police claimed she asked (and bear in mind, there is absolutely no evidence that she did, apart from the police say-so), it doesn't mean anything sinister at all!

Although the pathologist report put the time of death somewhere between 9pm and midnight, the possibility of Susan having committed the murder during this timescale is highly unlikely – like many of the other cases, she has a very short space of time to not only commit the murder, but to then also clean away all traces, and return to acting perfectly normally. At the same time, other, perfectly feasible suspects are allowed to disappear without examination or scrutiny.

As with all the other cases in this book, examination of the Susan May case against the "Twelve Points" needs, by now, no explanation:

- Susan May was convicted on purely circumstantial evidence (once the "bloodstains" evidence was discredited, there was no other concrete evidence)

- Reasonable doubt is more than glaringly obvious
- There was no DNA or forensic evidence linking Susan May to the crime (again, after the "bloodstains" evidence was discredited)
- Although Susan admits to being at her aunt's house at around 9pm that evening, there are no witnesses to testify that anything untoward happened at that time. Susan was not witnessed acting anything other than perfectly normally, and there were no reports of noise indicating that the house was being ransacked.
- There were other, credible suspects who were never followed up
- There was clear over-reliance on "expert testimony" to the detriment of Susan May
- There were serious questions about the ability of Susan to have carried out the crime within the timescale suggested
- Character assassination constituted a strong part of the prosecution's case
- There was evidence of forensics experts selectively interpreting evidence to the prosecution's own ends
- Susan May was a woman of previously exemplary character, with no convictions or psychological conditions.

Therefore, in this case, ten of the twelve points apply.

The similarities with the other cases, however, continue to accumulate.

Police procedures fail in almost exactly the same manner; altered police records, failure to record critical details, such as where the body was placed in the body bag, and by whom (Derek Christian, Simon Hall, Gordon Park); the suspect "targeted" by a police opinion that they knew something that "only the killer could have known" (Luke Mitchell); unidentified footprints found at the scene of the crime (Derek Christian, Simon Hall); the crime scene or evidence contaminated (Derek Christian, Gordon Park, Luke Mitchell); the jury misled by statements made by the judge (John Taft, Simon Hall, Luke Mitchell); incompetent and shoddy forensic procedures and experts (Derek Christian, Simon Hall, John Taft, Gordon Park, Luke Mitchell); the appointment of a "liaison officer" without the eventual suspect ever being advised that this officer is, in fact, a member of the investigating team (Luke Mitchell), and, of course, similar to all of these cases, we are asked to believe that Susan suddenly behaved in a manner which is completely out of character, and, within moments of such uncharacteristic behaviour, returned immediately to her normal self!

The most worrying issues raised by the Susan May case

- Standard police procedures are blatantly ignored.
- "Evidence" of a highly dubious nature, including restrospective alterations to written documents, is allowed
- Police use clearly unfair (and illegitimate) means to elicit information
- Once again, the use of innuendo and speculation, designed to discredit the suspect in the absence of other, more concrete evidence, is apparent
- The entire police operation demands further investigation (but, as with all of the other cases, is unlikely to be given even the most cursory examination)
- Certain evidence was not made available to the jury, and evidence which should have been made available appears to have been suppressed.

References:

Transcript: Summing up, Before Justice Hutchison, Thursday April 22nd 1993 to Tuesday May 4th 1993
Transcript: CCRC Statement of Reasons, referred April 1997, reported 24th November 1999.
Transcript: "Skeleton Argument," 20th November 2001
Transcript: "Judgment," 7th December 2001
"Judgment Response, Andrew Green, www.innocent.org.uk
Private Eye 1137, July 22nd 2005
Telegraph, "Woman Loses Appeal over Murder of Elderly Aunt," Feb 15th 1997
Guardian, "Town Fights to Free Jailed Carer," Tracy McVeigh, May7th 2000
Independent, "Jailed Woman Insists She did not kill Elderly Aunt," Robert Verkaik, Legal Affairs Correspondent, August 13th 2001
BBC News, December 7th 2001
Guardian Unlimited, "A Death in the Family," June 9th 2002.

Chapter Eight

The case of Sion Jenkins

IN SPITE of massive media coverage, very little factual detail concerning the case of Sion Jenkins has actually made it into the public domain. Although Sion Jenkins has been cleared of any and all wrongdoing since work on this book began, the inclusion of his case is both relevant and important. The fact that so many striking similarities exist between this and many of the cases highlighted in this book goes some way to showing that the inherent flaws and weaknesses in the criminal justice system *do* exist, and also re-inforces the difficulties faced by those prosecuted and imprisoned as a result of those flaws and weaknesses, in having their concerns acknowledged.

Billie-Jo Jenkins was fostered by Sion and Lois Jenkins (it is coincidence that the surnames are the same – there is no blood relation between the family and Billie-Jo) in 1992, following a "difficult" childhood, which had included some time spent in care. For five years, she lived as, and was treated as, a full member of the family, alongside the Jenkins' four natural daughters. According to both Lois Jenkins, herself a social worker, and the social work department, Billie-Jo flourished with the family, blossoming into a confident, happy teenager.

On Saturday February 15th 1997, at approximately 3.30pm, Billie-Jo was battered to death in the garden of the family home. The weapon, an 18 inch tent peg, was left beside her head. Billie-Jo had not been sexually assaulted, and there were no signs of the house having been broken into or burgled.

There had been several incidents in the Hastings area where the Jenkins lived, and where Billie-Jo was killed, in the months leading up to the murder. Two young girls were sexually assaulted and two people had been murdered in 1996. Billie-Jo's murder was immediately linked to these crimes, and also to the attack on the Russell family in Chillenden, Kent. The extent of Billie-Jo's injuries led police to describe the attack as "vicious and frenzied," calling the attacker "evil and deranged."

Early newspaper reports stated that police were looking for a man with a scar or birthmark across his face, who had been witnessed acting strangely in the area that day.

According to Sion, the day had been a typical, chaotic family Saturday. Lois took three of the girls shopping to Safeway, and telephoned Sion to say she couldn't pay the bill because she'd forgotten her chequebook. Sion drove to Safeway, realising when he got there that he'd taken a chequebook with no cheques left in it, so he had to go back and bring another. The family then returned home, with the exception of one daughter, Lottie, who had been at the cinema with a friend. Lottie was then taken to a clarinet lesson by her friend's mother, and it was decided that while Lois took the two youngest children for a walk on the beach, Sion would pick up Lottie from her clarinet lesson. After Lois left for the beach, Sion set the two eldest children some chores, for which they would earn extra pocket money. There was some disagreement about who was to do what chores, and a compromise was reached – Annie would clean out the storeroom and Billie-Jo would sweep the patio and paint the doors until 4pm, when Annie would take over the painting, allowing Billie-Jo to go to a local store to buy some trainers. When it was time to pick up Lottie, Annie decided to go with Sion, Billie-Jo opted to stay and continue painting. They collected Lottie and her friend, dropping off the friend on the way home at between 3.15pm and 3.20pm. When they got home, Sion realised he should have picked up some white spirit at Do-It-All. Taking Annie and Lottie with him, he drove to Do-It-All only to discover that, exactly as Lois had done earlier in the day, he had no means to pay.

They returned home, and all three entered the house. Billie-Jo was lying in a pool of blood on the patio. Sion went to her, crouched over her, then ushered the two other children into the house. The girls were hysterical, but Sion had to return to Billie-Jo, where he examined her more carefully, then made a 999 call for an ambulance. He then telephoned for a neighbour, and eight minutes after the first 999 call, he made another. When the ambulance men arrived, Sion went outside and got in his car, then got back out and returned to the house. Although this action was most likely the result of shock, it would later be used to devastating effect by the prosecution.

Sion Jenkins was charged with Billie-Jo's murder on March 14th 1997, having been arrested on February 24th, just 9 days after Billie-Jo was killed. He was sentenced to life imprisonment in July 1998. He always protested his innocence. His first appeal in December 1999 was rejected. The case was referred back to the appeal court by the CCRC in May 2003, the appeal succeeded in July 2004, and Sion Jenkins was released on bail, pending a re-trial, in August 2004. The retrial began on April 6th 2005, ending with a hung jury on 11th July that year. The prosecution immediately called for a *third* trial, which began on 31st October 2005. That jury, also, could not come to a unanimous decision and on February 9th 2006, Sion Jenkins was finally formally acquitted of murder.

The case, throughout the whole nine years from 1997 to 2006, was the subject of enormously intense media attention, almost entirely negative, speculative and prejudicial. As with so many of the cases in this book, Sion Jenkins was not tried and convicted on "the evidence," because, quite simply, there was none. Yet the treatment of the case by the media, and by those involved in the "investigation" effectively closed off any chance of a fair trial, and Sion Jenkins' right to be presumed innocent until proven guilty was denied from the off.

The Police Investigation and the Prosecution Case

Originally, police statements reported in the media claimed that Billie-Jo's murderer would have been heavily bloodstained, and would possibly also have paint stains on his clothing. He was described as "evil and deranged." They were looking for a man, they said, with a scar or birthmark across his face who had been seen acting strangely in the area that day. A man fitting descriptions by witnesses was traced, but his psychiatrist would not allow him to be interviewed, as he was "floridly psychotic" at the time of Billie-Jo's murder. It was always assumed that this man would be interviewed at a later date, but this never actually happened.

The case had received massive publicity, and the police were under extra pressure because of recent cases which had undermined public confidence in the Sussex force. Two "discoveries" would lead to the entire weight of the investigation being focused on just one person – Sion Jenkins. The first was a discovery that he had been less than truthful on his cv when applying, some 5 years earlier, for the job he currently held. With no regard to the glaring illogicality of their approach, the police assertion was that if he had lied on his cv, he was probably lying about what had happened to Billie-Jo. The second discovery was the return of forensic tests which showed that blood spots, so tiny as to be invisible to the naked eye, found on Sion's fleece, were Billie-Jo's blood.

In a blaze of publicity, Sion Jenkins was arrested for obtaining pecuniary advantage by deception, and for the murder of Billie-Jo Jenkins. The rumour mill went into overdrive – although police had made it clear Sion had "lied" on his cv, they did not (obviously) clarify *what* he had lied about, leaving speculation and innuendo to do the rest. The public perception quickly gravitated around a belief that he was somehow a bogus teacher, unqualified to hold the position he held. In fact, he was fully and completely qualified – the embellishments in his cv amounted to changing Glasgow Academy to Gordonstoun, and enhancing the teaching qualification he gained at Nonnington College of Education to a "degree from the University of Kent" (Nonnington College was later incorporated into the University of Kent). Whilst this is clearly wrong, it is also fairly common, and hardly an indicator of the likelihood to carry out a vicious murder. However, once the suggestion of Sion's ability to lie "convincingly" (so much so, the implication went, that he had managed to fool people into believing he was a teacher for all those years, to the point where he was about to be promoted to the position of headmaster), everything else was examined and evaluated against this backdrop.

The prosecution, with expert evidence to claim that there was no explanation for the blood on Sion's clothes other than that he had been the murderer, then produced the most remarkable series of claims to back their contention:

Sion, they claimed, had suddenly and inexplicably lost his temper with Billie-Jo, and beaten her to death with the tent peg. Being, however, extremely callous and controlled, he then composed himself, and set off on the trip to Do-It-All to cover his tracks, and to create a "window of opportunity" in which he could claim that an intruder had, in fact, been responsible. The proof that the Do-It-All trip was a sham, they contended, was that he had gone to buy white spirit that he didn't need, as there was already some in a cupboard in the house, he took no money with him, and he took an indirect route (presumably to buy himself more time).

The way he acted upon finding the body, and in the immediate aftermath was used as further "proof" that he must have been the murderer – he "acted strangely" by, at one point, getting into his car, closing the roof, and getting back out, his 999 calls were "not accurate" and "vague," he did not check whether Billie-Jo was dead (because, they claimed, having killed her, he already knew), and he seemed detached and calm in the face of the tragedy he had just discovered.

Further suspicion was raised by the claim that he was reluctant to wear his fleece that evening, and, in police interviews, he had first said that he did not go back into the house on returning from the clarinet lesson, and only accepted that he had done so after being shown his daughters' statements.

The extent of prejudicial reporting prior to the case cannot be over emphasised. Sion entered court already branded a "liar" because of the cv claims. As in the Luke Mitchell case, some 6 years later, the deception charge was left on file, having served its purpose in creating prejudice and suspicion during the lead up to the trial.

On the morning after Billie-Jo was found, the two daughters who had been with Sion at the time of the murder, Annie and Lottie, were interviewed by police, and their interviews video-taped. These interviews supported Sion's version of events. He had had an opportunity to speak alone with Annie prior to these interviews, but not to Lottie. However, police logs showed that, as there was very little to progress the case against Sion (particularly as the girls' account verified Sion's own account) a decision was taken, and logged in police records as "Feed into Mum." This followed on the heels of forensics testing which showed that the fine mist of invisible blood spots on Sion's fleece had come from Billie-Jo.

It must be pointed out at this stage that Billie-Jo had been brutally bludgeoned, her skull crushed by the tent pole. The whole scene was covered with blood, including the murder weapon which was left lying by her head. Yet at no point did the question arise as to how Sion's clothing came to have nothing but a fine spray of blood spots, which were invisible to the naked eye.

Indeed, experiments allegedly claiming to "prove" how such spots could only have appeared on Sion's clothing if he were the attacker (experiments involving striking the skull of an already dead pig) could not be completed even once without the striking arm of the assailant becoming heavily bloodstained!

But the decision to "Feed into Mum" was to have devastating effects for Sion's defence. He had been arrested on February 24th. On February 25th, during a two hour interview, police repeatedly told Lois Jenkins that they had scientific evidence which proved that her husband had killed Billie-Jo. Until this point, Lois had made no mention of any violent behaviour by her husband. Now she made another statement, claiming that he had hit her on a number of occasions.

Just over three weeks later, on March 20th, police spoke to the four children, in the presence of their mother, and informed them that there was forensic evidence to prove that their father had killed their foster-sister, and also that he had been violent towards their mother. A social worker who had been scheduled to attend had been unable to do so. In the weeks and months following this interview, the girls were to make significant alterations to their statements, often reported to police by Lois. This outrageous move on the part of Sussex police was later to be criticised by appeal judges. At the time, the testimony of these two girls was Sion's only alibi. Anyone else attempting to influence key witnesses in this manner would have been in grave danger of being charged with attempting to pervert the course of justice – no action was taken against the officers involved in this instance. Even the clear example of double standards appeared not to faze the police – on the one hand, they implied that the time Sion had spent alone with Annie on the evening of the murder had allowed him to "influence" her statement, going as far as to bring in social workers who suggested her recollection of events would need to be "deconstructed," yet on the other, failed to acknowledge any problem with feeding information to mother and children who would be spending a great deal of time alone together.

Yet, on closer examination, the prosecution's case simply does not hold up. The most immediate problem is that of time-scale. Sion is proven, without doubt, to have dropped Lottie's friend off after the clarinet lesson between 3.15 and 3.20pm. The first call to the emergency services was logged at 3.38pm. That leaves a window of between 18 and 23 minutes. The drive from the friend's home to the Jenkins home takes four and a half minutes. The window now drops to thirteen and a half to eighteen and a half minutes. The drive to Do-It-All and back would have taken an absolute minimum of fifteen minutes – the only unaccounted time left is three and a half minutes, and is dependent on Sion having dropped Lottie's friend at exactly 3.15pm, a time which was never positively confirmed. Any time after 3.15pm drops the amount of time available to Sion even further.

In this three and a half minutes, we are asked to believe that Sion experienced a volcanic eruption of temper, bludgeoned Billie-Jo to death, returned to his normal, calm state, and removed every trace of what had just occurred from his person, and still had the presence of mind to drive to Do-It-All to provide himself with a fake alibi. Further, we are to believe he carried out this attack with his other two daughters in the house, who could have wandered in at any minute. Billie-Jo was not killed by a single blow – her skull was "crushed" in a "frenzied" attack which consisted of several blows. Given the physical exertion, alone, required to carry out such an attack, it is highly unlikely that it would have been physically possible for Sion's heart rate, breathing and skin colour to have returned to normal within the timescale available, yet his daughters noticed nothing at all untoward.

The fact that he had initially said he had not entered the house on returning from the clarinet lesson can easily be explained as a simple oversight on what had been a chaotic day, with an utterly devastating end. However, this error makes no real difference, since Annie's statement makes specific reference to her speaking to Billie-Jo in this period. Yet, for the Do-It-All trip to have been a cover for the murder, it is in this time that Sion would have to have murdered her – the loss of

145

opportunity to use Annie's statement left the prosecution free rein to continue to assert that Sion had killed Billie-Jo in this period. Lottie's statement was equally important at this juncture, since she was adamant that the side gate to the garden, which had been closed when they left, was swinging open when they returned and found Billie-Jo. There had been previous difficulties in the area with prowlers, and the gate had been found open on several previous occasions when the family had already closed it. There had also been an attempted break-in in the weeks leading up to Billie-Jo's murder. The jury in the original trial did not hear either of the girls' statements, on the grounds that later information given to them by the police would, most certainly, have influenced their testimonies.

Despite Sion's long teaching career, dealing with children and teenagers, not a single incident of him losing his temper could be found, ever. The prosecution could offer no explanation as to why, now, he should suddenly behave in such an uncharacteristic manner – the best they could manage was that Billie's painting was not up to scratch, or that she had been playing her music too loudly. Billie-Jo had been fostered by the Jenkins family for five years at this point, yet no explanation was offered as to "why now?" Two other factors point away from the prosecution contention that this had been a sudden, explosive loss of control. Firstly, the tent peg which was used to batter Billie-Jo was on a coal bunker by the gate. There were other implements, including a hammer, which were immediately to hand, had Sion, indeed, suddenly "lost the rag," but he would have had to go out of his way to pick up the tent peg. Much more telling, however, was the discovery that a large piece of plastic had been inserted into Billie-Jo's nostril, and pushed deep into the nasal cavity, probably, according to the pathologist, with an implement. This not only raises immediate questions as to the psychological state of the attacker, it forces an extension of the time-frame, and even greater certainty that the attacker *must* have been visibly bloodstained.

In another course of action which would, in other circumstances, have raised concerns about tampering with evidence, and perhaps perverting the course of justice, photographs were produced in court clearly showing a half bottle of white spirit in a cupboard in the Jenkins house. This was proof, the prosecution claimed, that Sion did not need to go to Do-It-All for white spirit. However, these photographs were taken after everything in front of the half bottle of white spirit had been removed, making it appear that the bottle was clearly visible to anyone opening the cupboard.

An ambulanceman who attended the scene clearly remembered seeing muddy footprints on Billie-Jo's legs – he stated that it looked as if someone had stood on her. Sion's shoes had distinctive treads, and were not muddied, but nothing further could be led in this regard, because no photographs were taken of the prints, and they were lost when the body was moved.

Already, there are several pieces of information which point to the attacker being someone other than Sion – the opened gate, the piece of plastic, the footprints, and the timescale. Yet, rather than pursue these avenues, the police and the prosecution continued to concentrate on only that which could be used to "prove" that Sion had been Billie-Jo's murderer.

The existence of blood spots, even though they were invisible, appeared to be enough to convince them. The murder weapon, left lying beside Billie-Jo was heavily bloodstained, yet only three microscopic drops of blood were found on the right sleeve of Sion's fleece (he is right handed). The expert witness Adrian Wain would claim in court that the blood spray on Sion's fleece proved that he had been the attacker, and that this proof was "incontrovertible."

In fact, later experiments, carried out by Professor David Dennison would not only show that the original findings were far from incontrovertible, but that they had been acquired using somewhat crude and inappropriate methods.

For the prosecution, a pig's skull, with no blood circulating, but with blood on the surface, was struck to produce a spray which the forensic scientists claimed replicated the spray on Sion's clothing. The attacker, standing close to the victim, would have created this fine mist as he reined blows down on her head.

But, the new findings criticised these findings on several counts – a pig's skull is much thicker than the fragile human skull, and is of a completely different structure. Further, pigs' respiratory systems are completely different from humans', and the lack of circulating blood means that comparison is not accurate. Also, given the nature of the attack on Billie-Jo, scientists would have expected to find not only blood, but flesh and brain tissue, to have been displaced by the blows.

The defence claim that the blood could have been deposited on Sion's fleece after having been breathed out by a dying Billie-Jo was refuted in protracted, confusing and extremely technical testimony, so much so that the judge, himself, became confused with regard to two of the most significant terms. In short, the prosecution witnesses claimed that it would have taken a large amount of air being expelled strongly from full, healthy lungs to have carried the fine mist of blood the distance required for it to land on the fleece.

They pointed to the fact that Sion had not claimed that Billie-Jo was still breathing when he found her - a factor they claimed would have been "obvious." Professor David Southall, for the prosecution, claimed,

"Anybody approaching a child with an injury who is gasping would be in no doubt whatsoever that the child was breathing and still alive and would report that because it would be so obvious to an observer."

Yet, the previous year, following the attack on Lin, Megan and Josie Russell, professionals at the scene did not, at first, realise that Josie was still alive, and informed Dr Shaun Russell that all three were dead. If it is not obvious in such circumstances to professionals, such as police officers and ambulance crews, then it can hardly be claimed to be obvious to an ordinary person, with not even basic first aid training. Also, this evidence is based on a "gasping" child, backing up the contention that only a very strong breath could have carried the spots of blood the required distance, and appears to imply that this is the only circumstance in which Sion's fleece could have become spattered with the fine mist. Josie Russell was not gasping – indeed, her breathing was so imperceptible as to have gone un-noticed for almost 45 minutes, before a police officer noticed a slight movement and realised she was still alive. By 2000, Professor Southall had been suspended by his NHS Trust. In June 2004, Professor Southall appeared before the conduct committee of the General Medical Council, and two months later, was found guilty of serious professional misconduct.

Evidence

By this stage, it becomes fairly clear that there is nothing to link Sion Jenkins with the crime. The prosecution made much of the fact that he had been the last adult to see her alive, and the first to discover her dead. What was meant by this has never been clear – if those circumstances are taken as proof of guilt, then many parents who are involved in the hunt for their missing children would fall into the same category.

There was no evidence whatsoever to support the notion that Sion had suddenly and inexplicably lost his temper. The prosecution contention that Sion had killed Billie-Jo in the three and a half minute window available, then driven to Do-It-All simply makes no logical sense – if he had driven to Do-It-All to buy time, then surely it would have made more sense (and bought more time) to have taken money, and actually gone into the store and purchased the white spirit. Again, Annie's statement confirmed that Sion had turned back, having decided it was probably too late for Annie to start painting anyway, and had only turned around and headed back to the store at Annie's insistence – had that not been the case, he would have bought himself very little time at all. There is a complete absence of logical explanation as to how he managed to commit the crime in such a short space of time *and* to walk away without a single, visible trace of evidence on his person. The crime scene was covered in blood – it simply beggars belief that the perpetrator could have remained free of bloodstaining. Similarly, Sion is right handed, yet just three microscopic dots of blood were found on the right sleeve of his fleece, even though the weapon was heavily bloodstained.

Lois's claims that Sion had frequently been violent toward her and the children also raise some serious issues. Billie-Jo had been fostered by the family for five years. This would mean that Lois had knowingly allowed a vulnerable child to be brought into an abusive household. (She and Sion had only recently signed an order which represented the halfway stage between fostering and full adoption). Furthermore, it would also have meant the social services failed to pick up on the fact that a child they had placed in care had been placed with a violent foster parent, despite regular visits and reports. The only other evidence relating to Sion and violence came from Lois following the police decision to "Feed into Mum." This becomes more concerning when it is taken into account that Lois, herself, was a social worker.

The evidence concerning Sion's "strange" behaviour following the discovery of Billie-Jo is nothing more than speculation. In traumatic circumstances, people often behave strangely – there is not, and never has been, a proper, right or normal way in which the majority of people would react. The claim that he did not check if she was alive, because he already knew she was dead is nonsense – he had found a child in a pool of blood, her skull crushed, with blood everywhere, his two other children were present at the scene, screaming and hysterical, and, by his own admission, he had no first aid training, and no experience of having to deal with such an emergency. The 999 calls were described as "vague" and "inaccurate," with Sion saying Billie-Jo had fallen and that he had been out of the house "half an hour or three quarters of an hour." Once again, the prosecution suggested that Sion had tried to distance himself from the murder by exaggerating the time he had been away from the house. Yet another, equally possible explanation is that in his panic and distress, Sion simply said the first thing that came into his head. Indeed, a neighbour, whom Sion had called for assistance, admitted that when she spoke to the emergency operator, she knew she wasn't telling the truth, she just thought they would "come quicker."

The prosecution attempted to imply or insinuate some sort of improper relationship between Sion and Billie-Jo, to provide some sort of basis for motive. Even the judge referred to 'that complex relationship" between them. Yet there was absolutely no evidence to back up this claim – all of the pathology reports proved that Billie-Jo had never been sexually abused, or sexually active.

The prosecution claim that Sion had lied to police by stating that he had not entered the house on returning from the clarinet lesson also requires further examination – it was in the immediate aftermath of the murder, on the same day, that Sion is first claimed to have told a police officer that he did not enter the house. This officer did not write up his notes until three days later, using his own words, rather than recording Sion's words. Sion was not shown this statement, nor was he asked to confirm its accuracy. Also, he was not, at that point, a suspect, and his statement was not taken under caution. Yet there is another, equally plausible and innocent explanation for Sion's statement that he did not enter the house, if, indeed, that is what he said. He was questioned within hours of finding Billie-Jo. Amidst the shock, confusion and chaos of that afternoon, it is more than reasonable to suppose that he simply forgot. How many of us, even without such horrific circumstances, would be able to account for every single movement and action in a day, when asked to do so without warning, and without time to think about it? The timescale for entering the house, as has already been shown, was just three and a half minutes – given the enormity of the events of that day, an oversight of such a tiny fragment of the day is entirely within reason.

So where, then, is the evidence which convicted Sion Jenkins, beyond reasonable doubt?

He was not convicted by eyewitness testimony – indeed, eyewitness testimony which does exist supports his innocence.

He was not convicted in the absence of other suspects

He was not convicted on feasible forensic evidence linking him to the crime – what forensic evidence existed raised serious questions as to Sion being the killer

He was not convicted through association with the murder weapon

He was not convicted on the basis of a feasible "window of opportunity" to have carried out the murder

He was not convicted on the basis of a history of violent behaviour

He was not convicted by being proven to have "lied" about any of the circumstances of that day.

He was not convicted on the basis of an improper relationship having existed between him and Billie-Jo.

He was not convicted by any link with the piece of plastic inserted into the victim's nose.

Yet the jury found him guilty of the murder of Billie-Jo Jenkins, and he was sentenced to life imprisonment on July 2nd 1998.

After the trial

On September 15th 1999, 14 months after Sion Jenkins' conviction, Channel Four's '*Trial and Error*' screened a programme covering the case.

Professor David Dennison, an expert in heart and lungs, and an eminent scientist, carried out several experiments into the possibility of the blood spots on the fleece having been breathed out. These experiments were carried out under rigorous conditions, with findings being "minutely documented" and captured on slow motion film. Professor Dennison's consistent and clearly verified findings provided conclusive proof that a tiny, inaudible breath could cause two or three drops of blood to produce two thousand droplets. Billie-Jo need not even have been alive for this to have been the case – Sion had always claimed that he had lifted Billie-Jo's shoulder when he first found her – that movement alone could have caused a minute amount of air to be released from her airways, according to Professor Dennison's findings. Indeed, the high speed cameras used in the research revealed a consistent pattern, matching the drops on Sion's fleece.

These findings completely discredited the prosecution's scientific evidence, which had been the only real evidence available to them. In fact, Adrian Wain, the prosecution's forensic scientist who had carried out the "pig's head" experiments, claimed after the verdict that this was "central evidence" to the case, **without which there would have been no conviction.**

The programme also covered evidence relating to the psychiatric patient who had been reported acting suspiciously in the area that day, and witness statements, including one from a neighbour who heard a man in a state of distress, making strange noises and running along the passage behind the houses shortly after the time Billie-Jo was murdered. This statement was never followed up by police.

The First Appeal

The first appeal began on 29th November, 1999, and ran until 13th December 1999. The judges considered five points –

1. The issue regarding police treatment of the children whose original testimony provided Sion with an alibi
2. The admissibility of evidence by DC Hutt
3. The confusion surrounding the expert witness testimony, which had even confused the judge
4. Other points regarding the summing up
5. The fresh evidence produced by Professor Dennison

On February 16th, the day after Billie-Jo's death, both Annie and Lottie were interviewed by police, and their interviews video-taped. These two statements fit with Sion's version of events, in that the three had returned from Lottie's clarinet lesson, and gone back out almost immediately to purchase the white spirit.

On February 25th, the decision to "Feed into Mum" was taken, and the following day, police spent two hours convincing Lois Jenkins that the bloodspots on his fleece proved that her husband had killed Billie-Jo. One officer's pocket book entry "describes in vivid detail the distress that was being suffered by Mrs Jenkins and the children." This remark raises an interesting point. At a time when the police are, by their own admission, convincing Lois Jenkins that they have proof that her husband is the murderer, someone takes a great deal of care to log "in vivid detail" the distress being suffered at that time. The unspoken implication here is that the distress is as a result of the information being imparted, yet, at this stage, we are told that only Lois is given information, not the children. From this point, changes to the girls' statements begin to appear. A neighbour, on March 3rd claimed that Annie had changed her mind about what had happened that day, saying that she thought she had been outside with Lottie when her father came out (as opposed to the original statement that she had been indoors, talking to Billie-Jo.) On March 3rd and 4th, Lois Jenkins told police that Annie had "volunteered" further information, including that her father had been in a "bit of a funny mood," that he had been cross with Billie-Jo following an argument between her and Annie, and that Sion had stopped Annie from going back into the house.

On March 7th, Lois told police that Sion had been violent towards her, and had used a slipper and stick on Annie and Lottie, and that all of them were afraid of him.

Ten days later, on March 17th, three days after Sion had been charged with Billie-Jo's murder, the police consulted a consultant psychiatrist and his social worker and family therapist wife. This couple, Dr and Mrs Bentovim, concluded that Annie's thoughts had been "reconstructed" by her father, and she now needed to have them "deconstructed" in a "debriefing." It was on the strength of the reports from Dr and Mrs Bentovim that the decision to tell the children the details of the case against their father was taken. The reason for this, ostensibly, was that the children may have felt responsible for the prosecution of their father, so this extra information would help show them that this was not the case.

On March 20th, police officers spoke to all four children in the presence of their mother. Lottie referred to the "blood on his clothes," prior to the police mentioning this factor. Given that the blood was invisible to the naked eye, it can only be concluded that Lottie had been told about this evidence prior to the police visit of March 20th. The children were told that there was strong evidence that their father had killed Billie-Jo, that he had not been truthful when he got his job as deputy head teacher, that he had a "bad temper" and used excessive violence on them when they were naughty, and that he used to hit their mother.

Four months later, on July 17th, Lois Jenkins once again reported a conversation with Annie to the police. In this version, according to Mrs Jenkins, Annie claims that her father stopped her getting back into the house on three occasions, that she did not go into the house at all, that her father had come "running" down the steps, and that when they returned from the trip to Do-It-All, the door was open, because, she thought, they had left in such a hurry that her father had not had time to close it. (This, of course, takes us back to the timescale factor – within the three and a half minutes available to Sion Jenkins to have carried out the murder, we are now asked to believe that he also had time to stop another of his children entering the house not just once, but *three times*.)

On November 27th, Mrs Jenkins again reported a conversation with Annie, in which she claimed Annie had told her she did not recall entering the house after the clarinet lesson, and if she did, it was probably only as far as the hallway. She (Annie) also told her mother that she was "pressured so much" by her father that she was "unsure what to say."

Just under a month later, on December 22nd, Mrs Jenkins told a police officer that Lottie had said that she could not recall her exact movements when she returned home from her clarinet lesson, that her father had tried not to give his jumper to the police the day after the murder, and that she knew he had killed Billie-Jo.

Valerie Mellor, a consultant clinical psychologist criticised the meeting of March 20th, saying that effect of the information given to the children during that meeting "would be to influence the children's perceptions of their father." She went on to say,

> "….the effect of their evidence is very likely to be detrimental, i.e. to change their perception of their father. This in turn is likely to affect their recollection of the events of the day in question….."

The original judge, addressing the question of whether the loss of the evidence of two crucial witnesses cost Sion the right to a fair trial concluded that he was not satisfied, on the balance of probabilities, that it was the session of March 20th which had caused the girls to turn against their father. Even as he noted that between February 25th and March 20th (the period between Lois Jenkins being told that police had evidence to prove her husband had killed Billie-Jo, and the meeting with the children), Annie's statements had become "increasingly hostile to her father," he refused to infer that this may have been as a result of police "brainwashing" Lois.

The appeal judges concluded that

> "the good faith of the police has not been challenged, and their conduct was not unlawful. There was nothing unworthy or shameful about the conduct of the police."

Although the original judge had said that it

> "might have been better if police officers themselves had not conducted the session of March 20th, and if matters such as the appellant's alleged deception to obtain his teaching post, and violence towards the children and their mother had not been mentioned,"

and the appeal judges agreed with this, they then outright reject the suggestion that the police embarked on a

> "deliberate campaign to influence the children and taint their evidence so as to damage the defence of the appellant."

They also stated that the police were entitled to seek to persuade Mrs Jenkins that her husband was the killer, and concluded

> "We can find nothing to criticise in the manner in which the police conducted their enquiries of Mrs Jenkins."

The fact that the children's mother had already been "convinced" well before the session of March 20[th,] and the fact that they had spent the intervening period with their mother seems to have completely escaped attention. Lottie's comment regarding the blood on Sion's clothes goes some way to substantiating the notion that the children had already been negatively influenced, before the meeting of March 20th, as a result of the police handling of their mother. The appeal judges also conclude that because there is a lapse of four months, in Annie's case, and nine months in Lottie's case, between the March 20th meeting, and the children's statements becoming "hostile," the meeting of March 20th cannot be seen to be to blame. They also claimed that

> "even if the children had given evidence which was adverse to their father, this would not have been brought about by the conduct of the police."

DC Hutt was the officer who, following an interview with Sion on February 15th, had written up his notes some three days later, in his own words, rather than in the words Sion had allegedly said. This related to the question of whether Sion had gone into the house following the clarinet lesson – according to DC Hutt, Sion had said he did not go into the house, a factor the prosecution had claimed was a "lie." This conversation did not take place under caution, and the judge ruled the evidence supporting it as inadmissible. However, evidence of an interview on February 24th with DC Hutt, which made reference to what was allegedly said on February 15th was allowed! The appeal judges concluded that there had been nothing untoward in allowing the evidence of February 24th, because Sion had, at that point, been given the opportunity to "confirm its accuracy." What he had, in fact, said, was that if he *had* told DC Hutt he had not gone into the house, either he or the DC had made a mistake or been confused.

The appeal judges agreed that confusion which had arisen during the medical and scientific argument had not been cleared up, and had carried through to the summing up.

Regarding the new evidence of Professor Dennison, the appeal judges concluded that "his exhalation theory does not fit the facts of this case."

Their final conclusion was that

> "fresh evidence, though relevant and credible, adds so little to the weight of the defence case as compared with the prosecution's case that a doubt induced by the fresh evidence would not be a reasonable doubt,"

and dismissed the appeal.

What becomes immediately apparent is that the appeal judges have made a decision that should have been reserved for a jury – how could the judges "know" whether a jury would have considered such relevant and credible evidence to have raised 'reasonable doubt" or not?

The Second Appeal

The second appeal opened on June 28th 2004. It was adjourned almost immediately, following the serious illness of one of the judges, and resumed on June 30th.

There were three main grounds in the second appeal:

1. that the testimony of Annie and Lottie had never been heard
2. that there was fresh evidence concerning the blood splattering
3. that there was evidence suggesting an alternative suspect – Mr X.

Lottie Jenkins gave evidence at the appeal for the defence. Somewhat unusually, Anthony Scrivener, Sion's barrister at his trial also gave evidence, so as to explain why the girls' testimony had not been able to be heard at the trial.

Dr Ian Hill was the pathologist who had conducted the post mortem examination, and had given evidence at both the trial and the first appeal. In summing up the first appeal, the judges' conclusion that the "exhalation theory does not fit the facts of this case" was based on the fact that it was dependent on the existence of an obstruction of blood in the nasal valve. They stated,

> "We are satisfied from the evidence of Dr Hill that the only obstruction was in the lower airways."

However, the existence of the piece of plastic forced into Billie-Jo's nasal passage would have created just such an obstruction. At the second appeal, Dr Hill effectively retracted his evidence from the original trial. Clare Montgomery, for the defence, told the court

> "The prosecution scientists who swore on oath before the jury and the first court of appeal that there could be no innocent explanation for the blood on his clothing now accept it is a reasonable possibility that the blood was expirated as he tended Billie-Jo."

During this appeal, however, Lord Justice Rose made the following statement:

> "As to {Mr} X, there is nothing in the material before us to suggest that this aspect of the matter renders the appellant's conviction unsafe. It seems implausible that X could have walked from the park to the killing unobserved, arrived during the small window of opportunity in time, entered apparently occupied premises….and bludgeoned a girl with whom he is not shown to

have any connection for no reason. There is no evidence that he killed her."

This statement seems almost bizarre, in the face of the actual evidence:

1. Mr X was not "unobserved" – there were several witness statements reporting sightings of Mr X in and around the park, including the street where the Jenkins lived on the afternoon in question, at the relevant time. He was clearly reported moving about that area shortly before the murder, and there were witness statements of a bloodstained man seen running from the scene, and of a man who was "clearly distressed" running along the path at the back of the houses just after the time of the murder.
2. The "small window of opportunity" to which Lord Justice Rose refers is the 15 to 18 minutes during which Sion and the two girls were not at home. This is an enormous window of opportunity when compared to the three and a half minutes in which Sion is claimed to have carried out the murder, with his two other daughters close by, cleaned away any incriminating evidence from his person, and returned to a completely normal state.
3. "… and bludgeoned a girl with whom he is not shown to have any connection for no reason." Mr X had been in the Debenhams store the previous day, as had Billie-Jo. He had left writings in the restaurant referring to paedophilia and the protection of children.

Perhaps most tellingly, Lord Justice Rose is correct to assert that there is "no evidence that he killed her" – not because none exists, but because police never followed up this obviously plausible alternative suspect in order to gather what evidence there might have been.

However, if eyewitness testimony, timescale opportunity and psychiatric disorders including an obsessive habit which turns up at the scene of a murder are not enough to raise suspicion, then it begs the question as to how Sion Jenkins ever came under suspicion in the first place.

The second appeal found that Sion Jenkins' conviction was unsafe, and ordered a re-trial.

Not one but two re-trials followed, the first on opening April 6th 2005, and ending on 11th July 2005 with a hung jury, the second opening on

October 31st 2005, and ending on February 9th 2006, with Sion Jenkins finally formally acquitted of murder, just a week short of nine years after the event.

Although, by this stage, it hardly needs re-iterating, comparison of the Sion Jenkins case against the imaginary twelve points throws up the following findings:

- Sion Jenkins was convicted on purely circumstantial evidence
- There was no credible DNA or forensic evidence linking Sion to the murder – indeed, what forensic evidence *did* exist pointed away from Sion as the killer
- At the alleged time of the murder, Sion was not witnessed behaving in any way abnormally or unusually. Although he was in the vicinity of the crime (it was, after all, committed within the family home and garden), there is no feasible time during which he could have committed the murder.
- There was another, perfectly feasible suspect who was never followed up
- There was clear over-reliance on expert testimony, to the detriment of Sion Jenkins
- There were serious questions about the ability of Sion to have carried out the crime within the timescale suggested
- Clothing constituted a strong part of the prosecution's case
- Character assassination constituted a strong part of the prosecution's case
- There was evidence of forensic experts selectively interpreting evidence to the prosecution's own ends.
- Sion Jenkins was a man of previously good character with no previous convictions and no psychological conditions.

In this case, therefore, ten out of the twelve points are present.

In this final analysis, we witness once again, the consistent faults, flaws, and dirty tricks used to secure convictions in the absence of proper evidence and procedures.

And so we return to the question raised in the first chapter of this book. How can it be that so many cases, where there is no evidence to speak of, result in convictions? Now, though, we have to add some other questions;- why, for example, do all of these cases share very, very similar factors? In one case, such mistakes or flaws could be explained away as accidental, but when they appear again and again, in case after case, we have to conclude that there is something more than simple chance or coincidence at play. Is it possible that some quite deliberate and calculated processes are undertaken knowingly, and acceptably, within the various organisations which make up the criminal justice system in the UK? If so, on whose authority are these processes sanctioned? Why is the general public completely unaware that a "parallel universe" may exist within a system that same public believes to be completely transparent and incorruptible?

The remainder of this book attempts to answer these questions.

References:
Trial and Error, Channel Four, "The murder of Billie Jo," September 15th 1999
Transcript: Appeal Before Lord Justice Kennedy, Mr Justice Dyson, Mr Justice Penry-Davey
December 21st 1999
Daily Mail, "Why I Couldn't Have Murdered Billie Jo," Bob Woffinden, May 15th 2003
Sunday Telegraph, "Two years On; The Facts Reviewed", July 2nd 2000
BBC News "Jenkins defence 'impossible'- doctor" June 15th 1998
BBC News: "Legal Review of Southall's Cases" February 20th 2007

Chapter Nine

The Police

POLICE OFFICERS are human beings, just like everyone else. They are impacted by the same social processes, the same conditioning and influences, and, just like everyone else, perceive everything they experience through the filter of their own particular beliefs, thoughts, and experiences. However, because of the nature of their work, they are also likely to be influenced by particular factors which are not a consideration for people in other occupations. Generally, they are likely to spend much of their time dealing with people who have broken the law and committed crimes. Likewise, they are required to find, and examine, evidence which proves that the law has been broken and crimes have been committed. By default, therefore, there will be a subconscious expectation within police officers that those who come to their attention within the investigation of a crime are likely to have done something wrong – it is hardly reasonable to expect that the police spend vast amounts of time investigating clearly innocent people. There is also the self image of police officers as "defenders of the innocent" and "upholders of the law." Such a self image is likely to produce feelings of power and superiority, especially when coupled with the *actual* power in the hands of police officers. In reality, the police operate with a large amount of freedom and self regulation. It is rare to hear of police officers, particularly in the upper echelons, being dismissed from their positions, and, more often than not, enquiries into the conduct of any given police force are carried out by another police force. Since different forces often have to rely on one another during large investigations, the rigour and impartiality of forces investigating each other is very much open to question.

However we look at it, the police have a freedom and power which can be, and often is, misused, particularly in the case of the might of a given police force against one individual. Rather like the introduction of surprise evidence in court, if the police break the rules, or "get it wrong," it may be pointed out afterwards that this or that behaviour was unacceptable, but by then, it is too late.

In all of the cases highlighted in this book, the investigating teams appeared to take decisions regarding which person would be their main suspect, and then, rather than continuing to look at all of the evidence rationally, began to selectively collect or discard evidence according to their theory. What is most alarming is that, once the decision had been made, each of these teams clung to it tenaciously, even in the face of evidence which was clearly to the contrary.

The first question, then, is why this should have happened. What pushed each of these teams to the point where they had to decide on someone, and then defend that decision, even when it should have been apparent that they were mistaken?

Had the police simply pursued these individuals in the absence of any other evidence or suspects, then, even if, in the end, they had been pursuing the wrong person, their actions would have been understandable. But in every case, there was strong evidence to suggest that they were on the wrong track, and there were other people who would fall into the category of "suspect." What is also interesting to note is the fact that serious mistakes had been made in the early stages of these investigations; mistakes which would later prove to be extremely significant.

Following the discovery of Joan Albert's body, two police officers took Lynn Hall into the house to check if anything was missing. None of the three was wearing protective clothing, items were picked up and moved, and broken glass was trodden in, all before the scene had been forensically examined. The Home Office pathologist failed to attend the scene until some 10 hours later, by which time crucial forensic evidence, including the ability to estimate the time of death, had been lost. That "fibre evidence" would later form a central part of the prosecution case seems almost laughable, were it not so serious – Lynn Hall is Simon's mother. How could anyone ever know for sure that the fibres used to such devastating effect to connect Simon with the crime had not come, perfectly innocently, from his mother, whilst she was helping police to ascertain whether or not anything had been stolen? Further, a pubic hair found in Mrs Albert's bathroom was discovered to have come from a police officer working on the case.

Police failed to properly check the statement given to them by Barbara Taft and the Evans family. Barbara Taft's statement was proven to be incorrect on several points, and the Evans family's statement actually gave John Taft an alibi. By the time John's case came to court, two police officers who had been involved in the initial investigation 16 years earlier admitted that their original notebooks had been destroyed, apparently in line with police policy, yet this was an unsolved murder case.

At the scene of Margaret Wilson's murder, police failed to take photographs or casts of the tyre marks left at the scene. Later, two police officers would alter their original statements to "fit" Derek Christian's car, although no such statements were recorded at the time. Police records were not properly logged, so that it was impossible to say who had placed Mrs Wilson's body in the body bag, where fibres not attributable to Derek or Mrs Wilson were later found. No identity parade was ever carried out.

On the night Jodi Jones was murdered, the crime scene was not secured, or a tent erected. The forensics officer was unable to get to the body that night, so it lay out in the rain for a further 8 hours. By the time a second forensics officer arrived, the body had been moved, and items at the scene gathered up. No identity parade was ever carried out, and clothing from three of the four people who had discovered the body was not taken for forensic testing that night (although Luke Mitchell's clothing was taken).

Police lost the documents relating to Gordon Park's original statements and the missing person's enquiry at the time of his wife's original disappearance. Later, their labeling of items brought up from the lakebed investigation was criticised.

Officers investigating the murder of Hilda Marchbank failed to properly maintain records accurately, so no evidence was available as to who put the victim in the body bag, or where in the house this happened.

Muddy footprints on Billie-Jo Jenkins legs, reported by an ambulanceman at the scene, were not photographed, and this evidence was subsequently lost when the body was removed.

A pattern begins to emerge, then, of an investigation already back-footed by crucial errors in the early stages of the enquiry. Our perception of a highly trained murder squad following strict rules and guidelines is shown to be wildly inaccurate. In general, the first officers at the scene are likely to be "bobbies on the beat" - local police officers, on their usual shift. For the majority of these officers, a call out to a murder scene is most probably not a routine event, and while we would expect that they would know what was required of them, this appears not to be the case. It is also at this point that the cover-up culture becomes apparent, and perhaps even understandable. Whilst critical evidence may have been lost or contaminated, an investigation is still expected, and must be carried out. It would hardly be conducive to public confidence for a police force, following a brutal murder in the local community, to announce that the investigation would not be able to proceed because PC Plod unfortunately didn't know what to do with the crime scene. And so the investigation proceeds, albeit hindered, and perhaps terminally damaged by the procedures of those first few hours.

Whilst the inexperience, or even ignorance, of ordinary constables in extraordinary circumstances may go some way to explaining the errors and mismanagement at the very beginning of an enquiry, it is not the whole story. As is highlighted in the Luke Mitchell and Simon Hall cases, it is the more experienced and qualified participants whose failure to properly carry out their duties creates serious difficulties for the enquiry. For pathologists or forensic officers to fail to attend the scene, with no good reason, so that critical evidence is lost forever, must surely border on the criminally negligent? The very point of these professionals is that they get to the scene as quickly as possible, so as to acquire and preserve as much information as possible. In both of these cases, lack of an established time of death allowed the already flawed investigation the freedom to presume the time of death neatly into the time slot where the chosen suspects did not have an alibi, or at least, not a strong one. Here we witness the first examples of the investigating team "deciding" what "probably" happened, then adjusting the "evidence" to fit.

However, this still does not explain why all of these investigations (and many more like them) push on relentlessly in a particular direction, when there is a pool of evidence pointing in other directions.

When all of the evidence is pulled together, and it becomes apparent that there is nothing to link the suspect forensically, physically, or by eyewitness evidence to the crime, where there is no time of death, or the timescale for the suspect to have been the perpetrator is so tight as to be bordering on the impossible, and where there is clear evidence of another person or persons having been present at the scene, then surely there must be reasonable doubt. Why then, do the police continue to pursue such unlikely avenues of investigation in a manner that appears almost hell-bent on not just getting a result, but on getting their *chosen* result?

An ex police officer puts it this way:

"It is necessary to understand the role of investigating police officers and their own perceptions of right and wrong, truth and justice.

Initially, most people join the police service through a desire to serve the public, by making a contribution to society by helping to maintain law and order and protect the vulnerable from the criminal element. They join as honest men and women. It would be true to say the majority of police officers spend the best part of 30 years of their lives believing this and that they are doing whatever is necessary to achieve these objectives.

Doing what they believe is necessary, however, does not mean they are fulfilling a role in accordance with the expectations of the public. It does not mean they are adhering to the rules of evidence and procedure. The general public go about their business unaware that the police officers they have so much faith in, regularly and routinely abuse their powers. The public perception is that the police get it right most of the time, and that any failure is merely a blip, a tragic mistake that does not happen often. The truth is that police officers often get it wrong. Why do they so often get it wrong, and why do police officers adopt the attitude that whatever they do is in the best interests of society?

The artificial world you become part of when you join the police service becomes a way of life. You are surrounded by either the good or the bad, without realising it, you become prejudiced. The good you will perceive to be your colleagues, the victims of crime, or older members of society. The bad will be the younger element which you will further put in to categories by either race, creed, or where they live. These perceptions are reinforced by the people you meet every day.

You become part of a state controlled framework which endorses your actions as a police officer, whether those actions are within or outside the rules, providing the end result is perceived to justify the means. Winning is a result, losing is to fail, and a police officer is trained to win, whether that be an argument with a motorist or a court case. Not all police officers are bad, they are not, that goes without saying, but the problem arises in that some believe that in order to achieve their objectives they often have to bend the law to get a result. Obviously, officers who adopt this approach do so from a very early stage and as their career progresses they tend to deal with cases of a more serious nature. The corruption becomes more serious and the consequences for the victims of that corruption ever more devastating.

Truth is **not** an essential part of an investigation. All the investigating officer is interested in is getting a conviction. His skill is measured by his superiors on the basis of results. In any investigation, the police have the upper hand from the outset. They have access to all the initial evidence either from witnesses or documents. They have access to vast resources, such as expert witnesses and manpower. The defence, on the other hand, are constrained by receiving the evidence second hand from the police and only in documentary form. They have no access, prior to trial, of the police witnesses. What a witness says in a statement is all the defence gets, and from that, they have to try and establish the truth. Statements taken from witnesses will only contain those points relevant to the police case. The defence is also heavily constrained by the cost and resources they have available.

The police service is well aware of these constraints placed on the defence, and exploit that knowledge to the full. It is very easy for an investigating officer to take a suspect and a set of circumstances and fit those circumstances around the suspect. It is much more difficult to be faced with a crime and find the person who definitely did it, without there being any doubt. This is at the heart of all miscarriages of justice and police corruption....

...The defence has enormous difficulty in disproving what {a suspect} is alleged to have said to {a} police officer. Courts usually believe the police version of events...

...The police service is given enormous powers and is, on the whole, unaccountable for its actions. Judicial processes and legislation like the Criminal Procedure and Investigation Act which covers the disclosure of evidence, ensures that the odds are heavily weighted against those accused by the police and prosecuted by the state. The old maxim that you are "innocent until proven guilty" is entirely redundant in practice."

This takes us right to the heart of the matter. The "artificial world" to which this officer refers becomes a self fulfilling, self perpetuating whole, in which the means always justify the end, backed up with a legislative apparatus which actively encourages and endorses its activities. Morally, officers who, for whatever reason, are required to make the circumstances fit are not seen to be, and do not consider themselves to be, doing anything wrong.

This would go some way, also, to explaining why certain investigations will continue in the face of clear and obvious evidence to the contrary – the over-confidence of the officers involved that their result will be sanctioned by their superiors and the judicial system blinds them to the fact that contrary evidence will not simply disappear. However, the strength of such a system is obviously great, given the massive difficulties faced by those who have been wrongly convicted, in having their cases re-investigated.

For example, Craig Dobbie, the Chief Investigating Officer in the Luke Mitchell case told reporters that Lothian and Borders police had carried out a "first rate investigation." Clearly, if this is what Mr Dobbie truly believes, then there will be no examination of the areas of that investigation which were, unarguably, less than first rate – for example, the failure to secure the crime scene, the original forensics officer leaving the scene, and another not arriving for another 7 or 8 hours, and the fact that the body was moved and items gathered up. In many ways, this reinforces the claim that so long as the end justifies the means, the investigation is considered to be acceptable. In Mr Dobbie's view, there is no need to investigate these factors, because his team secured the necessary result. He backs up his claim by stating that "not a single factor was deemed to be inadmissible" – is that really the measure by which an investigation is evaluated? As will become apparent later, it is by no means guaranteed that judges will rule correctly, coherently or consistently on what they deem admissible or not – to attempt to claim that an investigation was "first rate" because the judge did not deem factors inadmissible completely misses this point!

Also, when it became apparent in the John Taft case that police statements taken from the Evans family not only gave John an alibi, but rendered the whole police contention impossible in the face of other evidence, the reaction was not to consider that the investigation had been at fault – after removing the jury, the prosecuting counsel tried to persuade the judge that that particular area of evidence should be deemed inadmissible, since John should have told the police that he had an alibi!

Bearing in mind the pressure on police to prove their worth by producing statistical evidence of their clean up rate, and given this inbuilt mindset, whose values and methods, however far removed from the public perception, have a validity and credence of their own within the police service, it is not too difficult to see how an investigating team could quite easily decide in advance what it believes to be the case, and set about systematically gathering data to support that case. Within their own culture, these officers are doing what they believe is expected of them, both from their paymasters, and from the public. They need not be aware that what they are doing is, in fact, *constructing* a case, rather than investigating and uncovering evidence, what matters is that, from their own standpoint, they are following a logical and methodical procedure. (The logic, of course, being, if the evidence can be made to fit, it will be retained, if it cannot, it will be discarded. Once enough evidence which fits has been acquired, they have a case – the discarded evidence is not then evaluated, because, in this scenario, there is simply no need – the objective has been attained.)

It seems to be this, more than anything, which explains some of the more outrageous factors in the cases highlighted here, and in many others like them.

In every case, there is a wealth of evidence which could just as easily have been used to (a) exonerate the person who was convicted, or at least raise such reasonable doubt as to have the case dropped, and (b) convict another person or persons.

In Derek Christian's case, eyewitnesses all describe a man who is clearly not Derek. Eleven out of fourteen witnesses describe the car at the scene as white – Derek's car was silver. Footprints at the scene did not belong to him.

In John Taft's case, several men, who were definitely not John, were identified. An unidentified fingerprint was found on an open window in Cynthia Bolshaw's bedroom. A man (not John) was seen with her car in the early hours of the morning. John was positively identified in his own back garden at 11.30pm – against other concrete evidence, this alone destroyed the prosecution case against him.

Footprints and fingerprints found in and around Joan Albert's home did not belong to Simon Hall. Both the gastro-enterologist report, and witness statements suggest Mrs Albert was murdered at around 2 or 3am, when Simon had an alibi. Although the killer entered and left Mrs Albert's home through a broken window, there were no traces of glass on Simon's clothing or in his car. The break in the window was just 14" wide, and Simon is 6'1" tall, and well built.

DNA found on the clothing of Jodi Jones belonged to two other people, neither of which was Luke Mitchell. Two other people were positively identified at the scene of the crime, at the presumed time of the murder, Luke was not.

Carol Park was seen on the driveway of her home after the family had gone out for the day. A Volkswagon car, which has never been identified, was parked on the driveway for 20 minutes that same day, and the driver was not Gordon Park. A prisoner who had been convicted of the murder of Carol Park's sister, and an attack on her mother, was being allowed "weekend liberty" in the area at the time of Carol's disappearance.

Two witnesses saw a car outside Hilda Marchbank's house the night she was murdered, and another witness claimed that her brother, a local burglar, had told her about the murder *before* Susan May discovered her aunt's body, and unidentified fingerprints and a footprint were found at the scene.

Several witnesses reported a man acting suspiciously in the vicinity of the Jenkins' family home at around the time Billie-Jo was murdered. One account tells of a man clearly distressed, and making "odd noises" running away from the area of the Jenkins' garden. Police appear to have completely ignored or discounted evidence regarding the piece of plastic pushed into Billie-Jo's nostril, although this was obviously extremely important in identifying the perpetrator.

On our premise that police investigations examine all the evidence and deduce from that the most probable scenario, we would be inclined to believe that all of the above factors would raise such reasonable doubt as to cast a serious shadow over the continued direction of these investigations. But with a glimpse into the existence of the "artificial world" from which police procedures emanate, we can begin to understand how the concept of reasonable doubt slips through the cracks. Once the course has been set, the objective is *only* to gather together that which supports the course. In this instance, what we, the general public, see as evidence which should raise reasonable doubt, investigating officers see as irrelevant to their objective. Indeed, it may even be argued that the concept of reasonable doubt is a concern for the jury, not the investigating team.

It is this difference in perception as to what is actually being pursued that creates both the climate in which miscarriages of justice occur, and the methods and means by which they are kept concealed from the public in general.

Outside of the drama and emotional engagement of the whole investigation and trial process, in so many cases, the facts just do not add up.

Certain themes emerge over and over again, appearing to back up the notion that fitting the circumstances to the suspect is not an occasional, desperate move in the case of a police force in dire need of a result, rather, that it is common, and perfectly acceptable practice within the police service.

Not only in the cases highlighted in this book, but in many others already in the public domain, there is a startling similarity and repetition of these themes – the first and most obvious is how so many investigations completely ignore or discount what should be very relevant evidence. Next, there is the "fudging" of police records – they are lost, or incomplete, they get altered at a later date, or information is "accidentally" filed where it is unlikely to be uncovered. Another theme is that which takes a theory, however ludicrous or unlikely, and builds a case around it. This is one of the most important recurring themes, because it lies at the very centre of every miscarriage of justice, along with the initial poor investigative procedures at the beginning of the investigation. It is worth looking at some examples where the police have constructed a theory, and stuck with it to the bitter end, even though it can quite easily be proven to be not just wrong, but impossible.

In the case of John Taft, the line of reasoning was that he had killed Mrs Bolshaw in her home, taken her car some five miles away and abandoned it, walked eight miles back to his own home, where he had burned and buried the clothing he had been wearing. Clothing fibres, claimed to have come from John's clothing, were found on the driver's seat of Mrs Bolshaw's car. So far, so good. The police even found witnesses who testified to having seen John, in his back garden, digging, at 11.30pm that evening (the implication being that this was when he buried the clothes). This is where the problem for the police case arises. Pathology reports show that Mrs Bolshaw died somewhere between 3 and 6am the following morning. John is now cleverly burying the clothes he plans to use some 4 hours later! In an attempt to wriggle round this problem, the judge introduced the possibility that John had killed Mrs Bolshaw, gone home, then returned to the scene later to remove her car. That being the case, how did the fibres from clothes the prosecution insists he has burned and buried, come to be on the driver's seat of the car?

Simon Hall is claimed to have driven to Mrs Albert's home after dropping off a friend at 5.30am, and killing her at "around 6am". The pathology reports state that the killer continued to inflict wounds on Mrs Albert's body for up to 30 minutes after death, yet Simon was in his own home by 6.30am. Since no DNA, no shards of glass, indeed, nothing whatsoever was found to link Simon with this crime, it also has to be accepted that during this time frame, he also managed to clean away every microscopic trace of evidence before returning to his own home?

One of the other recurring themes which helps divert attention away from these inconsistencies is the use of very detailed, very complicated scientific evidence which, on closer inspection, actually reveals nothing at all relevant to the case. However, the sheer complexity of this evidence, and the fact that it is claimed to be based purely in science (ie, in logic and reason, and therefore not easily influenced by personal opinion or recollection) not only diverts attention away from the much weaker aspects of the case, it gives an impression of strength and credibility.

Police and public make the same assumption in the John Taft case – his DNA was discovered at the scene, therefore he must have been the killer. This, of course, is nonsense. DNA belonging to another person was found on Mrs Bolshaw's pillowcase – if the presence of DNA is proof of murder, then this other person must, by the same reasoning, also be guilty!

The use of "fibre evidence" has become increasingly popular and, as a result, increasingly dangerous. The term "microscopically indistinguishable" is used to devastating effect. Expert witnesses claim that fibres found on the body or at the scene are "microscopically indistinguishable" from those taken from the accused's clothing. Whilst this may be perfectly true, it is of no real significance, since those same fibres (that were found on the body) could also be microscopically indistinguishable from literally thousands of other articles. The term does not mean "the same," in the context that those fibres must have come from that item of clothing.

In Derek Christian's case, the fibres found with the body were found to also be "microscopically indistinguishable" from clothing belonging to two officers working on the case, and a brand new garment bought from a local store.

In both John Taft and Simon Hall's cases, the link between fibres and those men as the perpetrators was even more tenuous – no items of clothing belonging to these men were *ever* shown to produce "microscopically indistinguishable" fibres – the mere suggestion that fibres from clothing belonging to them had been found at the scene was sufficient.

In Gordon Park's case, extremely lengthy, immensely complicated testimony as to rock composition was given by two separate geologists. What all of this eventually amounted to was that the rock in question probably *did* come from the Park's garden. However, the police claim that it had come from the lake bed was completely discredited, in that the rock had none of the characteristics normally found on one which had been immersed in water for such a long time. Hours and hours of technically stultifying testimony to say "this rock, probably from the garden, has somehow "found its way" into a list of exhibits allegedly brought from the lake bed, even though this particular rock most probably did not come from the lakebed."

Once again, however, the *actual* meaning is lost amidst the science and jargon.

Even where the scientific findings *clearly* show that the data is not linked to the accused, the language and approach used by these witnesses is clearly designed to confuse and mislead.

The specialist who had been examining DNA in the Luke Mitchell case told the court that "parts of DNA" from a stain on Jodi's clothing matched "parts of DNA" from Luke Mitchell. In its most understandable form, this statement means "a match was not found" - for a match to be claimed, there are a specified number of points which must match up, otherwise, the two specimens are concluded to be a "no match."

Similarly, the forensic scientist who claimed that the killer would "not necessarily" be heavily bloodstained was stating a literal truth. When cross examined, however, he conceded that it was "highly likely" that the killer *would* be heavily blood stained.

Another theme with dangerous undertones is what is allowed to pass for "identification." The man seen by witnesses in and around the area where Margaret Wilson was murdered was described by all of the witnesses as clean shaven. Derek Christian had a "pronounced" goatee beard. No identity parade was ever held, and not one of the witnesses was asked if Derek Christian was the man they had seen. Some would claim later that he was *definitely not* the same man, but, since they were never asked in court, this information was not available to the jury.

The man seen with Cynthia Bolshaw's car was "definitely not" John Taft. Nor was the man seen with her three weeks previously in an estate agents'. Nor were any of the men in Buff's Lane that evening. None of these men was ever traced.

The photographs shown to Andrina Bryson highlighted Luke Mitchell as the only one with long hair, and on a light background. No identity parade was ever held. Ms Bryson failed to identify Luke Mitchell in court, in spite of the fact that his picture had been in the newspapers for more than a year.

Obviously, there is something more than simple, occasional error at play. What is suggested by the examples cited here is that there is an inherent, unchallenged acceptance that logic, in its more generally accepted context, need not apply. So long as enough information which may be used to persuade the Crown Prosecution Service and a jury can be found (regardless of how this information is acquired), the investigating team have fulfilled their duties. Considerations such as relevance to the actual facts of the case, whether or not the "evidence" actually supports any of the charges (an excellent example of this is the citing of bottles of urine found in Luke Mitchell's bedroom – no-one, it seems, ever stopped to ask what, exactly, this had to do with the case against him), or if the evidence has been properly and fairly acquired simply do not arise.

How, then, do the Crown Prosecution Service, the media, jury members and the public generally, end up convinced that the case against the accused is sound? The answer to this lies in a complex series of interactions, between all of the parties involved – the police, the media, the judicial system, the public, the accused, and the families and friends of the victims. All of these will be examined in later chapters. For now, we will remain with the police.

One mechanism for reducing opposition in the face of contrary evidence is the use of rumour and innuendo. Whilst it is notoriously difficult to prove, there are many examples of the public somehow becoming convinced of the badness of a given individual. As a result, the public are much less sympathetic to claims of injustice or unsafe conviction, simply because of an underlying feeling that there's "no smoke without fire." This is not a new phenomenon, and it is deployed in many different ways, the power of suggestion serving to allay doubts or undue interest from the public as to just how any specific conviction has been secured.

Older examples include the case of George Kelly, who was hanged in 1949 for a double murder at the Cameo cinema in Liverpool. Over the years, many, many irregularities surfaced, casting doubt on the conviction until, following two books and a documentary, hardly anyone remained convinced that the conviction was safe. However, Liverpool and Bootle Constabulary let it be known that Kelly was a petty thief, dealing in black market goods. The result was a public perception of Kelly as a "criminal," and, as such, probably implicated in some way. Three judges finally deemed his conviction unsafe in June 2003 – 53 years after Mr Kelly was hanged.

Derek Bentley, who was hanged in 1951, at just 19 years old, is another example. Although the unsafety of his conviction was highlighted over and over again, (he was eventually posthumously pardoned by Jack Straw) Ken Clarke, as Home Secretary in the early 1990s said Derek Bentley should not have hanged, but he should not have been on the roof of the warehouse either! In other words, he might not actually have done the thing that he was hanged for, but neither was he a "good boy" otherwise, he wouldn't have been on the roof.

In the sixties, James Hanratty was accused of killing a man and raping his partner in Bedfordshire. Even though Hanratty could account for his movements, he was hanged. Later, Peter Alphon confessed to the rape and murder. The police let it be known that James Hanratty was a petty thief.

The very same tactics were used in some of the cases highlighted in this book – the portrayal Sion Jenkins as a cold, emotionless man who had lied on his cv, or Luke Mitchell as a Satan worshipping "Goth" with psychological problems, being used to create doubt as to their "goodness" in the public mind.

The case of Shirley McKie, the police officer who fought for nine years to clear her name after being accused of perjury, displays just how far-reaching this particular tactic can be. Having finally forced an admission from Strathclyde police, her previous employers, and the Scottish Criminal Records Office (SCRO) that they had wrongly identified a fingerprint at a murder scene as hers, a union spokesperson for the SCRO appeared on television the following day with a statement declaring that the officers who made the original identification **stood by their findings.** Just one day after being forced to admit they were completely in the wrong, the same group continued to cast doubt on Shirley McKie's honesty.

One of the most telling examples of this particular tactic is the case of the so-called "M25 gang". Following the quashing of their convictions by the European Court of Human Rights, on the grounds that they had not had a fair trial because evidence had been withheld from the defence, the appeal judge actually stated, "This does not prove that they are innocent."

Too much confidential information seeps from police investigation into the public arena for this to be accidental or coincidental. Whereas public opinion often calls for "previous record" to be revealed in court cases, the implicit involvement of the police, themselves being party to the dissemination of local rumour and innuendo, meets this perceived need in a much more covert and insidious manner. It also serves to raise the police service in general, above direct criticism – if the accused can somehow be painted as having previous form, then it's not such a bad thing – maybe he didn't commit this crime, but at least if he's in prison, he's prevented from pursuing his criminal career. In this circumstance, the public perception begins to mirror the "artificial world" of the police perspective.

References:
BBC News, *"Print Experts Stand By McKie ID,"* May 30th 2006
"Character Assassination," Ronnie Williams, reproduced at www.portia.org, March 15th 2006
"Wrongful Convictions," Michael Naughton, Observer Crime and Justice Debate, July 28th 2002
"Cutting Crime, Delivering Justice," HM Government, CJS, A Strategic Plan for Criminal Justice 2004-2008
Edinburgh Evening News, *"Clues that Snared a Murderer,"* Nicola Stow, January 21st 2005

Chapter Ten

Expert Witnesses

THE use of expert witnesses is an everyday occurrence in modern day court cases. Expert witnesses have been used to explain everything from "ear print analysis" to "facial expression analysis." But just how reliable is such testimony, and why do we need it in the first place? Does it, in fact, serve the purpose for which it is intended – to clarify information for a jury whose members most probably do not, in their everyday lives, come across the type of information held by these experts?

There are two types of expert witness. The first is the *forensic pathologist*. There are around 35 Home Office accredited pathologists. Surprisingly, (some may say shockingly), these are the only experts who are required to be qualified. In every other branch of expert testimony the expert giving that testimony need not have any qualifications or credentials whatsoever. This *includes* areas such as forensic science – blood analysis, DNA testing and results, fingerprint evidence, toxicology, glass fragment identification – in short, everything that we have come to believe is based in a solid foundation of scientific discipline. The truth is, anyone can practice in any of these fields, and call themselves an expert. A further sub-group of this section of expert witnesses are those whose areas of expertise are not quite so readily identified as scientific, although the manner in which they are presented in court often provides a very strong illusion of a scientific basis or justification. Areas such as facial mapping, body language experts, lip-reading, ear print analysis, detecting dishonesty from facial expressions, and so on, fall into this category.

The obvious problem with experts who need not be qualified, and whose findings need not be backed by rigorous scientific testing, is that we then have no way of evaluating just how accurate, likely, or even possible such evidence is in reality.

The supposition that these experts are needed to clarify certain factors for the jury is not borne out in actual court cases. For example, when Darren Suturan was tried in 2002 on a manslaughter charge, **ten** medical experts gave evidence concerning just two issues – how many bruises were on the victim's face, and did she acquire these in a fall, or were they inflicted by the accused. The experts gave hugely conflicting views, and the conviction was later quashed on the grounds that the jury could not have been other than thoroughly confused by such clear disagreements amongst the experts.

The Gordon Park case is another example of this – testimony from knot experts was confusing, complicated, and conflicting – some said knots used to truss the body were similar to those used by Gordon Park, some said they were nothing like each other, and one expert withdrew after viewing the defence findings! By the time the experts had trawled through the knot testimony, then the hammer testimony (was it possible that Gordon Park's hammer had made the dents in the lead piping found with the body), could the ordinary men and women in the jury be expected to understand and evaluate what they had just heard? Worse, this was followed by the rock testimony: what follows is just a small quote from the judge's summing up of the rock testimony:

> "Dr Pirrie identified the calcium bearing rare earth element, now named by him as synchysite in PDB 5/19 and in the Bluestones rocks but not in the Coniston rocks... In the Coniston photographs Dr Pirrie identified a rare earth element in each case without calcium. Two contained phosphorous and one had neither calcium or phosphorous.... A Coniston sample could, he thought, show diagenetic rutile with post dated monazite in association with each other."

The judge's summing up of this area of evidence (and in the same type of terminology) runs to *twenty* pages. Not only do we have the question of whether the jury could reasonably be expected to understand this evidence, we also have the question of whether it was, in fact, absolutely necessary to the case.

As it happens, the findings of the defence geologist did cast serious doubt as to whether the rock had ever been immersed in water for many years, as the prosecution had claimed, but it has just taken only two lines of text to say so!

This process of completely overwhelming the jury with expert testimony is not unusual, and often deflects attention from the more pressing factors of a case, and also from weaknesses in the prosecution's case. In cases where the evidence is purely circumstantial, such as the cases highlighted in this book, the number of expert witnesses appears to increase, and as a result, the sheer volume of this type of testimony. It is not so much, then, a case of the jury being required to understand and evaluate the information, as a form of almost bludgeoning jurors with information to create the illusion that "there must be something in it" - basic reasoning suggests that the court wouldn't spend three days, or whatever, leading evidence that was of no relevance or significance. Sadly, in many cases, this is exactly what happens – the fibre evidence used to such powerful effect in the case of Simon Hall, Derek Christian and John Taft ultimately proved *nothing* of relevance to these cases.

Once again, it is the power of suggestion which may be seen to sway the jury. If the evidence is extremely complex, lengthy and confusing, jury members may simply default to the belief that it must be important, somehow, or it wouldn't be getting so much attention. This takes us back to the bias introduced by the Crown Prosecution Service's position of deciding whether or not there is enough evidence to secure a conviction. At the back of juror's minds will be the assumption that all of this evidence has already been evaluated by more able minds than their own, and has made it into the court room, therefore it must be relevant or important.

Also, it is not just the content of such testimony that can be used to devastating effect by the prosecution; the wording of particular parts of testimonies can be used to sound as if one thing is being said, when, in actuality, exactly the opposite is true.

The DNA scientist in the Luke Mitchell case who claimed that "some parts" of DNA found on Jodi's clothing matched "some parts" of Luke's DNA has already been discussed. This is a clear example of misleading wording – this witness could simply have stated that this particular sample of DNA, found in Jodi's clothing, did not match Luke's.

Why, then, would an expert witness construct their testimony in such a way? If the truth is that there was no match, then why not just state this, in simple, understandable terms, rather than muddy the waters in this manner?

The answer to this lies in the procedures for defence and prosecution calling expert witnesses in the first place.

Up until 1989, the Forensic Science Service was part of the Police Department of the Home Office. Each police force paid an annual fee, related to the size of the force, and not the amount of forensic work that force required to be carried out. Then, police forces submitted their cases to the Forensic Science Service for whatever work was needed, as and when these cases arose.

In 1989, however, this arrangement was changed. The Forensic Science Service was, to all intents and purposes, privatised. Each police force was now required to pay the full cost of forensic work for every case it submitted. The result was that police forces now also had the freedom to use other, independent forensics laboratories. This change in 1989 brought about fundamental changes to the way forensic, and other expert witnesses were engaged.

Rather than submit a case for forensic examination, the police (as well as prosecuting and defence lawyers) could now approach independent experts for evaluation and evidence. However, by this stage, those asking for such evidence know what they need the evidence to support. Since these independent experts are being paid for their findings, it is not in their interests to produce findings which go against that which they are being asked to support. This need not imply outright dishonesty. Limited, or selective testing, strictly within the boundaries of that being requested, can be argued to be honest and fair, in that the experts have done precisely and exactly that which they have been asked to do, and nothing more. This, of course, will not be known to the jury, whose members are likely to be under the impression that such scientific findings have come about as a result of testing all of the information for all of the possibilities.

What we have, then, is a system whereby expert witnesses who may have no qualifications, and whose competence or even honesty are not, and cannot be assessed, are paid to provide evidence for one side or the other. If their evidence is satisfactory for the purposes of those who pay them, they are likely to be consulted for future cases; as a result the pressure to continue to find what they are asked to find actually increases. If, on the other hand, their findings are *not* satisfactory for the purposes of those who are paying for their services, it is highly unlikely that they will be consulted again. How do we square the concept of "independent and impartial" findings, with the knowledge that the financial survival of the investigating expert is dependent on those findings meeting a predetermined outcome?

Another problem with expert testimony is the tendency to present only *part* of a fact as the whole fact. For example, it may be stated that research has shown that 85% of girls who have been abused in childhood are likely to self-harm in their teens. Faced with a teenage girl who is known to be self harming, the conclusion may be drawn that she is highly likely to have been abused at an earlier point in her life. This reasoning, though on the surface, quite compelling, is completely flawed. For example, if 100 out of 1000 girls are abused in childhood, we would be justified in predicting, on the basis of that research, that 85 of these girls are likely to self harm in their teens. However, another 100 of these 1000 girls may also go on to self harm, for other reasons. Therefore, to conclude that one of these girls has been abused in childhood is completely wrong. Out of the 185 girls self harming, we do not know which ones may have been abused in childhood and which were not. Yet this type of presentation of "facts" is common in many cases, and often slips by un-noticed. The obvious examples in the cases highlighted in this book are those involving fibre evidence and the term "microscopically indistinguishable." If this evidence was being presented fully and rationally, the expert witnesses would be required to explain that the same fibres are likely to be microscopically indistinguishable from literally thousands of other garments. In truth, it is left to the defence to understand this factor, and to force the expert to admit it in court.

The official line is that we need expert witnesses to explain that which is not readily understandable to members of the jury, but, as has begun to become clear, this does not seem to be the reality. Expert witness testimony, in many cases, creates more confusion than it alleviates. There is also the problem of expert testimony being introduced in cases where other evidence to support the prosecution case is weak. The suggestion seems to be that expert testimony is sometimes factored into cases to provide extra evidence where the evidence which already exists would be insufficient to secure a prosecution. If this is, indeed, the case, and such witnesses are paid to produce results conducive to such a result, then our confidence in the fairness, or indeed, the reliability of the criminal justice system must be severely eroded.

The examples given already, covering so-called fibre evidence, fall into just such a category. In all of the three cases involved, it was shown, quite clearly, that this evidence was of no relevance to the case, as it effectively proved nothing, and, in at least two cases, no garments from which fibres may have been shed were ever produced as corroboration. Yet it was still led, and a great deal of attention afforded it. Rather than proceeding from a basis which considers a suspect innocent until proven guilty, the use of this type of evidence appears as an almost underhanded method of suggesting that the suspect really is not innocent, without actually having to prove it! The effects on jury members, although subtle, are likely to be extremely powerful. Reliant as they are on authority figures for their guidance, jury members will be unaware of the drip feed of negativity being conveyed by these testimonies. This could be seen, in some ways, to be balanced out by the fact that often the experts cannot agree amongst themselves – that being the case, is the jury not likely to simply discard the evidence? Whilst this seems like a logical suggestion, it misses the underlying psychological influences – as we have already seen, juries do not make their decisions based on just the facts, but on a multitude of other factors, including impressions and assumptions arising from what they see and hear. A convincing but flawed testimony from an expert who is 'attractive' in some way to jury members may, in the final analysis, carry more weight than a factually sound testimony from a less convincing, or less attractive witness. Although the random selection method of choosing jurors is supposed to counter such a possibility, it is difficult to ignore the influence of collective cultural beliefs and prejudices – there are certain factors within our culture which can be shown to be generally attractive or believable, regardless of whether they are factually correct or not. In the Luke Mitchell case, for example, two factors (neither of which had any factual bearing on the case) highlighted such collective cultural influences. The discovery of bottles of urine in his bedroom provoked an almost uniform reaction – that there was something seriously amiss, not just with the boy himself, but with his whole family set up. In our culture, we simply do not urinate into bottles and then keep those bottles. The other factor was the emphasis on his "satanic beliefs." In a predominantly Christian influenced area, such claims created a wide reaction of both shock and fear. Since the jury is supposed to be a miniature reflection of the wider community, it is easy to surmise that the jurors would react in a similar manner.

It is also quite a revelation to discover that there are actual registries of expert witnesses. Anyone who has a need to do so can log into several websites and acquire themselves a "registered" witness on just about anything under the sun. What is not obvious, however, is just what, precisely, defines the expertise of these expert witnesses.

What, though, of the more traditional experts – the pathologists, the medical profession, forensic scientists, and so forth. Surely these are more credible, and more reliable, given that they are required to undergo rigorous formal training and qualification? In many cases, unfortunately, this is not the case. There is no escaping the fact that, with or without formal training and qualification, we are all subject to influences which shape our beliefs and assumptions, which in turn create prejudices and mindsets from which we draw our conclusions and interpretations from the information we receive. Although training can make us aware of the existence of such filters to our perceptions, it does not necessarily follow that we will be able to observe the effects of these filters on our own personal perceptions and conclusions.

If, for example, as a trained psychologist, I have an unshakeable belief that failure to make eye contact is a high indicator of untrustworthiness, and I have been proven correct on this belief many, many times, then it is reasonable to assume that the next person I am required to deal with, who fails consistently to make eye contact, will trigger the assumption within me that this person is not to be believed at face value, and that further checks on everything that he or she tells me will need to be carried out. I need not be aware that I have pre-judged this person – I am simply acting upon a deeply embedded belief that is valid for me because I have seen it borne out in reality over and over again. The weakness in this approach is that there may have been other cases in my experience where failure to make eye contact has turned out not to be as a result of untrustworthiness, but I am unlikely to have paid them much attention. Since they do not fit with my expectation, I am likely to have dismissed them as quirks, or as possibly examples which, for one reason or another, could not be *proven* to be caused by untrustworthiness. (Note that my basic assumption has not changed – I still believe that untrustworthiness is the root cause; I rationalise that I simply could not get to the evidence to prove this to be the case. In this instance, I have not concluded that untrustworthiness is *not* a cause, only that I have been unable to produce conclusive proof).

This approach is, in fact, one of the foundations on which science precariously balances. In order for something to be proven as fact we must be able to produce concrete, tangible proof which can then be reproduced uniformly and repeatedly. This expectation causes us to focus in one direction – ie in finding those factors which can be produced uniformly and repeatedly to prove something we initially only believed or observed to be true. Where such proof cannot be produced, the world of science has traditionally done one of two things; either it dismisses the object of investigation as irrelevant or "unscientific," or it holds to its original assertion on the basis that proof will eventually be found, it just has not been found yet.

At its base level, this leads to the notion that that which cannot be proven scientifically does not exist (ghosts, God, the supernatural, etc), or, when something unequivocally, undeniably exists, in that we can observe it with our physical senses, but cannot explain it in scientific terms, then it is "still under investigation." Because of huge leaps in technology, we have come to believe that science *does* have all of the answers, it is only a matter of time until it finds them.

It is from this school of thought that our trained and qualified expert witnesses are drawn, and so, once again, we are forced to face the fact that they are neither impartial nor independent. Additionally, those witnesses drawn from, for example, the medical profession, have the added influence of their perceived status. Great prestige is bestowed upon those at the top of the scientific professions – fame, recognition and respect are afforded those whose expertise and research bring us ever more, ever greater breakthroughs in technology, medicine, understanding of the universe and so forth. The pressure on these people to 'get it right' is enormous, and there are emerging examples of some who have come to believe in their own infallibility.

The difficulties with these expert witnesses is that their knowledge and expertise, whilst far more widely accepted than those experts already discussed, are even more difficult to question. So select and elite is the group at the top of these professions that only "one of their own" could ever be in a position to point out errors or flaws in their reasoning and conclusion. Indeed, the general image is that there *are* no errors or flaws – that these people are so highly skilled, so completely immersed in their professionalism and perfectionism that it is, at best, extremely unlikely that they will get something terribly wrong. They are perceived, generally, to have spent lifetimes ironing out the problems and difficulties, accessing vast amounts of information and research, so as to have reached a state of near perfection within their chosen field. As a result, they are also generally perceived to be above the day to day weaknesses inherent in the rest of us mere mortals. They do not have "bad days." Their professionalism insulates them from allowing domestic difficulties, for example, to influence their work. They are able to cut off from the usual mish-mash of emotional, personal, financial and domestic rabble that clamours for attention at the most inopportune moments for "ordinary" people.

Of course, we know this simply cannot be the case, and that they are as human as the rest of us, yet the image remains remarkably resilient to common sense.

The case of Professor Sir Roy Meadow is one of the most high profile examples of how our unquestioning reliance on these experts leads to the most appalling mistakes being allowed to pass un-noticed. Sir Roy Meadow is a retired paediatrician whose evidence was instrumental in gaining several convictions which were later overturned. More important, however, is how the courts came to rely so heavily on evidence from this expert witness. Sir Roy Meadow invented the condition Munchausen Syndrome by Proxy (MSBP), which, his research tells us, causes some women to inexplicably harm children (as a means of gaining attention for themselves). His paper "Munchausen Syndrome by Proxy: The Hinterlands of Child Abuse," published in the Lancet in 1977 created a huge amount of interest, and he was employed by social services, the CPS, and family court prosecutors for his expertise. He gave conferences around the world, and regularly commented in the press. For twenty five years, Sir Roy Meadow's findings were cited as proof of wrongdoing in many, many cases, until he claimed, at the trial of Sally Clark in November 1999 that the odds of two unexplained cot deaths in one family were one in 73 million. The Royal Statistical Society wrote to the Lord Chancellor to complain, and eventually, Sally Clark's conviction was quashed on the grounds that Sir Roy's figures were wildly inaccurate, and that the chances were actually much closer to 1 in 200. Also, Sally's children were not, in fact, victims of "cot death" (or Sudden Infant Death Syndrome, as later evidence would prove.)

Lord Howe, in 2003 is on record as having called MSBP:

> "one of the most pernicious and ill-founded theories to have gained currency in childcare and social services in the past 10 to 15 years. There is no body of peer-reviewed research to underpin MSBP. It rests instead on the assertions of its inventor. When challenged to produce his research papers to justify his original findings, the inventor of MSBP stated, if you please, that he had destroyed them."

In family courts, Sir Roy Meadow was often the only expert called to give evidence, and his evidence has been accepted across the country, almost without question. We can only begin to wonder how many families have been ripped apart, children removed from parents who have done nothing wrong, and innocent women imprisoned for the most awful crimes imaginable – those of deliberately damaging their own children, all on the say-so of this one "expert," whose expertise, it turns out, is nothing more than over-confident repetition of his own opinion. Sir Roy Meadow had claimed that one sudden infant death in a family is a tragedy, two is suspicious and three is murder, unless proven otherwise – this became known as "Meadow's Law," so influential had this one person become. What is incredible is the willingness with which Professor Meadow's findings were embraced within the various agencies which used his services. Whereas, previously, it would have been difficult to accuse a parent of harming a child in the absence of any history or evidence of such behaviour, a diagnosis of MSBP in the mother provided a blanket justification. The more he lectured, the more he was asked to lecture, so compelling was his oratory. His claims provided neat, almost tailor made solutions and explanations for many previously unexplained circumstances. Yet once again, this drags the presumption of innocence until guilt has been proven, back into question. Without an underlying air of suspicion regarding unexplained infant death, Sir Roy Meadow's findings may have been less readily embraced. The fact remains that, however much we tell ourselves that our justice system runs on the basis of "presumed innocent until proven guilty," the reality is that in so many cases, the suspicion of guilt is the over-riding presumption. Sir Roy Meadow's findings may have arisen from just such suspicions, and certainly helped justify those suspicions in others. No matter how suspicious jury members may have been of mothers whose babies had died unexpectedly, without the critical testimony of Sir Roy Meadow, there would have been little other evidence to bolster those suspicions. The very wording of "Meadow's Law" brings this sharply into focus –

"...three is murder, unless proven otherwise" – how can anyone be "presumed innocent" on the basis of a law which requires them to prove that innocence from a position of "proven" guilt?

Another factor in Sir Roy Meadow's case is that he gave lectures to judges on how to interpret medical evidence presented in court cases. This, in any other profession would amount to a serious conflict of interests, yet, as with so many other factors in the criminal justice system, it was allowed to pass unquestioned.

Professor David Southall, whose evidence in the Sion Jenkins case was criticised for being inaccurate and misleading, was suspended by his NHS Trust in 2000. However, having watched a documentary in April that year, questioning the safety of the conviction of Sally Clark, Professor Southall, despite his suspension, called the police and informed them that, in his opinion, Stephen Clark, Sally's husband, had murdered the children. With not a shred of evidence to back up his claims, and without any involvement in the case whatsoever, he wrote up a report setting out his theory. This was completely discredited by everyone who came into contact with it, from the CPS and police, to twenty plus medical experts, the CCRC and appeal courts, and Stephen Clark was completely exonerated. It would take another four years for the GMC to find Professor Southall guilty of Serious Professional Misconduct. He was not 'struck off," however – he was restricted from working on child protection cases for three years. Seven other complaints against him were, at that point, still outstanding. As late as February 2007, it was reported that the Attorney General is to review cases in which Professor Southall gave evidence for the prosecution, going back some ten years. It is impossible to even begin to guess how much agony Professor Southall's unwarranted, self appointed intervention must have caused to a family already suffering so enormously at the hands of the British Justice System.

The murder conviction of Kenneth Fraser was overturned when it was alleged that Home Office pathologist, Dr Michael Heath had given "flawed" evidence in the case. Dr Heath had concluded that Mr Fraser has killed his girlfriend by hitting her over the head. Four other pathologists concluded that she had, in fact, died falling down stairs.

A second conviction, that of Steven Puaca, was overturned in 2005. Dr Heath claimed that the victim, Miss Tindsley, had injuries consistent with being held face down into bed clothes, and had been asphyxiated. The perpetrator, it was claimed, was Mr Puaca. Three other pathologists, however, concluded that Miss Tindsley died from an epileptic seizure following a drugs overdose.

Dr Heath's work was also called into question in the case of the man found dead in Michael Barrymore's swimming pool. He concluded that the man had drowned, yet three other pathologists found that marks on his face indicated that he had died of asphyxia, possibly from having an arm clamped over his throat during a violent sexual assault. Steven Taylor spent 10 months on remand facing a charge of strangling his wife, based on Dr Heath's findings. It was later found that marks on Beatrice Taylor's neck were caused by procedures carried out by a mortuary technician.

Dr Heath was the pathologist in the Simon Hall case, who did not attend the scene until some 10 hours later, at which point, time of death could not be established. One of the most shocking factors is that, should a tribunal find against Dr Heath, he would lose his Home Office approval, *but could still practice privately.*

The Steven Puaca case gives us a clear insight as to the extent to which evidence given by this type of expert witness is trusted, almost without question – the judge, after hearing evidence from other pathologists at appeal said,

> "We confess to a certain surprise that the deceased could have been suffocated in this way, but that was the evidence which Dr Heath gave."

Another senior Home Office Pathologist, Paula Lannas, came under investigation when concerns were raised about her findings. Her methods of investigation had been described as "demonstrating a continuing pattern of inadequate and unsatisfactory examinations and breaches of accepted forensic pathology practice." A Home Office enquiry into 18 complaints against her was abandoned in September 2002, - although the Home Office refused to say why, it was reported that colleagues who had been brought in to assist with the enquiry felt "unhappy" about sitting in judgement of one of their own.

Dr Lannas claimed that bruises on a child's neck were the result of strangulation by the mother's boyfriend. Dr Ian West, a leading expert in forensic pathology, told the court that the bruises were almost certainly caused by Dr Lannas herself, and that there was no way that the neck could have been dissected the way she did it.

In the case of Veydat and Serena Keyretli, both convicted of manslaughter in 1998 on evidence from Dr Lannas which claimed the victim had died of a single stab wound, and had no other injuries, it emerged during the appeal that the victim had a potentially fatal skull fracture, which Dr Lannas had not disclosed.

During the trial of Jeffrey Cattell, she stated that she had carried out a post-mortem examination eight and a half hours after death, when rigor mortis had fully passed. She offered no explanation when it was put to her that rigor mortis takes 24 – 36 hours to pass. The trial judge, however, would not allow her professional opinions to be questioned, on the grounds that she was a witness "of exceptional professional integrity and a leading expert in her field."

Kevin Callan was convicted of shaking his girlfriend's four year old daughter to death, on the evidence of pathologists Jeffrey Freeman and Geoffrey Garratt. Four other experts in child neuropathy found that the child had died from injuries sustained from a fall from a slide earlier that day.

These are just a few of the cases that have come to light in recent times. What is worrying is that, even when doubts are cast over the evidence given by these experts, they continue to give evidence in other cases. In the case of Sir Roy Meadow, for example, after the convictions of Sally Clark and Angela Cannings had been overturned, a CPS spokeswoman, when asked if Sir Roy would be called again as a witness, responded "There is no professional body that has found against Professor Meadow that we are aware of." Yet, following the quashing of Sally Clark's conviction, it was revealed that another 298 cases involving Sir Roy Meadow were to be re-examined.

Professor Southall continued to work for four years following his intervention in the Stephen and Sally Clark case, and was still practicing in 2007, even though he is facing another GMC hearing in November.

Dr Heath, despite facing a Home Office disciplinary tribunal, continued to give evidence in other cases, and remained on the Home Office approved list of pathologists.

Dr Paula Lannas was investigated in 1996 and "placed under close monitoring," yet she was not suspended from duties until 2000. It was reported, following her suspension, that dozens of cases in which she had given evidence would need to be re-examined.

Given the relatively small number of this type of expert within the judicial system, and the correspondingly high number of cases which may become subject to their influence (for example, Paula Lannas carried out more than 7000 post mortem examinations between 1990 and 1998), errors of the magnitude reported here are nothing short of catastrophic.

The attitude of the judge in the Jeffrey Cattell case shows just how influential these experts really are in cases – in disallowing questioning of this expert, the judge actually reinforces the sense that these experts are answerable to no-one, and that their findings are above question.

These are just four experts, yet their evidence has been used in literally thousands of cases. There is no way of finding out what level of mistaken conclusion or inaccurate finding exists. After the Home Office enquiry into Paula Lannas collapsed, the case was referred to the General Medical Council for investigation. The GMC "could not say" when the investigation would take place, and Nat Cary, a senior Home Office pathologist is quoted as saying, "It may be a cynical view, but I think they want to keep the lid on things."

The Crown Prosecution Service made no comment, and there was no suggestion from that organisation that any sort of investigation or enquiry would be forthcoming, nor that *it* would review any of the cases which may have been affected.

Of course, it is not just the personalities upon which we have become so dependent and trusting. There are procedures presented as expert evidence which have become so commonly and routinely used, that we believe them to be irrefutable and conclusive. The two most obvious examples are fingerprint matching and DNA profile matching. The odds of a fingerprint or DNA match being wrong are minute, we are told. Whilst this may be true, it misses a crucial point – the match will be evaluated by a human being, using specific techniques. Since we have no real way of knowing exactly what these techniques are, or if they have been properly carried out, we take it on faith that this is, in fact, the case. In the case of Shirley McKie, it took several years, and several independent experts to prove that the fingerprint found at the murder scene, and claimed to be hers, was not. During the enquiry, it emerged that a senior officer claimed to have found the requisite number of matching items to declare a true match. Other, less senior officers, were initially unable to find the required number of matches. Because of the determination of the senior officer that they did, indeed, exist, the pressure was on the other officers to "find" what was required. This brings us once again to the pressures brought to bear on individuals working within organisations which require specific results. An officer who, for example, repeatedly fails to find the desired matches may very quickly find his or her continued employment in serious jeopardy.

A report in the Observer in 2002 refers to a study carried out in Austin, Texas, into the accuracy of DNA tests. The study found that as many as one in every hundred tests may give a false result. Researchers had asked labs (anonymously) to match a series of DNA samples – in over one per cent of cases, the labs either falsely matched samples, or failed to notice a match. Statisticians then calculated that "substantial human error" had occurred in 12 out of every 1000 tests.

Yet the response from British government scientists to these findings was to deny that errors are possible.

Professor Derek Pounder, of the Department of Forensic Medicine at the University of Dundee said, "The increased quality controls that have been introduced to laboratories over time are a reaction to errors being found." This surely suggests that errors can only be found if they have been made in the first place! It also suggests that all labs will have introduced the "increased quality controls" to which he refers, but, as has already been shown, there is no monitoring body to check whether or not this is actually true.

The Forensic Science Service denied that mistakes made it into court. Chris Hadkiss, manager of the DNA laboratory at the FSS said, "People make mistakes – no one is disputing that – but we have a quality system here and have external auditors. The mistakes are not allowed to go to court." This can only be true, however, if the mistakes are recognised as such. Also, the official sounding "Forensic Science Service" is the organisation that was privatised in 1989, opening the doors for prosecutors and defence alike to use other, independent, forensic services. Even if it is true that the FSS itself ensures that mistakes do not make it into court (and we cannot be certain that this is, in fact, the case), it is only one of many organisations providing such information for court cases.

Once again, we find ourselves dependent on blind faith rather than transparent, provable fact.

References:
"Why Experts Make Errors," Itiel E Dror and David Charlton, University of Southampton, February 2006
"False Result Fear over DNA Tests," Nick Paton Walsh, Observer February 2nd 2002
Justice Without Science Isn't Science, Frank Ward, September 17th 2003, reproduced at www.portia.org.uk
"DNA Evidence," Crime Busting, Chapter 20, Jenny Ward, Published by Blandford Press, ISBN 0 1737 2639 3, reproduced at www.portia.org.uk
"When Science Opinion Outweighs Science Fact," Alex Wade, Guardian, October 3rd 2003
reproduced at www.innocent.org.uk
BBC News "Print Experts Stand by McKie ID May 30th 2006
BBC News "Profile Sir Roy Meadow" February 17th 2006 (eg)
Times Online: "Pathologist's Work under Scrutiny," Stewart Tendler, November 14th 2005 (eg)
Inside Time No 39 "Pathologist's Integrity Dealt Fatal Blow," winter 2000 (eg)
BBC News: "Legal Review of Southall's Cases," February 20th 2007 (eg)

BBC *"Inside Out," Alison Duberry, 1999.*
Science and the Law, Dr Zakaria Erzincliogu, reproduced at <u>www.innocent.org</u>.uk
Transcript: Summing Up. Before; The Honourable Mr Justice McCombe, Regina –
V- Gordon Park, 26/01/05.

Chapter Eleven

Investigation procedures, rights, and the role of juries

THE flaws already highlighted in the investigatory stage of any case will, of course, impact on all of the other areas of the case. That, in itself, is bad enough, but when we add the flaws inherent in the other stages, quite independent of the police procedures or the input of expert witnesses, then the true scale of the problem becomes frighteningly apparent.

For example, we have an unchallenged assumption that a person who is suspected of having perpetrated a crime will be treated in a particular way, following set procedures, and will have certain undeniable rights. We imagine that they will be cautioned that anything they say will be taken down and may be used in evidence against them. We imagine that they will have the right to remain silent until they have a solicitor present, and that their solicitor will give the best advice in the circumstances, in order to protect their client. The solicitor, we assume, will have access to all of the information he or she requires in order to best advise their client.

From these assumptions spring still more: that we would "know" who our solicitor is, that we would "know" that we were being treated as a suspect by the police, and that the advice we would be given would, indeed, be the best advice available to ensure we would be properly protected in law. We further assume that anything which has been "taken down" will be shown to us, or read back to us, for our signature in agreement.

The point at which these assumptions begin to unravel is when we realise that the line between a person being treated as a witness or a suspect often becomes blurred. The Police and Criminal Evidence Act, in 1991, contained the paragraph:

> "*a written record shall be made of any comments made by a suspected person, including unsolicited comments which are outside the context of an interview but which might be relevant to the offence. Any such record must be timed and signed by the maker. Where practicable, the person shall be given the opportunity to read that record and sign it as correct or to indicate the respects in which he considers it inaccurate. Any refusal to sign should also be recorded.*"

In the case of Susan May, the police log clearly showed the point at which they began to consider Susan as a suspect, yet she continued to be treated as a witness. She had no way of knowing that the questions she asked, and the responses she gave to questions put to her were being used to gather "evidence" which would later be used against her. Although PACE does not apply in Scotland, the same problem arose in the case of Luke Mitchell. The Chief Investigating Officer admitted to the press following conviction that he had considered Luke as a suspect "from July 3rd," yet the following day, Luke and his mother attended the police station to give what they believed to be *witness* statements.

John Taft, on the advice of his duty solicitor, responded with "no comment" to any questions other than those which asked directly whether he had been involved in any way with the murder of Cynthia Bolshaw. Reforms to the criminal justice system had essentially taken away the right to remain silent, by allowing such action to be presented to juries who were advised that they could draw "negative inferences" from a person's refusal to answer questions. In John's case, this is exactly what happened in the end, even though he had acted on the duty solicitor's advice.

In Simon Hall's case, confidential information was imparted by investigating officers to potential witnesses *before* Simon had been told he was considered a suspect.

Clearly, those who have never had any dealings with the criminal justice system are at an immediate disadvantage. They may *think* they know what their rights are, and what procedures should be followed, but if events do not follow their pre-conceived ideas, they are at a loss as to how to rectify matters. For example, during the questioning of Luke Mitchell on August 14th 2003, with no solicitor present, Luke requested the presence of his solicitor several times, and stated that he did not wish to comment further until his solicitor arrived. The police officers concerned simply ignored him, firstly telling him that he had *no right* to talk to anyone, then continuing to question him, in spite of his stated desire to answer no further questions without a solicitor present. As a fifteen year old child, what could he possibly have done to rectify such a situation? Also, it does not immediately follow that someone who has been assigned a duty solicitor will know that they have the right to source a solicitor of their own choosing. Indeed, in many cases, choosing a solicitor to defend themselves is as random a matter as looking through the Yellow Pages, or accepting a recommendation from a solicitor that they may have had reason to access previously – perhaps one who has prepared documents for a house sale or other domestic matter. Because of the reliance upon and belief in the fairness of the system, it simply does not occur to some people that their legal representation may not, in fact, be the best they could have secured. Although this particular case is not one of those highlighted in this book, the following is a quote from an interview with Chris Danks:

> 'I never saw my solicitor. I couldn't pick him out on an identification parade, and he couldn't pick me out. My family never saw him. The person we thought was my solicitor turned out to be an unqualified clerk. After I was convicted, I told him I wanted to appeal. He said he would sort it out. A few weeks later, he came to see me and told me I could not appeal. Only after that we found out that he was not a solicitor at all. He was an ex-police officer.'

It is immediately apparent, then, that knowing our rights, and being able to ensure those rights are properly afforded us, are two completely different things. If investigating officers choose to ignore our rights, there is, quite simply, nothing we can do. However, when the case finally reaches the courtroom, the jury will be completely unaware that these breaches have occurred, and will proceed on the basis that the accused has been afforded all of the rights available, in law, to him or her.

There is the further belief that safeguards are in place to ensure that whatever a suspect is claimed to have said is provable, transparent and fair. Yet there are several examples where this is far from the case. Changes to the Police and Criminal Evidence Act decreed that suspects are supposed to be shown everything they have said that will be used against them, and to sign their agreement. Further, interviews with suspects are supposed to be recorded, to ensure, in part, that they are not led, bullied or harassed into saying things that they otherwise might not. Yet, as has already been shown, these safeguards only come into play *after* a person has been advised that they are, in the eyes of investigating officers, a suspect rather than a witness. This leaves a gap in which exactly the sort of behaviours that PACE is supposed to safeguard against can take place, and frequently do.

Susan May had no idea that she was being "backed into a corner" by police who had information that she did not. Derek Christian made a perfectly innocent alteration to his initial statement regarding the moving of boxes, which was later used as evidence that he had "lied and lied and lied." Luke Mitchell was alone with officers at the police station where he was stripped and questioned without a responsible adult being present, in spite of the fact that he was just fourteen years old, and was questioned a further twice for six hours each time, without a solicitor present.

It is not just the suspect him or herself who is likely to be subject to such treatment. Crucial witnesses do not have the same protection under

PACE, because they are not suspects and therefore do not have to be cautioned, or to have their interviews recorded. Officers investigating the Simon Hall case were claimed to have given confidential information to witnesses and others, which may have impacted on the evidence they would later give. Simon's mother, Lynn Hall, came under particularly intense pressure because she was the only witness who could place Simon in his own house between 6.15am and 6.30am. Claims that she had "lied" to cover up for her son were never substantiated, but were allowed to be led in court – even the judge made reference to Mrs Hall's possible dishonesty. The same was true of Corrine Mitchell, Luke Mitchell's mother. Although no evidence was ever offered in court to prove that Mrs Mitchell had been dishonest regarding her son's whereabouts and her own actions that evening, the implication that she had lied was made repeatedly throughout the trial.

The family of Sion Jenkins provides perhaps one of the most shocking examples of such manipulation of witnesses. Firstly, police made a conscious decision to feed information to Lois Jenkins, Sion's wife, that they had "proof" that he had killed Billie-Jo. Three weeks later, his four daughters, two of whom provided Sion's alibi, were told by police officers that he had murdered their foster sister and had been violent to their mother. The only other adult present was the girls' mother.

These examples draw our attention to some of the initial areas where our perception of investigative procedures and their reality begin to part company – once we are caught up in an investigation, without access to the "outside world," the fact is that the investigators hold all of the cards. No matter what we may previously have believed our rights to be, or the processes we assumed would be followed to the letter, once the ball has started rolling, we are completely powerless to either stop it, or to change its direction. It is possibly this factor, more than any of the others, that ordinary people find so difficult to accept. Yet even something as simple as "the caution" – something with which we all believe we are completely familiar, and would recognise immediately – does not live up to our perception of it. The following is an exact quote of what was later claimed to be a caution:

> "Okay. Right, what, the purpose of our visit here today, eh, is to , as you're well aware, Luke has provided an inter, ehm, has been interviewed and provided a, a statement in relation to the circumstances eh that we found on, on Monday and the sad loss of Jodi Jones, ehm, now today we're intending to facilitate a further interview with Luke ehm in relation to the, the statement

that's been provided by you wi the purpose of going into more detail eh in relation to your observations at that particular time and also another aim of the interview is to facilitate herein a lot more information in relation to, to Jodi, and her, her ehm immediate friends, the backgrounds and eh movements and hobbies. Now that's all gonna be vitally important to the investigation and I think because Luke you're one of the immediate, immediate friends, close point of contact with eh Jodi, it's vital that we, we get as much information in relation to the immediate people in cont, that have contact wi Jodi so that we can eliminate from the investigation and that's, that's important for yourself as well, I'm quite sure you agree wi that. Ehm, I've made you aware of a warrant {*warrant to search the family home*} eh, and I've also made you aware that we're hoping to invest, eh bring you here for the purpose of facilitating this, this interview and yous have both agreed to attend the police station for the purpose of completing a declaration of voluntary attendance form..........{*followed by instructions about how to fill in this form*}.........then......

"Okay, in fairness as well it's a, a procedural thing I've got to caution you that you're no bound to answer any of these questions that we say today but if you do your answers will be tape recorded, video recorded, may be noted, and may be used in evidence."

Would any of us, in reality, far less a fourteen year old child, have been able to understand from the excerpt printed here, that we were being questioned under caution as a *suspect*, and that our answers may one day be used in evidence against us? The entire implication here is that he is there, voluntarily, to help investigating officers to better understand Jodi's normal activities, friends, and general personality. Within that understanding, it is patently obvious that information he gives may be used as future evidence – there would be no point in police obtaining it if they did not intend to use it. This "suspect" has been clearly and completely misled – even the "caution" itself omits to mention the fact that the answers he gives may be used in evidence *against him!* The actual caution is introduced in such a casual, unimportant manner ("*…in fairness as well, it's a procedural thing…*") that its significance is completely missed.

Our concept of the caution – *"Joe Bloggs, you are being arrested on suspicion of the murder of Jack Black. You do not have to say anything, but anything you do say may be taken down and used in evidence against you,"* is nowhere to be found. Rather, we have misleading, ambiguous and, in some instances, downright dishonest statements, cobbled together in a rambling, almost incoherent narrative which seems, by design, to be intended to confuse the issue, rather than clarify it.

To quote the officer in this instance, *in fairness,* the caution should be absolutely clear and unambiguous, so that there is no doubt in anyone's mind what is occurring.

What we are faced with, therefore, is the uncomfortable suggestion that once the police have a suspect "in the system," behind closed doors, "procedure" becomes anything investigating officers need or want it to be, and those caught up in that system can do nothing about it.

However, even if this is the case, surely procedures once a case comes to court would highlight these failings, and immediately right these particular wrongs?

Unfortunately, this is not the case – many of the procedures in place in the court setting are carried over from the flaws and errors which arise in the original investigation.

For example, one of the most difficult factors to address is that of what the jury does not hear. Information that could make a clear difference to the outcome of many cases simply never makes it into court. There are several reasons for this – the defence is unaware that such evidence exists, or fail to use such evidence through incompetence, genuine human error, or a combination of both; evidence which should have been available to the defence is deemed "irrelevant" by the disclosure officer, and relegated to the unused evidence schedule, where it is likely to be labeled in such a way as to conceal its relevance; evidence is lost, either deliberately or accidentally, by being mis-filed, removed, or altered, or judges decide that certain evidence should not be seen or heard by the jury. These are not occasional glitches in the system, they are common occurrences, in spite of our tenacious belief that trials are based on the concept of "all of the evidence," and that juries do, indeed, hear everything of relevance before being asked to make their decisions.

The gastroenterologist's report in the Simon Hall case *could not possibly* have been deemed irrelevant by the disclosure officer, yet it found its way onto the unused material schedule, and was only discovered due to the particular diligence of one of his defence team. There has never been any explanation as to how such a critical piece of evidence should have come to be lost in this manner. Similarly, witness statements referring to the "loud, crashing noises" at around 2am met a similar fate – they were not made available to the defence team.

The witness statement from Wendy Price in the Derek Christian case was not made known to the defence until just a few weeks prior to the trial, even though the police had known about it for several months.

The rock in the Gordon Park case, so crucial to implicating his involvement, somehow found its way into a group of exhibits taken from the lakebed where his wife's body had been found. Expert testimony which cast serious doubts as to this rock *ever* having been submersed in water, far less for many years, was led in evidence, but the significance of this testimony is likely to have been lost in the protracted, extremely confusing and highly technical nature of the evidence.

Because Sion Jenkins' daughters had been given information which claimed police had "proof" that their father had killed their foster sister, their video-taped statements, which provided Sion with a clear alibi, could not be led in court. The defence concluded that any evidence in cross examination could not fail to have been tainted.

Evidence regarding another, extremely credible suspect in the Luke Mitchell case was first held onto by police for several months, and then, when the defence team finally obtained access to it, the police claimed that they had not acted upon the evidence because the case was officially "closed."

In the case of Susan May, the jury was never made aware that two separate witnesses had reported a car outside Mrs Marchbank's house that night, its engine running, both with and without occupants. Neither was the jury advised that Susan's sister was mentally ill, a factor which should have had a significant impact on the weight given to Ann's testimony.

Clearly, once again, there is something more than simple human error at play here – there are too many cases in which evidence detrimental to the prosecution's case is never heard by the jury. Perhaps, as suggested earlier, within a mindset which strives to gather only that which supports the prosecution line, this evidence is not so much lost as deemed unimportant. However, this raises a serious issue regarding the conclusions juries draw, and the beliefs juries hold. There is no doubt that the jury is led to believe that it is hearing "all of the evidence" – indeed, judges guide jurors that they must find *only* on the evidence that has been presented in court. Somewhat confusingly, jurors are told, on the one hand, that if there is any doubt regarding the "facts," or if events could have another innocent or plausible explanation, they must find for the defendant, yet on the other hand are told that they must not "try to guess" possibilities other than those led in court. Since they are actively encouraged *not* to try to "fill the gaps," so to speak, jurors are unlikely to even consider the possibility that there may be other evidence which would provide a more complete, or feasible, explanation. Like the early police investigation, jurors are in the position of having to make sense from the information they have available to them – unlike the police, they have no idea that this is what they are having to do, because they have been led to believe that what they have heard is "all of the evidence."

There is also an assumption that what constitutes evidence is clearly defined. The Oxford Dictionary of Law defines "evidence" as "that which tends to prove the existence or nonexistence of some fact. It may consist of "testimony," "documentary evidence", "real evidence" and, when admissible, "hearsay evidence."

What is important here is the first sentence – "…that which tends to prove the existence or nonexistence of some fact." If information is introduced which does not prove the existence or nonexistence of some fact, on what grounds can that information reasonably be included? In each of the cases highlighted in this book, information was presented to the court which did not prove anything relevant to the case, yet it was allowed to be led, and was given a disproportionate amount of attention and significance, clearly to the detriment of the suspect. The "fibre evidence," already discussed in some detail, falls into this category. In each of the cases, it proved nothing of any significance whatsoever – in the cases of Simon Hall and John Taft, there was not even an "originating" garment from which the fibres were claimed to have come. The contention that John Taft had disposed of the originating garment was completely discredited by other, more concrete evidence, but in Simon Hall's case, the prosecution does not even offer such an explanation. There is simply no evidence to support the theory that he had ever owned or worn an item of clothing of the type that would have shed the fibres found on Mrs Albert's body.

The "financial evidence" in Susan May's case was of no relevance to the murder charge, to the extent that the judge had to *remind* the jury of that fact. One is left wondering, if even the judge admits certain evidence is of no real bearing, why was it ever allowed to be led?

The introduction of evidence regarding bottles of urine and a Mariyin Manson cd in the Luke Mitchell case did not receive quite such a thorough examination by the judge, who failed to recognise, for example, that incidents which occur *after* an event cannot possibly have been causally influential – the Marilyn Manson "evidence" was proven to have been acquired by Luke Mitchell after Jodi Jones had been murdered!

Another issue regarding what constitutes the definition of evidence is that of corroboration. In many cases, including several of those highlighted here, "evidence" is presented with little or nothing to back up its validity. In cases which rely heavily or solely on circumstantial evidence, the corroboration of two independent sources is supposed to be required, yet more often than not, this does not happen, and, as a result, much of what is presented in court is not, in fact, evidence, but suggestion. The prosecution will suggest that a person is evil, or calculating, or lying, without necessarily having to back up such suggestions. Without a clear definition of evidence, and with information being introduced which does not prove anything of significance to the case, it is hardly surprising that members of the jury, and even witnesses themselves can be heavily influenced by these suggestions which are allowed to intermingle with fact, conjecture, and irrelevant information. Rather than a clear cut presentation of the facts, backed by concrete, relevant evidence, prosecutors weave a fairy tale (or a horror story) of speculation and innuendo, often requiring jurors to suspend the observations of their own senses in order to maintain the illusion. The place where this becomes most obvious is in the prosecutions' summing up speeches.

Andrew Campbell, in the case of Derek Christian told jurors

"Don't be misled by his behaviour. Pathological killers don't wear a sign on their heads or have five ears. They are as, in appearance, just like you and me. Don't be misled that because Christian did not attract suspicion in the days afterwards, the killer can't be him."

This is, in fact, in direct contradiction to the guidance given to the jury by the judge – that they must find only on the evidence presented to them. The evidence presented in court, in this case, pointed to Derek Christian's behaviour, psychological make up, and history showing a man with *no* psychotic tendencies whatsoever, yet the prosecutor invites jurors to conclude exactly the opposite.

Summing up the Gordon Park case, Alistair Webster QC, prosecuting, told the court:

"Whoever killed and disposed of Carol Park would have the following characteristics; a person who knew her sufficiently well to come across her in her short nightdress; a person who had reason to strongly dislike her or to lose his temper with her; a person who was thoroughly familiar with knots, both as a sailor and a climber; a meticulous person; a person with access to a boat and familiarity with Coniston Water. One man fits this description: Gordon Park."

This is patently nonsense – several men could, in fact have fitted that description, but only *one* who was in court that day.

Alan Turnbull, summing up the Luke Mitchell case claimed that the fact that Luke Mitchell had "gone through the V in the wall, and had known to turn left, rather than turning right or going straight ahead" proved that he "must have known where the body lay – something only the killer could have known." All of the evidence presented in court completely discredited such a course of events, down to the fact that the other members of the search party could not possibly have seen what was going on on the other side of the wall, yet jurors are asked to ignore the obvious facts before their own eyes (a reconstruction of the wall was actually built in the courtroom), and accept instead, an explanation which was not simply implausible, but actually impossible.

Jurors in Sion Jenkins' case were asked to accept that he had carried out a brutal and bloody murder in an impossibly small period of time, without getting a single trace of blood on himself, and without even showing signs of physical exertion.

How, then, can jurors be duped in this way? In every day life, faced with a choice between the possible and the highly unlikely, we believe we are able to make clear distinctions – if someone tries to persuade us a green light is blue, for example, we will be quite adamant that the light is green. What is it about the courtroom setting that sees this everyday logicality put aside in favour of the implausible, unlikely, or downright impossible?

There are, of course, many factors to consider. In this age of information technology, it is naïve, to say the least, to imagine that jurors have not been subject to outside influences prior to a case. With twenty four hour television and radio, mobile phones and the internet, it is virtually impossible to miss a high profile news story. Even if the eventual defendant is not named, the details of the crime itself create opinions and prejudices in potential jurors – the widespread horror and revulsion over the case of the Russell family, in which only nine year old Josie survived the hammer attack which had killed her mother and sister, or the murder of two year old Jamie Bulger by two ten year old boys, are such examples.

The tendency of the media to link factors which have no logical link is an early stage in the process of leading potential jurors in particular directions. Sion Jenkins was charged with "obtaining pecuniary advantage by deception" as well as the murder of Billie-Jo. There is no logical link between the two, but this factor is hidden in the barrage of intense publicity, and an implied link eventually becomes an accepted link, – in this case, the reasoning runs thus: he lied on his cv, therefore he is a liar, therefore he must be lying about killing Billie-Jo. Gordon Park, having given an interview to one newspaper in an attempt to stem the barrage of negative and hostile reporting then found himself in the position of being accused of being prepared to profit from his wife's death. (The fact that the two "witnesses" who claimed that Gordon had "confessed" to them also stood to profit from Carol Park's death, was not given any consideration whatsoever). The link here, that being prepared to make money from his wife's death only goes to show that he must have killed her, has no basis in logic, but served to raise even greater suspicion.

As previously stated, jurors are aware that a case has been through both a police investigation, and CPS vetting, before it even reaches the courtroom. Where a particularly horrific crime has been committed, is it reasonable to expect ordinary people to be able to separate their emotional reactions to what has happened from the non-emotional, purely reason-based faculties with which they are required to evaluate the evidence put before them?

All of the political parties place crime and punishment high on their agendas, feeding into and from the public perception that crime is "on the increase," and steps must be taken to ensure the guilty are caught and punished (with the underlying assumption that this is not happening, or at least not often enough). Against this backdrop, the pressure on jurors not to be seen to be helping a vicious criminal to "get away with it" is great. As already discussed, the perception that the system is geared to weed out those cases which do not have enough evidence to secure a conviction leads to a situation where jurors cannot help but be biased towards the assumption that the person in the dock is not there without good reason.

One influence which may have some bearing on why jurors are swayed by the summing up speeches, especially of the prosecution and the judge, is that of television and film. Crime fiction invariably depicts the "good guys" cleverly and meticulously outwitting the "bad guys," often winning on a very clever, or very subtle last minute point. Whilst this may seem simplistic, it is, in fact, from just such sources that many people have learned what they believe are their rights, and the correct processes of legal procedures.

Two other factors which have to be taken into account when establishing how juries are persuaded to come to certain conclusions are the makeup of the jury itself, and the procedures governing the actions of juries.

The jury is supposedly a random selection of members of the public, a miniature representation of that greater public. However, this is not entirely accurate, in that professionals in certain fields are often excused jury duty. Doctors, surgeons, lawyers and scientists are some of the professions where it could be claimed that their absence would cause difficulties for others. As a result, a certain intellectual stratum is rarely a component part of juries – the very stratum which is best equipped to evaluate and analyse data relatively dispassionately. In reality, jurors are drawn from a group of people whose life experience is likely to be less broad, and for whom tackling important issues on a day-to-day basis is not a part of that experience.

Once a jury is selected, we have no way of knowing what prejudices or beliefs are held within those twelve or fifteen people. Also, jurors in any trial are most likely to be drawn from a specific area – ie, an area which is within a reasonable distance of the court where the trial is to be held. Although this is a factor which is hardly ever noted, this is a *financial* as well as a practical consideration – the cost of ferrying jury members several hundred miles, or accommodating them in local hotels, etc, is not one which the judicial system is often disposed to incur. Immediately, we can see a problem. If jurors are drawn from a certain locality, then collective prejudices or beliefs common to that locality will be amplified. Normally, as a safeguard, high profile trials are held outwith the locality of either the crime itself, or the home area of the suspect, but this is by no means always the case – Luke Mitchell was tried just seven miles from his and Jodi Jones' home towns, and the area of the murder, and Sion Jenkins was tried in the same area in which he lived and worked, and where Billie-Jo was murdered.

But the question of prejudice in general remains – it would be naïve to believe that everyone serving jury duty will be without prejudice, of a certain intellectual ability, or capable of rational and logical reasoning. Jurors do not have to give reasons for their findings, and this leaves us with the inescapable fact that we can simply never know how many jury decisions are based in prejudice, ignorance, or simply the inability to differentiate between fact and supposition.

The jury, following summing up from the prosecution, the defence, and the judge, retires to consider its verdict. What this means, in essence, is that twelve to fifteen people, having heard everything that was led during the trial, have to agree one way or another (or in Scotland, another still, given the Not Proven verdict). In an ideal world, these people would reasonably and rationally discuss their differences, and eventually come to some sort of consensus. That the judge can accept a 10 – 2 majority, should the jury fail to reach a unanimous decision, is the first warning bell that all may not be as it seems. (This is even worse in Scotland where the term "majority" is taken literally – a majority of *one* is sufficient to convict – from a fifteen person jury, up to seven members may vote Not Guilty, and the defendant will still be convicted!) On any jury, there will be the possibility of those who have listened to all of the evidence, and have the intellectual capacity to evaluate and analyse this evidence rationally, and those less able in these respects. Without the ability to evaluate and analyse, there are those who will go with what "feels right," based on their own beliefs and prejudices. Neither side will be able to convince the other using their own particular approach, because the two approaches are mutually exclusive. What happens next comes down to personalities. There is enormous pressure for juries to reach a verdict. They may have been kept away from family, work and normal life for several weeks. There may be a great deal of public pressure to see a conviction secured. Even with a 50/50 split, only four jury members need to be "persuaded" to change their stance for a majority verdict to be brought. The reality is that the bombastic, the opinionated and the intimidatory are much more likely to force through agreement than the timid, the thoughtful, or the disinterested. There is no getting away from the fact that we simply do not know, and are not allowed to know, what brings juries to their conclusions. So many apparently irrational jury findings point up the fact that it is by no means a given that deliberation, evaluation or analysis play even the smallest part in reaching those conclusions.

Interestingly, in most circumstances, a decision made under duress would be deemed legally invalid, yet the whole set-up of the jury decision-making process is one of duress. Once "in deliberation," jury members are theoretically isolated from everything and everyone until a decision is reached. Once the 50/50 balance is unsettled, the pressure on the dissenters becomes greater and greater – for example, imagine a jury is split 9 – 3. Only one of those three need change their stance for a majority verdict to be brought, and for the trial to be completely over. There are additional factors which also come into play – Fridays are notoriously fraught days for pressuring jury members into agreement, since, if such agreement is not secured, they will have to spend the weekend in a hotel, away from home, family and friends. In particular, following lengthy or complex trails, a natural desire to "get it over with" is likely to come into play, and those who perhaps did not stick with their original decision can always claim to have "just gone along with everyone else."

There is also the unspoken expectation that a jury *will* come to either a unanimous or majority decision, indeed, that they *must* do so. The fact that the dissenters can hold out and refuse to change their mind is not a fact that is particularly well highlighted – we rarely see or hear about cases where the jury has had to say, "Sorry, we just can't get enough of us to agree one way or the other," even though this is a perfectly reasonable and acceptable outcome. When the jury retires to consider its verdict, the judge will advise them that they must, if they can, come to a unanimous verdict. The judge in the Gordon Park case, for example, told jurors, "I ask you to reach a verdict on which each one of you is agreed." The possibility of *not* being able to reach a verdict on which everyone is agreed (or at least ten of the twelve agree) is simply not addressed. Jurors are given no advice or guidance as to what they should do if such agreement cannot be obtained, or even as to how long they will be left to "slug it out" without agreement. The very fact that they believe they *must* reach a unanimous decision appears to be one of the main influences in such a decision being reached.

We can see, then, how the whole idea that the trial is an arena where all the facts and evidence are laid out, and the jury makes its decision based on what it sees and hears in this arena, is far from the reality.

Suspects do not always have the information or knowledge to ensure that they are treated fairly – often, the system is used against them before they have even had a chance to begin activating their own defence. From this point, the many unexamined assumptions – that a defendant in a case will have had legal representation, that all of the facts have been presented in court, and that correct procedures have been followed, for example, become the bedrock on which the jury builds its framework of reference for the information presented during the trial, and from which it will eventually reach its conclusion.

We fail to recognise or understand that a legalised collusion, couched in the terminology of "co-operation" between various aspects of the prosecutory system produces "evidence," information and circumstances which are heavily weighted in favour of the prosecution case, before that case even makes it into court. Jury members believe that what they are witnessing is the presentation of facts on a level playing field, and that information provided from each side carries equal weight.

Finally, we cannot even begin to guess how much bias a jury might bring to a case, based on what members may have seen, heard or read, both prior to and during the trial. We have a view of juries being taken off to some secret venue, night after night, deprived of television, newspapers or contact with the outside world. This is, of course, complete nonsense – jurors in the Luke Mitchell case, for example, went to their own homes every night, including following a few hours deliberation on the Thursday afternoon, before returning to the court the next morning and delivering their verdict. That any one of these jurors had access to vast amounts of prejudicial media coverage, and was open to persuasion by anyone minded to exert such persuasion, throughout both the trial and the deliberation phase, is a fact that many people choose to ignore, and one of which many more are completely unaware.

The appeal judges in the case of Sion Jenkins did recognise such a risk, however, and insisted that a website dedicated to clearing his name be closed down in the period between Sion's release on bail and his re-trial. The reason they gave was that potential jurors might visit the website and gather information prior to the trial. This action seems odd, given the massive media coverage of the case from the beginning, almost all of it negative and prejudicial. There were many internet sites discussing Sion Jenkins case, and literally hundreds of media articles available on-line, but the only one the judges wanted closed down was one which clearly and unequivocally supported Sion Jenkins' innocence. In a breath-taking display of double standards, this decision seemed to say, in effect, it is acceptable for jurors to be exposed to that which is negative or unsupportive towards a suspect, but it is not acceptable for them to be exposed to that which might bias them in favour of a suspect.

Jurors in the Gordon Park case were told by the judge, following almost four hours deliberation,

> "I am going to let you go home now, but it is important that after you leave the court, you should not discuss the case with anyone else or allow anyone else to speak to you, just the same ways I have told you many times before.......
>
> ...Once you have left the court, do not try and deal with this case in any way at all looking for further evidence or trying to contact each other to discuss it. Just go home, enjoy a quiet evening and come back refreshed and ready for work tomorrow again, please."

Realistically, how many jurors can be expected to obey such directions? These people return to their own homes, families and friends, in the midst of high profile cases, with the accompanying blaze of publicity, local gossip and speculation, and they are expected to have closed eyes, ears, mouths and minds.

We can only guess how much outside influence impacts the final decisions of jurors in these circumstances. In the Luke Mitchell case, for example, the jury retired on the afternoon of Thursday 20th January 2005, and was sent home some four hours later, having indicated to the judge that jurors were "nowhere near" a verdict. The following morning, the verdict was delivered within one hour of the jury's return. There are two possibilities – that something in that one hour moved them from "nowhere near" a verdict to a confident, majority decision of a guilty verdict, or that other influences came into play during the intervening period. Quite simply, we will never know.

What is clear, however, is that the flaws inherent in the initial police approach carry over into investigation procedures with regard to the treatment of suspects and witnesses. Some of the most basic rights are completely ignored, and there is nothing an individual can do if this happens to them.

The role of juries, and the part played by the judges who instruct them, often amplify the difficulties already highlighted. Jurors are led to believe certain things – that they are hearing all of the evidence, and that both the suspect, and all of the witnesses, have been fairly treated, and that all of the evidence has been fairly obtained. The impact of these beliefs on the jury's final decision is obvious – should the jury become aware that any one of these "truths" is, in fact, completely false, then, plainly, the conclusion reached by that jury is likely to be very different.

References:

Christopher Danks at www.innocent.org.uk

Transcript, Interview, ADS Fulton, DC Steven Quinn, Luke M Mitchell, July 4th 2003

Transcript: "Charge to the Jury", Lord Nimmo Smith, January 20th & 21st 2005

Transcript: "Summing Up." Before; The Honourable Mr Justice McCombe, Regina –V- Gordon Park, 26/01/05.

"The British Jury System," www.portia.org.uk

Justice for All, JUSTICE's Response to the White Paper, October 2002

"Cutting Crime, Delivering Justice," HM Government "A Strategic Plan for Criminal justice 2004-2008"

Criminal Procedures (Scotland) Act 1995

Chapter Twelve

Court procedures, prosecution and defence, and judges

WE WOULD hope that the roles of prosecuting and defending QCs, and the judges themselves, would go some way to righting some of the many wrongs already discussed in this book. After all, it is they who know all of the rules, and who know what should and should not be allowed. Yet, as we have witnessed in so many other areas of the criminal justice system, our perception of what *should* be the case, and its reality, are far removed from one another.

One particular QC offers a fascinating insight into the differences in what we perceive to be happening, and what is actually going on.

Alan Turnbull QC, was quoted in a newspaper interview following the verdict in the Luke Mitchell case as saying:

"It's not the prosecutor's function to get a conviction at all costs, it's the prosecutor's function to present the facts to their best effect."

He then goes on to explain, somewhat bizarrely,

"That doesn't stop once you have got the case to the jury, because there is still the jury speech to be done. I think that if a prosecutor were to say, "Well, I've got the case to the jury – I don't need to put a lot of effort into what I'm going to say because they've heard it all themselves," then that would be the prosecutor not doing their best job. Many cases are influenced upon, if not decided by, the jury speech."

Just what, exactly, is Mr Turnbull trying to say here? If the facts, during the trial, have been presented to "their best effect," then surely that will be what the jury decides upon? To suggest that some cases are decided by the effects of the jury speech, then there must be something else, something not present during the presentation of the facts in the course of the trial. Obviously, the jury is not aware that something else is at play – jurors believe that each counsel, and later, the judge, is simply summing up all of the aspects of their side of the case.

What might this "something else" be? One clue is in Mr Turnbull's claim that the prosecutor would "not be doing their best job" if they decided not to put a great deal of effort into the jury speech because jurors have "heard it all themselves." The implication here is that the jury cannot be depended upon to come to the right conclusion based only on what it has heard, even though this is supposed to be the *actual* role of the jury! We are left with the uncomfortable suggestion that the jury speech is an opportunity to persuade jurors to interpret what they have heard in a specific way. It is not enough to consider the fact that the defence counsel has an equal opportunity to so persuade the jury. First of all, the basis of our judicial system is that the jury comes to its conclusions based on the **evidence,** as it has been presented during the trial, and it does so in a rational and impartial manner, unencumbered by influences outwith the presentation of that evidence. Secondly, we have to consider that the prosecution has far greater resources from which to pull its persuasions than does the defence.

As previously discussed, the close co-operation between prosecutors, the CPS and the Senior Investigating Officer introduces an element of unease – given the influence of any one of these parties in its own right, for the three to join forces at "the earliest possible stage" must, at the very least, introduce the risk of manipulation of information or circumstances towards an agreed outcome, even though this outcome may only be implied. In some ways, this mirrors the problems raised by Sir Roy Meadow lecturing judges on how to interpret medical evidence – each of the three parties in this case (prosecutor, CPS and Senior Investigating Officer) have a common vested interest in their work agreeing, or being interpreted in the same ways.

In a further, and perhaps more worrying statement, the same article from Mr Turnbull carries the footnote; "How I forged a bond with Jodi's grieving family."

The testimony of this family was used to great effect in the case against Luke Mitchell, even though, as has been shown in this book, it was flawed, and in some cases, impossible. There is also a suggestion that, in order not to further alienate a jury already expected to be hostile, following media coverage, the defence took a strategic decision *not* to "be too hard" on Jodi's family during the trial. What we have here is not a case decided on the evidence at all. The prosecutor, who has been involved "right from the start".... "even before {Luke Mitchell} first appeared in court," has had access to all of the police and CPS information, and all of the witnesses, including a "bond" with the victim's family. At the same time, the effects of media coverage forced the defence team to adopt a damage limitation approach, which meant that much of the evidence would be nodded through, rather than being vigorously cross-examined, so as not to put the jury even more off side. If nothing else, this is an implicit admission that this was never going to be a fair trial from the very start.

The contention that it is "not a prosecutor's function to get a conviction at all costs" does not sit comfortably with the actions of many of the prosecutors of the cases highlighted in this book.

The prosecution in the case of John Taft, rather than accept that their case was completely flawed, attempted to have the evidence of their own witnesses, which provided John with an alibi, ruled as inadmissible. Not only did this evidence provide John with an alibi, it completely destroyed the prosecution case against him, in that he could not have been the person who carried out the murder and removed the car *at the time the prosecution claimed he did so*. This factor remained unexplained and unaddressed until the judge's summing up. At that point, the judge introduced a new possibility, one which had not been led during the trial, as to how John may still have been the murderer, in that he may have returned to the scene at a later time. Such a possibility meant that other, more concrete evidence (including the pathologist's findings, and the evidence of the GP and the first police officer on the scene), had to be ignored, or disbelieved. Once more, we face a certain uneasiness with regard to the close co-operation of the different parts of the prosecution machine – in this instance, the supposedly impartial judge appears to be shoring up weaknesses in the prosecution case- becoming, in effect, another cog in that prosecution machine!

In Derek Christian's case, not only does the prosecution push the unlikely to an extreme degree; for example, the prosecuting counsel trying to persuade the jury that silver and white are the same thing; not one witness was asked at any point if the man in the dock was the man they had seen that day. Prior to the case coming to court, no identity parade had been carried out, and witnesses would later admit that Derek was not the man they had seen, but they were never asked in court. However, what is most disturbing about this is that his *defence* failed to ask this question. So much time and effort was spent on what was ultimately irrelevant testimony (i.e. fibre evidence, and car colour), yet this critical and fundamental question slipped past without ever having been asked.

There has been much made of the unfairness of dock identification as a stand-alone tool in the prosecution approach – too many witnesses are going to feel pressured to point to the person in the dock, simply because he or she is so obviously the person they are supposed to be identifying. However, in Derek Christian's case, *failure* to use this particular approach, along with the failure to use an identity parade as corroboration robbed Derek of a fundamental right – the right to be eliminated by eye witness identification.

It seems almost impossible to believe that such fundamental errors or breaches of procedures make it into the courtroom in the first place – that they not only make it there, but are then allowed to pass un-noticed and unquestioned beggars belief.

Remaining with Derek Christian for the moment, the incident involving the recall of a witness raises several questions. The prosecution had known about this witness for months, but the defence had only been informed of her existence a few weeks before the trial began. It was the *prosecution*, however, which asked that this witness be recalled. When the judge agreed (despite objections from the defence), it became apparent that the prosecution had already had this woman informed by police that she should return to court the following morning. If nothing else, this is an indicator of the level of confidence held by the prosecution that the judge would agree with their less than usual request.

Further, when the first witness returned to the stand and retracted all of her evidence, the defence requested that the trial be re-started with a new jury, as those who had heard the retracted evidence could not have been anything other than negatively influenced by that incident. This would appear to be a perfectly reasonable request, yet the judge turned it down flat, and allowed the trial to continue with the same jury.

As with so many other factors in the judicial system, our belief that there are clear and recognisable procedures which kick in the moment a case reaches the courts, and that any serious deviation from these procedures will be corrected immediately, is shown to be wildly off the mark.

The master of ceremonies in any court case is the judge him or herself. It is the judge who is responsible for ensuring that events in court follow proper procedures, and are fair and correct. In order to do so, the judge must remain completely impartial, applying interpretation of the law so as to maintain scrupulous fairness and transparency of events. To all intents and purposes, the buck stops with the judge, or so we are led to believe. Yet, once again, we have a wealth of examples of judges completely failing in this most fundamental of their duties.

The above example in the Derek Christian case raises an obvious question – why? Why did the judge refuse the application to restart the trial with a new jury? Why did the judge allow the recall of a witness to which the prosecution had had access for months? Why did the judge not point out to the jury that the man in the dock had never been identified by anyone, and none of the witnesses had ever been asked if this was the man that they saw? Given the self appointed responsibility of the judges in some of the other cases, in which other explanations or interpretations were introduced, apparently at the whim of the judge involved, we are left with the clear implication that judges are free to introduce whatever bias or opinion they choose. The strict impartiality we imagine to be observed by judges is, as with so many other aspects of the legal system, not as we believe it to be.

Certainly, in many cases, certain judges display a remarkable lack of understanding of what, to the ordinary person in the street, would seem self evident.

All of the judges in the John Taft case fall into this category. A very simple, very clear fact – that John could not be in two places at once – completely escapes their understanding, to the extent that they conclude that they can't see why that's *not* a possibility, not can they see why other people might think it's not a possibility!!

There are several clear examples of judges allowing information into the courtroom under the guise of evidence, when it is either nothing of the sort, or where other factors in law should have deemed it inadmissible. The very definition of what constitutes evidence is often stretched to ridiculous lengths, and information which cannot be made to fit even these definitions is still allowed to be led.

For instance, an agreement had been made in the Gordon Park case that payment for the interview given to a newspaper would not be raised in court, as it had nothing whatsoever to do with the case itself. Yet the prosecution *did* raise the matter, using it to claim that Gordon was prepared to profit from his wife's death, and the judge allowed this line of "reasoning" to be presented to the jury. Why, when previous agreement had been reached *not* to use this information, on the grounds that it was of no real relevance to the case, did the judge then allow it to be used simply to blacken Gordon Park's character?

The so-called cell confessions in this case should, one would have imagined, have backed each other up in order to be credible or believable. Yet, in the event, two "witnesses" claim three separate confessions have been made, and all three are allowed to be led as evidence of Gordon's "confession." Indeed, there is a question as to whether these two witness testimonies amount only to hearsay (which should be inadmissible) – each tells his own story, (or, in the case of Glen Banks, "stories") with no other evidence to back them up. Therefore, they are not used as corroboration for each other (although that is how they were presented in court). Other evidence completely discredits their claims – once we examine this logically, we realise that we just have to "take their word for it" that the stories they are telling are true, as there is nothing, anywhere to provide proof. Normally, we would imagine, for a statement to qualify as evidence, it would require something a little more concrete than simply the witness's word that their statement is true!

John Taft's case provides three clear examples of similar procedural anomalies – although the Evans family's statements are led as corroboration for Barbara Taft's statement, on closer inspection, they corroborate only a tiny fragment of her statement. However, the rest of the statement, with nothing to back it up whatsoever, is led as "evidence."

The "new evidence" concerning the semen stain, again, is not what it seems. DNA testing shows that it did, indeed, come from John Taft (who had already admitted having sexual intercourse with Cynthia Bolshaw.) However, the stain could not be dated, other than to say it was "old," therefore, its significance and relevance to the case is absolutely minimal. It cannot prove anything other than that to which John had already admitted, and it is certainly not proof in any form of John having been involved in Mrs Bolshaw's death.

It is not at all clear why the prosecution was allowed to lead information regarding the fire canopy and ripped diary page as evidence, when it is abundantly clear that this is not the case. The statement by Barbara Taft referred to a work's diary – there was no evidence to corroborate the prosecution's switch to Mrs Bolshaw's diary. Fingerprints on the fire canopy were not John's, and there was no other evidence of any description to tie John to the fire canopy. Yet the "connection" between these two items was allowed to be led, and was repeated on several occasions.

The tattoo evidence in the Luke Mitchell case should never have been allowed, in that it was not disclosed to the defence prior to these "witnesses" being called. Proper corroboration – copies, for example, of the id these witnesses claimed to have been shown – was not available. Once again, we have only the word of these witnesses that their statements are true, even though their existence was not made known to the defence before they were called to give evidence during the trial. Not only did the judge allow this, he later pointed out in his summing up that this evidence had been introduced purely *to discredit Corinne Mitchell.*

We believe that it is up to the judges to take control of what goes on in their courtrooms – to ensure that "evidence" actually meets the correct definition, and is led fairly and within the rules. Yet these examples appear to suggest that judges allow whatever it suits them to allow, based, in some cases, on their own beliefs and perceptions. The impartiality we believe judges are so careful to apply to their every decision in a case is, quite simply, not as rigorous, obvious, or commonly employed as we think.

When a judge is happy to admit that he has allowed information which does not meet the strict definition of "evidence," and which breaks all the rules and agreements regarding disclosure, simply to allow the prosecution to discredit a crucial witness for the defence, the whole issue of the power of judges, and their perceived impartiality, is brought into sharp focus.

Perhaps the most common failure of judges in maintaining impartiality, however, is where they appear to *lead* the jury in a particular direction through prejudice, bias, or simply personal opinion. It is one thing to allow information masquerading as evidence to be led, and leaving jurors to make up their own minds about it, it is quite another still to actually make direct suggestions to the jury regarding ways in which information should be interpreted.

The judge in the case of Susan May dismisses, almost laughingly, the possibility that animal blood may have been deposited on the wall, essentially encouraging jurors to ignore this suggestion. Yet later testing of various items, including a dress, gives a positive result for bovine blood, as a result of food preparation.

In the case of Simon Hall, the judge makes the absolutely critical error of referring to the "window of opportunity" as being the hour between 5.30 and 6.30am, when Simon did not have an alibi. The facts of the case, as presented in court, prove categorically, that the *actual* window of opportunity was between approximately 7pm the previous evening, and the finding of Mrs Albert's body on the morning of December 16th. What the judge presented to the jury as fact, in this case, was actually the prosecution's contention, and worse still, other evidence led during the trial placed the time of death between midnight and 3am, well before what the judge referred to as the window of opportunity. To further compound the issue, this same judge then went on to provide another "possible" explanation for noises reported in the vicinity. There are two problems with this. Firstly, the jury is supposed to decide only on the evidence presented in court. The suggestion that these noises may have been made by "clumsy cats" had not been led in court. Even if the judge only intended to provide another, equally plausible explanation for these noises, this possibility still bolstered the prosecution case, and detracted from the defence case.

Often, judges appear to be completely out of touch with reality. Sending jurors home in the Gordon Park case, the judge instructs them to go home, have a relaxing evening and put the case out of their mind until the following day. This was an enormously high profile case, and the judge seems completely unaware that what he is asking of jurors is virtually impossible. An even clearer example of this arises in the case of Luke Mitchell.

This was the longest single defendant trial in Scottish history. It had received massive and relentless publicity, yet Lord Nimmo Smith told the jury:

> "....we have had very little experience of the kind of problems that might arise when {*the jury is sent home*}. I suppose one obvious problem in some cases is that a juror might be approached by a member of the public who would seek to influence a decision. **I don't think there is any risk of that in the present case.**"

This is the same trial in which a juror, when the jury returned with their verdict, made a clear and obvious "thumbs up" gesture to the family of Jodi Jones *before* giving the verdict to the judge, and in which an anonymous member of the public contacted Luke Mitchell's defence team to advise them that he had heard someone in the public gallery discussing the fact that they were apparently in communication with a juror.

Given the enormous power in the hands of our judges, it would seem self evident that decisions need to be clear, consistent, and logical. In so many of these cases, quite the opposite is true.

Susan May's case was referred to the CCRC (Criminal Cases Review Commission), whose report has been described as "one of the strongest it has ever written." This report found that there had been serious breaches of PACE, and that the police had failed to disclose relevant information. Then the Police Complaints Authority found that police officers did not caution Susan correctly, in that the point where Susan had become a suspect was quite clear, yet D. Supt Kerr continued to have her interviewed as a witness.

The response of the appeal judges, following these findings by other bodies, was to dismiss the appeal. In spite of the findings of the CCRC and the PCA, the appeal judges stated that they were "unable to detect any breach of any provision of any code which was then in force."

The same judges rejected new evidence regarding the "bloodstains." Evidence concerning marks on the wall, the judges concluded, was "damning," even though expert findings had raised serious questions about the source of these stains, and even whether they were human blood or not. In fact, later independent testing would return negative results for blood, concluding, in fact, that these were not bloodstains *at all.* The question, in this case, is simply, how? How did the judges come to the apparently illogical conclusions they did, when the available data makes things perfectly clear at even the most rudimentary level of understanding?

A similar issue arose at the appeal of Sion Jenkins, when a statement, claimed to have been made by Sion, was written up by a police officer some three days after the event, and in the officer's own words. This initial report *was* ruled inadmissible by the judge, on the grounds that it may have constituted a breach of PACE. However, the appeal judges then upheld the decision to allow a later interview to be used in evidence, even though this interview made specific reference to the report which had been disallowed. Again, to the ordinary person, this seems obvious – what is the point of disallowing something, and then later allowing something that depends, for its validity, on the disallowed item?

In the case of John Taft, the appeal judges conclude that it was not "unfair" of the judge to have included the new possibility because John's counsel had been asked, and had agreed, that this particular information could be used. Clearly, that was an error on the part of John's defence team, yet the appeal judges were completely unwilling to allow for such an error, and used the agreement as blanket justification for concluding that the trial was "fair" and the conviction "safe." Having made that decision, they then go to extraordinary lengths to show how the new possibility could be a possibility!

This is, perhaps, where the role of judges as they perceive themselves, and as they are perceived by the general public, diverges. Judges quoting specific laws, or precedent from other cases, appear to be applying logical, rational and impartial interpretation of "the law." In too many instances, however, they are simply sifting through data to find that which agrees with their own opinion or interpretation, and applying their findings selectively. Because we still allow the nonsense of "legal speak" to dominate our courts, much of the time, it is almost impossible to understand exactly what these judges are actually saying, and once again, ordinary people are left to believe, by default, that the judges "know what they are talking about."

An outstanding example of selective application of the law, rather than what we would imagine to be common sense, or basic fairness, arises in the Luke Mitchell case. Shane Mitchell, Luke's brother, was questioned on three occasions as a witness, before being questioned and then charged with attempting to pervert the course of justice on April 14th 2004, the same day that Luke was charged with murder. Serious questions were raised by the defence as to the manner in which Shane was questioned on that day, including the claim that the interview was "a sham or pretence by police," in that there was no attempt to gather evidence about the alleged attempt to pervert the course of justice. Instead, the defence claimed, the interview was "an attempt by police by a variety of means to secure evidence against the appellant."

Lord Nimmo Smith, responding to the application to appeal on this particular ground, stated:

> "…I said that I proceeded on the assumption that the evidence of what he {Shane} said would be inadmissible against him if he were the accused at a trial against him. In my opinion, however, the concept of fairness operated quite differently when he was a crown witness….. while there were limits, in general terms the police were entitled to cross examine a witness and put pressure on him which might be regarded as unfair if he were the accused."

He also said,

> "If the Advocate Depute chose to use {this material} and treat Shane Mitchell as a witness, the concept of fairness which would have applied to him if he had been an accused no longer applied."

The point being made by the defence was that "this material," as referred to by the judge, was unfairly obtained by police using a variety of methods. Rather than address the issue of fairness in the manner we would all expect and understand – ie, was the material fairly obtained, and then fairly used against the accused, the judge takes the extraordinary route of first re-defining the concept of fairness, and then resorting to an overly strict application of "precedent" to dismiss the defence's concerns. This whole issue becomes a game of legal points scoring – the judge stating that

> "Mr Findlay was unable to point to any authority except the principle of fairness," (begging the question, isn't that enough in itself?)and

> "The underlying requirement of fairness to an accused was that he was not obliged to incriminate himself. This principle had no application to someone other than the accused."

It is worth noting, however, that this judge accepts that "Shane Mitchell was refused the presence of a lawyer, despite asking for this," and also that "Shane Mitchell was a suspect."

Therefore, even the most basic of reasons for Lord Nimmo Smith rejecting defence concerns – that Shane was a witness rather than a suspect – does not stand up under scrutiny. The same blurring of the lines between witness and suspect is once again used to devastating effect, and this judge, amidst pages of legal gobbledygook, either completely ignores, or fails to notice this factor.

This judge made a series of remarks at the end of the trial, and also when sentencing Luke Mitchell, which were widely reported. They included comments about the effects cannabis consumption may have had on Luke's mental state, and its contribution to his "being unable to make the distinction between fantasy and reality which is essential for normal moral judgements." Two further comments from this judge, in response to the application to appeal, need no further explanation:

"By the time the appellant appeared before me again," {*ie*, **before** *the above comment regarding Luke's mental state*} "...the psychiatric report...available to me...concluded that the appellant was not suffering from a mental disorder....he was sane and fit to plead.....there was no significant abnormality of mind present at the time of what was then the alleged offence..."

and

"I felt that the occasion called for some attempt on my part to identify factors which might go some way towards explaining why he had committed such a wicked murder. These were not intended or expressed to be aggravating factors: they simply represented an attempt by me, in the public interest, to give expression to such insights as I had been able to form."

This is an absolutely clear and unequivocal example of a judge expressing nothing less than prejudice. All of the evidence available to him underscores the fact that this young man's "mental processes" have not, in any way, been rendered abnormal, by cannabis or anything else. Yet he (Lord Nimmo Smith) feels perfectly at liberty to express his "opinion" that they have, knowing that his every word will be faithfully reported and repeated as fact by the media. He later tries to play down his comments by claiming that they were not intended to be "aggravating factors," yet at the time, he used phrases such as "your lack of emotion may account for the callous charade in which you pretended to help search for Jodi....and ".....I think that it is a sign that you found evil attractive......" Following the verdict, he was quoted as saying "it lies beyond any skill of mind to look into the black depths of your mind......" and "....you have been convicted of a truly evil murder."

In order to believe that fairness and impartiality are maintained in our courts, we are often disposed to accept that "the accused" ceases to be a real person in the eyes of the prosecuting and defence teams. The "facts" are all that matter, we believe, and both sides battle it out using just the facts – emotional considerations are not given any value whatsoever.

The judge is the "referee" who holds it all together, reprimanding those who break the rules, and strictly enforcing procedures so as to ensure fairness and uniformity.

Yet, as this chapter has attempted to show, judges, who are the final authority in all of these proceedings, are as open to the influences of bias and prejudice as anyone else, and frequently allow these influences to impact their decisions and actions.

The power wielded by our judges is enormous. It is sobering to realise that they are answerable to no-one.

References:
Daily Record: "My Luke Torment," Gordon McIlwraith, February 14th 2005
"Scots Law and the Issue of Dock Identification," Michael Bromby and Amina Memon, 2005
"Eyewitness Testimony", Dr Amina Memon, Institute for Cultural Research February 2002
"Why experts Make Errors", Itiel E Dror and David Charlton, University of Southampton February 6th 2006
JUSTICE's Response to Auld Review, January 2002
"Wrongful Convictions", Michael Naughton, The Observer Crime and Justice Debate, July 28th 2002
"Unreliable Confessions and Miscarriages of Justice in Britain," Gisli H Gudjonsson, International Journal of Police Science & Management, Volume 4 Number 4, 1st August, 2002
"Tinkering or Transformation? Proposals and Principles in the White Paper, Justice for All'," Ben Fitzpatrick, University of Leeds, 2002
Transcript: "Charge to the Jury", Lord Nimmo Smith, January 20th & 21st 2005
Transcript: Opinion of the Court, November 14th 2006
Transcript: "Judgment," December 7th 2001

Chapter Thirteen

The Media

MEDIA coverage of criminal proceedings is, we believe, restricted by law to ensure fairness. Whilst supporting the right to freedom of information, such restrictions are necessary to prevent unfair treatment of suspects, and to be certain that sensitive information is heard by the jury directly, rather than being disseminated through the media.

However, this is not always the case, and often, media coverage can, and does, have a direct impact on cases. The people whose arrests, trials, and appeals are covered negatively or in a sensationalist manner by the press often have no means to correct what is being reported, and a public image emerges which, in so many cases, has virtually no basis in truth. But it is to this image that other members of the public respond; where a prisoner is released, particularly in cases where a miscarriage of justice has occurred, he or she is already perceived in a certain, often negative, way, by members of the community to which he or she is returning. Having a conviction quashed does not necessarily deem a person innocent in the eyes of the community, even though they have been deemed innocent in the eyes of the law.

Perhaps worse than this, is the effect of media coverage on investigations and trials themselves. The spectre of "trial by media" is by no means a figment of the imagination – in some of the cases highlighted in this book, media coverage bordering on hysteria has undoubtedly impacted negatively on the whole legal proceedings.

Luke Mitchell, for example, was just 14 years old when his girlfriend Jodi Jones was murdered. When he was re-questioned four days after the murder, his house was searched and articles removed in a blaze of publicity. Within the first week, media articles suggesting that Jodi's murder had been linked with the satanic, or ritualistic, began to appear, alongside comments insinuating that these were "interests" of Luke's.

Within the first two weeks, Luke's credibility was in tatters. Police statements to the press contained thinly veiled hints that they were only looking for one person – on July 6th, a spokesman reported that they were awaiting results of forensic tests which would conclusively prove their "main line of enquiry," and if they did not, the enquiry would be "back to square one." (Scotsman 6th July 2003).

In those first few weeks the repetitious reports of Luke's questioning, his brother's questioning, the searching of his house, etc, were strategically placed alongside statements such as 'no arrests were made following the search,' 'no-one has yet been charged,' DNA evidence is 'central to proving or disproving the main line of enquiry being pursued' Luke being treated as a 'key witness,' all carrying the unavoidable implication that Luke was the "man" (albeit, a very, very young man) police suspected as being the killer, and it would just be a case of the evidence proving the fact. Almost every report ended with the claim that Jodi had left to meet Luke, but had never arrived, when, in fact, this was never proven.

Six weeks later, on August 14th 2003, police arrived at his home at 7.25am, handcuffed him and took him away for further questioning. His face was not covered, and a huge media presence had gathered prior to the police arrival. Luke had just turned 15. There was never any official explanation as to how so many reporters and photographers knew to be gathered at the Mitchell family home so early that morning, nor as to why, when it became apparent to police officers that there was such a large press contingent, no attempt was made to conceal his identity. Whilst the media were later to hide behind the defence that Luke was not, at that time, part of an active case – ie, he had not been charged with any offence, the police had no such defence – they did not protect a child from being photographed, in handcuffs, and his image splashed across every newspaper and television news bulletin that day.

To further compound the situation, the Education Department decided that Luke should not be allowed to return to school at the start of the new term in September, 2003, "for his own safety." The head teacher, Marion Docherty, wanted some time, apparently, to discuss with pupils "appropriate behaviour." At that stage, Luke had not been charged with any offence, or even accused of any wrong-doing. All of the pupils had been on holiday for the summer, so the head teacher simply could not have had any idea how pupils would respond. The question remains, then, as to why she concluded that Luke's safety may be compromised – and the answer to that question appears to be that she was acting on information obtained from the press. At this stage, any possibility of Luke being "presumed innocent until proven guilty" dissolved. The media portrayals of Luke in handcuffs, of officers emerging from his home with dozens of bags of items, the relentless repetition of how Jodi had left home that evening "to meet Luke Mitchell," but never arrived, and now his exclusion from school, on the basis that he would somehow be viewed by other pupils as a hate figure all combined to create one very definite picture – that Luke Mitchell had murdered Jodi Jones, and it was only a matter of time before police proved it.

It was reported in the Edinburgh Evening News on November 23rd that a dossier had been sent to the Procurator Fiscal, naming Luke Mitchell as the only suspect, even though he was still only 15 years old. The Aberdeen Press and Journal also printed the story. Both papers faced court action accused of breaching the Criminal Procedures (Scotland) Act, by naming 'a child.' However, both papers were *cleared* because they had named him before he appeared in court – since he had not been charged with an offence, the newspapers were not deemed to have breached the Act.

By the time the case came to court, newspapers and television had been free to report that Luke was "the only suspect" for some six months prior to his arrest, and in the immediate run up to the trial. Indeed, the only time they could not name him was during the early part of his detention following arrest – he turned 16 two weeks and two days before the end of the 110 day detention period, and the press were once again free to name him.

Reporting in this case was sensationalist, negative, and relentless. Even the most innocent actions were reported in a negative manner – a photograph clearly showing the boy reaching back for his seatbelt was accompanied by the claim that he was "making an obscene gesture" in one tabloid.

What appeared to be collusion between the police, the media and the education authorities made matters worse – Luke was allegedly excluded from school "for his own safety" yet reporters somehow found out where he was later being educated, and printed details. Photographs of Luke's bedroom appeared in one newspaper, even though reporters had never been allowed into the room – the only people who had access to such photographs were the police themselves.

By the time the trial began, Luke Mitchell had been branded a murderer for more than a year. Press reporting did not improve during the trial. In many publications, the prosecution case was reported in fine detail, with only the most cursory references to defence proceedings. The picture of a cold blooded, remorseless figure which had emerged in the run up to the trial was reinforced throughout every day of the 40 plus days of the trial. Video footage of Jodi messing about in her bedroom and garden heightened the stark comparison – on the one hand a young, pretty, carefree teenager, and on the other, a callous and vicious youth. The trial was held in Edinburgh, just a few miles from the homes of both teenagers. It is inconceivable that jurors, or witnesses, could have escaped the months of negative publicity. Indeed, one witness was even to admit that she had "recognised" Luke from a picture in the newspapers, even though, in court, she failed to identify him.

After the guilty verdict was returned, the Chief Investigating Officer, and the prosecuting QC both gave interviews to the press. Why they chose to do so is unclear, but both interviews make interesting reading – Alan Turnbull QC says "no-one would want to think that they had been involved in a miscarriage of justice," then goes on to explain why he believed Luke Mitchell was guilty! Craig Dobbie, the senior investigating officer in the case, explains in his interview why he became "convinced" that Luke was the murderer, based on his theory of motive, even though that "motive" could not, in reality, have been the case, and the evidence led in court completely undermined it. The need for these two senior figures to justify, in the press, their actions during such a high profile case seems rather strange. At the very least, these interviews could be seen to jeopardise any future appeal or retrial.

The negative reporting continued for many months after the conviction, with newspapers carrying stories about the expense of the trial, details of Luke's dinner menu from the prison, and letters he had written being printed. The demonisation of Luke Mitchell began within days of Jodi's murder, and continues to this day. Should an appeal overturn his conviction, what possibility is there of a fair retrial?

Sion Jenkins faced a similar "trial by media" which undoubtedly affected his original trial, and subsequent appeals.

Aside from the hugely prejudicial and sensationalist reporting in the run up to, and during the original trial, Sion's case received sustained, intense media attention at every stage of appeal and subsequent retrials. The insinuation that an improper relationship existed between Sion and Billie-Jo had nothing whatsoever to support it, yet the newspapers ran with the speculation. Shortly after his conviction, the News of the World ran a completely untrue article claiming that Sion had "confessed" to a cellmate in Belmarsh prison. There was nothing Sion could do to refute the allegation. The failed appeal in 1999 also made headline news, the obvious implication being that the appeal had failed because Sion Jenkins was guilty as charged.

Perhaps the most damaging media coverage, however, was that of his former wife's claims that Sion had been violent towards herself and the children. These claims were deemed inadmissible at the time of the second appeal, and the press was, at that time, refused permission to publish them. Within days of his acquittal, the newspapers ran details of "evidence the jury had not been allowed to hear." Most of this "evidence" was in the form of claims made by Lois that Sion had had a vicious temper, and would "snap" without warning. It is important to note that Lois did not give this information at the time of the original trial, nor at the first appeal. On February 9th, 2003, however, the Sunday Times printed an article in which Lois makes mention of Sion's "violent outbursts" – although she makes no specific allegations against her ex-husband, the article is riddled with innuendo. At the time of this article, Sion's case was being reviewed by the CCRC, and the following year, his conviction was quashed, and a retrial ordered. The printing of Lois's article, one would imagine, could have seriously undermined his chances of a fair retrial. In the event, the jury could not reach a verdict, and a second retrial was ordered. Following the jury's inability to agree on a verdict, Sion was formally acquitted. He was attacked whilst waiting in court by members of Billie-Jo's natural family, and the press reported extensively the attack, and the accusations hurled by his attackers, rather than reporting the *fact* that an innocent man had been unlawfully attacked. The Sun, on February 11th, ran the headline "You Coward", with the statement "Jenkins won't take our lie detector test." This was a man who had spent nine years battling the legal system to finally clear his name, a man who had endured three trials and two appeals, and had spent more than six years in jail.

Lois once again went into print, with further allegations and bitter claims. That none of the allegations printed were substantiated, and had been disallowed by appeal court judges goes unnoticed – it is almost as if the media are hell-bent on "proving" Sion Jenkins' guilt where the legal system has failed so comprehensively to do so! The Sunday Express printed

> "…although a judge has ruled that the outwardly respectable father of four is innocent in the eyes of the law… the unique position he now holds in criminal history has effectively sentenced him to life under a shadow of suspicion."

Who is casting that shadow? If the law says he is innocent, then there should be no shadow, unless those with dubious motivation decide to create one.

What these two cases alert us to is the damage caused not only to the presumption of innocence, or the right to a fair trial (or appeal), but the longer term damage. Once the media has reported in such a damaging manner, how can an individual return to "normal" life?

Sally Clark faced just such a dilemma following the quashing of her conviction.

Prior to, during, and after the trial, the media utterly destroyed this woman's reputation. She and her husband were portrayed as indulging in a "champagne lifestyle," Sally, herself being presented as "a selfish, alcoholic, depressive, career obsessed woman." Her motive, they claimed, for first "abusing" and then "murdering" her children was that they ruined her figure, and were holding her back in the pursuit of her career.

How tragic, for a woman who would ultimately be proven to have done absolutely nothing wrong, that this image of her had been permanently and indelibly imprinted on the public mind, without so much as a single shred of evidence. Indeed, all of the evidence which did exist supported the fact that Sally was a loving, caring, and devoted mother.

The media who had gained so much from the lurid, sensationalist, negative and downright dishonest coverage of the case made no effort to right the wrong. There was no coverage of the truth – a young woman suffering the unimaginable agony of not only having lost two babies, but of having then been wrongly accused of murdering them. Sally Clark died on March 16th 2007, aged just 42. A statement from her family, announcing the sad news, stated that Sally had never fully recovered from the effects of "this appalling miscarriage of justice."

The situation has not improved since Sally Clark was cleared. Indeed, because technology has advanced so rapidly, the situation would appear to be getting even worse - every damaging or negative statement can be reported almost immediately, whether that statement is backed up by evidence or not. For example, following Sion Jenkins' acquittal, the Mail alleged that the so-called "missing evidence" (that the jury were not allowed to hear) included "details of his alleged adulterous sexual encounters with teenage girls, one of them described as a 17 year old Billie-Jo lookalike." This is pure speculation – there has never been a shred of evidence to suggest Sion Jenkins was ever involved in any such encounters, yet the Mail feels perfectly at liberty to report it immediately following the court decision which finally cleared his name.

Sion Jenkins was a school teacher prior to his arrest. The fact that he has been cleared should mean he is free to return to teaching, yet, given the nature of media reporting, how possible is that ever likely to be? Even the suggestion that "disturbing questions remain" is reported in a biased and speculative manner – of course there are disturbing questions, such as why another, more credible suspect was never pursued, why the police investigation was so flawed, and why an innocent man had to endure three trials and two appeals to *prove* his innocence (in a country where the state is supposed to prove guilt). The implication in the Mail article is that the only disturbing questions concern why the "missing evidence" was not heard by the jury. These questions had already been answered – the "missing evidence" did not meet the required standard for evidence and was, in fact, unable to be substantiated.

This determination in the media to maintain guilt where innocence has been proven, and to presume guilt *before* it has been proven sets dangerous precedents. Innocent, law-abiding citizens are entitled to live their lives without threat, harassment or character assassination. Those newspapers who insist on reporting in the manner adopted in the cases of Sion Jenkins and Luke Mitchell and Sally Clark deny that right, and encourage others to deny that right. What is so alarming is that many ordinary members of the public are completely unaware that it could happen to any one of them!

The naming of Luke Mitchell, and the subsequent court ruling that the newspapers had done nothing wrong because Luke was not (yet) charged with any offence must, at the very least, be seen to be a very narrow application of the law. He was a fifteen year old child, and the Criminal Procedures Act (Scotland) 1995 makes it abundantly clear that children are entitled to the full protection of the law. Several newspapers ran the story of Luke visiting Jodi's grave with a photograph of him, his mother, and a female friend. The girl was the same age as Luke, and had her face blanked out from those pictures, and her name withheld, yet Luke did not. How can such behaviour be justified, or tolerated? In both the Luke Mitchell and Sion Jenkins cases, the innuendo of "improper relationships" (Luke with his mother, and Sion with Billie-Jo) were reported in an extremely damaging manner, yet there was never any evidence that such "relationships" had ever existed. In a somewhat bizarre development in the Luke Mitchell case, Jodi Jones's mother Judith was arrested for driving whilst some three times over the limit for alcohol, and the Daily Record called for readers to be "understanding" and "compassionate." This was the same paper which had, for almost three years, vilified a *child*.

One of the most powerful claims printed repeatedly in the Luke Mitchell case was that his mother had "lied" to cover up for her son. There was no evidence whatsoever to back up this claim – indeed, charges of attempting to pervert the course of justice were *dropped*, and no charge of perjury was ever brought. However, this claim, so often repeated in the press, led to Corrine Mitchell being targeted as a figure of hate in the local community, with attacks on her home and her business.

There were few depths to which the media would not stoop in the reporting of this case. Luke's brother Shane had been "viewing pornography" on the internet, at around the time Jodi Jones was believed to have been killed. Alan Turnbull, QC, forced Shane to tell the court "what he had been doing" whilst viewing this pornography, in order to then suggest that Shane would not "have been doing that" had he believed there was someone else in the house. This utterly humiliating exchange was faithfully reported on Scotland Today on January 12th 2005, and carried by some of the tabloids. In fact, this particular piece of "evidence" still proved nothing – Luke could have been in the house or garden without his brother being aware of his presence. Not content with completely demolishing Luke Mitchell's character, the media seemed determined to destroy the characters of his mother and brother as well, even though neither was ever convicted of any wrongdoing whatsoever.

Another case where media influence is apparent is that of Gordon Park. The sensationalist "Lady in the Lake" coverage pointed the finger relentlessly at Gordon Park. The original charges, in 1998, brought forth a raft of sensationalist, negative reports, portraying Gordon as cold, calculating and violent. The press would not let it lie, even after charges were dropped due to insufficient evidence – new reports emerged insinuating that Gordon had "got away with it" purely because of the passage of time. By the time he was brought to trial some six years later, much had been printed regarding the case that could only have prejudiced his right to be presumed innocent – various claims as to what had been done and how it had been done had been printed in the intervening years, and a documentary about the case had been shown on television.

There remain, then, many questions to be addressed about media coverage of cases such as these, and the rights of the individuals involved.

When someone has been portrayed as evil, murderous, violent, and so forth for many, many months, or even years, and it later emerges that they have not, in fact, committed the crime which led to that portrayal, what can realistically be done to right the wrong?

Certainly, in cases where appeal is a possibility, it would seem that some restraint needs to be applied, yet quite the opposite seems to be the case.

It is one thing for the press to report "the facts" of any given case; it is surely quite another for information which may seriously damage or undermine appeal proceedings to be published in advance of such proceedings. In the interests of justice, perhaps some more stringent controls require to be in place in cases such as these. For example, following the conviction of Luke Mitchell, a series of articles appeared claiming that he had attacked other girls in the past. Because he had just been convicted, there was nothing Luke could do to refute these claims, so the suggestion remains, unchallenged, unquestioned, unable to be denied.

But, having passed into the public domain, with nothing to refute them, these claims are likely to become part of the "common knowledge" which will shape perceptions of Luke Mitchell. Jurors in a retrial may not even know that these claims are unfounded, but it is easy to see what sort of impact such information could have.

There are those who would point to the fact that individuals have recourse to the Press Complaints Commission, or to legal action against untrue publications. Yet neither of these is, in reality, of much use. The PCC can order a newspaper to print a retraction or apology, but often this is such a tiny article that it is almost un-noticable. Pursuing legal action is a lengthy and expensive process, particularly if several newspapers have printed the same "information." When an individual is fighting to be released from an unjust conviction, from inside prison, the majority of their energy and resources must, of necessity, be devoted to that cause, leaving little left over for "taking on the press."

Many people wrongly convicted have never had any dealings with either the legal system or the media. Often, they are taken completely by surprise, and have no way of knowing how to deal with the situation. Susan May and Corrine Mitchell both expressed similar sentiments – that it was just a huge mistake or misunderstanding, and in any moment, "they" would realise that, and sort it out. By the time the truth dawned, that the system was going to pursue the cases right to the bitter end, so much of the damage had already been done. At that stage, as happens in so many cases, attention becomes completely locked onto proving innocence, the rest is simply left to be sorted out "later."

The sheer horror of what these people and their families have to endure is almost impossible to portray in words – lies, innuendo and speculation about every aspect of their own and their loved ones lives, splashed across pages of newsprint and photographs, with no way of correcting or even addressing them. At the same time, having to deal with the knowledge that only they, and perhaps a very few close friends and relatives know that they are innocent, must be one of the worst nightmares anyone has to endure.

Do we have a responsibility to ensure "freedom of information" does not cause such further suffering? Should we make our newspapers and television companies more accountable, particularly when what they print or screen can actually undermine an individual's basic rights? We have become so used to sensationalist reporting that it almost feels like a "victimless" activity, but nothing could be further from the truth.

The effects of media reporting on public opinion are immense, and as such, those publishing such reports need to be aware of the responsibility they carry. The "we print it because it sells" mentality is unacceptable, yet there are those who argue that it is not the newspapers or television companies that are at fault, but the customers who buy what these organisations produce. This argument misses the point that we cannot be sure that more balanced, more fair reporting would not sell just as well.

Although there have been some notable exceptions, with programmes such as *Rough Justice* and *Inside Out*, and journalists like Bob Woffinden and the late Simon Regan, attempting to redress the balance, there are simply too few of them to counter the constant and relentless flow of sensationalist and untrue reporting.

Perhaps most noticeable is the correlation between the rise in popularity of so called "reality tv," and the insatiable demand for the sort of coverage we have seen in the cases highlighted here.

Somewhere in the hype and hysteria, not just media reporters, but also ordinary members of the public appear to have forgotten that their "subject matter" consists of real human beings, with real feelings, and real rights. The media machine has become so out of control that even the most basic of these rights are being eroded, and our justice system is rapidly becoming one of trial by media.

References:

"*Unbalanced Newspaper Coverage of Homicide*" Amanda Hinds, *Economic & Social Research Council* January 22nd 2003

"*Media and Crime,*" (Speech to Nacro Conference), Richard Garside, Director, Crime and Society Foundation, November 19th 2003

"*A Murder Mystery: Why do Some Killings Dominate the Headlines?*" Colin Wilson, *The Times*, January 28th 2006

Chapter Fourteen

The Appeal System

THE appeal system, we believe, exists in acknowledgement of the fact that mistakes are sometimes made, and decisions to convict are sometimes wrong. We assume that access to the appeal process is automatic, following any suggestion that a conviction may be unsafe. Whilst this is generally true, it is by no means as automatic, nor as accessible as we tend to think.

Firstly, there are rules laid down as to which precise conditions must be met before an application to appeal can be made. The most important of these is that new or fresh evidence must have been found – an application cannot proceed to appeal unless this is the case. The difficulty is that the definition of "new" evidence is:

> "that which was not known, or could not reasonably have been known, at the time of the original trial."

Whilst this might seem quite straightforward, closer examination shows just how difficult it can be to establish – for example, if the defence fails to interview a witness, and it later emerges that this witness has new information, that would not be sufficient grounds for appeal. The precise application of the definition of 'new evidence' would hold that this information *could have been known* at the time of the trial – that the defence failed to uncover it is an error on their part- and therefore is not "new" evidence within this context.

One example of this is the first appeal in the Sion Jenkins case. In 1999, Channel Four instructed Professor Dennison to carry out experiments into the possibility of the blood on Sion's sweatshirt having been breathed out. When Professor Dennison's findings were presented to the appeal, the prosecuting counsel stated that the appeal judges should not even hear the evidence because it "represents no new breakthrough in scientific knowledge. It is simply fine tuning of a defence which was run unsuccessfully at trial, and in reality, the evidence of Professor Dennison could have been obtained just as easily before trial as after it."

The judges responded, in part, with the following:

> "We were not, and are not, satisfied that there is a reasonable explanation for the failure to adduce the evidence of Professor Dennison....... at the trial,"

although they did allow the evidence, in the end, to be heard.

In the case of Susan May, the appeal judges stated that evidence concerning the Craftsman Baker paper bag

"… was available at the time of the trial."

Yet in the same summary document, it is stated

"It {the bag} was intended to be examined further to see if the marks on it were of blood and what its contents were but those tests were never carried out."

In other words, the evidence was available *in theory*, and as such, would not have fulfilled the required definition of "new evidence." It has to be noted in this case, that this particular piece of evidence had been filed with the unused evidence, and labeled "paper bag" – its significance was completely lost until much later.

This reinforces the devastating effects of suppressed or lost evidence, and brings the role of the disclosure officer back into focus. Evidence which can be deemed to have been available at the time of the trial, but which has been processed in such a way that the defence is unlikely to discover its significance, cannot later be used as grounds for appeal, because it does not meet the definition of "new' evidence. The uncomfortable question, of course, is how much impact might this awareness have on the disclosure officer's work?

The admitted close co-operation between chief investigating officers, CPS and prosecuting QCs creates an opportunity for cases to be selectively constructed, however unwittingly. Within these selective constructions, we might conclude, are processes which preclude future exposure of what has been achieved – in other words, as part of the "selective evidence" process, that which is not "selected" is effectively removed, in terms of immediate or future possible use. Clearly, physical removal of evidence would be visible, and open to criticism and possible legal ramifications. Rendering evidence useless in a legal sense is a much more covert, and much more effective strategy for maintaining the legitimacy of a conviction. As was seen in the Sion Jenkins appeal, however, judges do have the power to allow evidence which may not strictly meet the definition of "new evidence," if they think it is in the interests of justice to do so. The question, then, is not so much how many judges exercise this discretion, as how many do *not*?

In fact, the admissibility of new evidence can have an even earlier starting point. In the case of Luke Mitchell, the emergence of new evidence was dealt with, primarily, by Lothian and Borders Police. Having apparently lost this information first time around, this police force was faced, some two years later, with the witness who had originally reported the new evidence coming back to ensure that it had been properly investigated. At that point, (August 2006) Lothian and Borders justified their lack of action on the basis that the case was closed!

There is the further difficulty of the defence team having to decide what may or may not be allowed as new evidence. Once again, we cannot know in how many cases applications to appeal on certain grounds are *not* made, because defence solicitors believe that they would be rejected summarily on the grounds that the evidence available does not constitute "new" evidence.

This, of course, is only one factor in the whole appeal process, but it is significant in that without evidence which meets the criteria of "new" evidence, applications for appeal are unlikely to make it past the first hurdle.

Once the definition of "new evidence" has been met, appeal judges have open to them several options:

1. They may conclude that the fresh evidence makes such a profound difference to the case that a guilty verdict is clearly not safe, in which case the conviction will be quashed, and no re-trial ordered.

2. They may conclude that the fresh evidence is not reliable or credible enough to make any significant difference to the case, in which case the appeal will be dismissed, and the conviction will stand.

3. They may conclude that the impact of the fresh evidence is not conclusive, but gives rise to enough reasonable doubt as to the safety of the conviction that the conviction should be quashed, and the option of a re-trial considered.

What is important to note here, however, is that these are the conclusions of a panel of three judges, and not a jury. The power in the hands of appeal judges, therefore, is enormous. Unlike juries, appeal judges are required to give reasons for their findings, and as such, this should offer some sense of confidence that, at least, we can know *why* an appeal has been dismissed (and we may, in fact, presume that these reasons will be based in careful consideration of facts and points of law.) Unfortunately, as has happened in so many of the cases highlighted in this book, appeals are often dismissed *in spite* of the facts, or points of law, or because of a rigid adherence to the letter of the law – the very "technicality" so beloved of those who continue to assert that the criminal justice system is weighted in favour of the criminal.

For example, in Sion Jenkins' first appeal, the judges concluded that the fresh evidence was "credible and relevant" (which would seem to rule out the option of dismissing the appeal, given point (2) above) then went on to dismiss the appeal on the grounds that it

> "adds so little weight to the defence case as compared with the prosecution's case that a doubt induced by the fresh evidence would not be a reasonable doubt."

This raises some interesting questions. How can the appeal judges know what a jury might have made of this "credible and relevant" evidence? There is an assumption in this decision that a jury would not have decided that the new evidence raised reasonable doubt, yet no jury had ever been allowed to hear that new evidence. As has already been ascertained, jurors do not have to give reasons for their conclusions, so no-one, including appeal judges, can have any idea what may or may not convince a jury of reasonable doubt.

Next, there is the question of reasonable doubt itself. There is no actual definition of the term, although guidance to jurors tends to instruct that if they are in any doubt as to the "facts," or if they believe there are other, equally credible or plausible explanations, then they must find for the defendant. In this decision, the judges appear to have their own idea of what constitutes reasonable doubt, and the evidence presented is not it! There is no explanation as to why they have come to this conclusion (that the new evidence would not constitute reasonable doubt), so we are left none the wiser – whatever these judges understand to be reasonable doubt is not disclosed. Yet they then project this undisclosed understanding of reasonable doubt onto potential jurors (or previous jurors, as the case may be), and make a further assumption – that those jurors would have the same understanding of reasonable doubt as do the judges.

In truth, this is nothing more than an opinion on the part of the judges themselves. It has no real basis in law, or in fact, and they are not required to explain specifically *why* this is their conclusion. This is often missed amongst the legal technicalities which *are* explained, and once again, we are faced with fact and opinion riding side by side.

Perhaps the most compelling example of opinion outweighing fact or legal requirement is the appeal of John Taft.

During summing up, the original judge introduced a new possibility, a possible explanation which supported the prosecution's approach, but which had not been raised by either prosecution or defence during the trial. This new possibility was that the murderer had left the scene of the crime, and later returned to drive away the victim's car. The prosecution had claimed that the car had been driven away directly after the murder, and that the murderer had left clothing fibres identical to those in the victim's house, on the seat of the car.

The appeal claimed that the introduction of this new possibility may have influenced the jury detrimentally, and, indeed, it is not part of the judge's responsibilities to offer such an explanation in the first place. The single judge, who first considered the appeal application concluded:

> "It is difficult to see in what material respect the trial would have taken a different course if the prosecution had suggested that the applicant had driven the car away some time after the murder."

The crux of the case was that John Taft, having murdered Mrs Bolshaw, and taken away her car, had returned to his home and burned and buried his clothes in the garden. If the clothing had been burned and buried *prior* to him returning for the car, then he would not have been able to leave fibres from those clothes on the car seat. Further, this scenario would have meant that the victim must have been murdered much earlier than the pathology reports stated. It is, in fact, quite plain to see that the trial would have had to have taken a completely different course, had this been the prosecution's assertion. Yet, once again, the judge appears to pre-judge what a *jury* might have made of a differently presented prosecution argument.

The panel of three judges compounds the errors of the initial judges. Firstly, they make the assumption that

> "the possibility voiced by the judge was one that inevitably any jury would consider for themselves."

Why would this be so? The jury is directed, with a great deal of emphasis, that they must find only on the evidence as it is presented in court.

The judge in the case of Gordon Park, for example, told jurors at the beginning of his summing up:

> "You must, of course, <u>decide the case only on the evidence which you have seen and heard in this court</u>....... You are, however entitled to draw inferences. That is, come to common sense conclusions upon the evidence which you accept. <u>You must not speculate about evidence you have not heard or that you wish had been available. You must not be drawn into speculation.</u>"

Yet here we have three judges assuming that the jury will consider an alternative possibility, one which has had no evidence led, either to support or discredit it, one which is, clearly, nothing more than speculation. This undermines the very purpose of the jury – to decide, from the evidence led in court. Further, the possibility is more than likely *not* one that the jury would consider for themselves, given that it simply cannot be made to fit, in any way, with the evidence that *was* led in court. To consider this possibility, they would be required to dismiss or ignore other, more concrete evidence, such as pathologist reports, testimony from the GP and the first police officer at the scene, and, in fact, the central evidence of the prosecution case – the disposal of the clothing.

Because the possibility was introduced by the judge, however, it is reasonable to expect that jurors would automatically give credence to it, perhaps explaining away the discrepancies by surmising that the judge was in a position to perhaps "know" something that they, themselves, did not.

The appeal judges go on to say,

> "We cannot see that the inference that the judge said was a possibility that had to be considered, was one which could remotely be characterised as not being a possibility, even having regard to the totality of the evidence, as we have been invited to do."

The immediate question which arises from this statement is – *what the hell does that mean?* The use of legal jargon to confuse, to muddy the waters, to buy time or space, once again raises its ugly head.

In ordinary language, the judges appear to be saying

> "the idea that the murderer came back later *is* a definite possibility – we can't see how anyone could claim it is *not* a possibility, no matter how you interpret all of the evidence."

Yet, with regard to the totality of the evidence, returning to the car at a later time is *not* a possibility, within the claims of the prosecution case. In fact, it is really very simple. The prosecution contend that John Taft murdered Mrs Bolshaw, leaving clothing fibres at the scene of the crime, drove her car away, leaving the same clothing fibres on the seat of her car, returned to his own home, and burned and buried his clothing. If the order of events is changed, so that John returns home first, disposes of the clothing, then returns to the scene to drive away the car, how did fibres from the destroyed clothing come to be on the seat of the car?

Worse still, the judges back up their "conclusion" by pointing out that the prosecution case shows John embarking on a "cover-up," and make specific reference to "burning or hiding clothes." They stated :

> "....if he had his car with him (which is at least a possibility) he would want to remove that as quickly as possible from the

scene. He was then going to embark on a cover-up, nobody being likely to have discovered the body by that time. It required him to go back the short distance and remove the car."

Again, with regard to the totality of the evidence, the appeal judges clearly accept that the hiding of the clothing was part of the "cover-up," yet this was "witnessed" at 11.30pm, and pathologist reports put the time of death of the victim at between 3am and 6am the *following* morning.

The final conclusion of the judges in this appeal is a stark example of opinion which is in no way related to the facts:

"We have carefully considered the safeness of this conviction........ we... can see nothing that suggests to us that the verdict was unsafe."

And that, in many cases, is the end of the matter. The judges have made their decision, and it is legally binding and final. Unless further "new" evidence can be found, a further appeal is not a possibility.

Yet, we have to ask, what is the point in finding "new" evidence, if it is to be subject to the sort of examination received in John Taft's case?

The requirement for appeal judges to provide a written report of their reasons for finding one way or another in a case is utterly worthless – even if, as in John Taft's case, that written report makes it abundantly clear that they have completely missed the point, the decision remains. One cannot then appeal to a higher authority that the judges got it wrong, because there is no higher authority. Referral to the CCRC is a tortuously slow process, with just one in every twenty five cases being returned to the courts.

One notoriously difficult area for appeal is that of police breaches of procedure. In the first instance, providing "proof" of such breaches is extremely difficult, and secondly, the interpretation of the law by appeal judges in such cases is often technical and selective.

For example, Susan May's defence team claimed at appeal that there had been two serious breaches of the Police And Criminal Evidence Act (PACE). Susan was claimed to have made a statement to a police officer, in the presence of another officer, which made her a suspect in the eyes of the police. This was a question allegedly asked by Susan regarding "scratch marks" on her aunt's face. However, the police did not, at that stage, tell her that this question had made her a suspect, (as they are required to do under PACE), since they contended that she could not have known about the marks unless she was the murderer. They continued to question her as a witness, and as a result, the interviews were not recorded. Consequently, there was no record of how the questioning was conducted. Susan always denied having made the statement, and the notebook of the officer concerned was "lost." Also, details of the "statement" were not logged anywhere else, such as in the crime log, or on the computer database.

Yet, at appeal, the judges "accepted that there were no grounds to suspect May of having committed an offence such as to require that she be cautioned in the earlier stages of the inquiry".

"They said that they were unable to detect any breach of any provision which was then in force."

This was in spite of the fact that the CCRC had found that several breaches of PACE had taken place during the investigation.

At appeal, it was submitted that:

> "the police were dealing with a woman who was known to be a good carer, and of entirely good character. Despite her proximity to the deceased, there was initially no real reason to suspect her when she spoke as she did to Sergeant Rimmer......"

Yet the officers concerned, Sergeant Rimmer included, had stated at the original trial that it was precisely the fact that Susan had "spoken as she did" which made them suspect her. Given that the line between witness and suspect is so often blurred, it is more than disappointing to discover that appeal judges are actually prepared to back up those officers who manipulate the "grey area" between the two. The suggestion that Susan's "good character" was somehow a contributing factor in the decision not to caution her is strange, to say the least – if, by the police's own admission, she had become a suspect, PACE makes it abundantly clear that she should have been advised to that effect, and all future questioning should have been under caution, and recorded - character traits and personality simply do not come into it.

In Sion Jenkins' first appeal, which was dismissed, the judges concluded that police were "entitled to seek to persuade Mrs Jenkins that her husband was the killer," and that the decision to tell the children that there was "proof" that their father had killed their sister was not "a deliberate campaign to influence the children and taint their evidence so as to damage the defence of the appellant."

The two children provided Sion's alibi, and as such were key witnesses, yet the appeal judges see nothing wrong with a police decision to "feed" information to the mother, and the two children. Even where it is clear that police procedures have not been as professional as they might have been, some appeal judges still stop short of fully admitting and accepting this – to remain with Sion Jenkins, the appeal judges accepted that it "may have been better" if the meeting with the children had not been carried out by the police, and certain information given to the children by the police, yet they concluded that there had been no wrong-doing, either in intent or action, by investigating officers. Do we really have room in the criminal justice system, and particularly within the appeals system, for the schoolboy equivalent of "could do better"?

Simon Hall, in spite of glaring inconsistencies in the case, has, to date, been unable to secure permission to appeal. Two applications have been rejected, and the case has been taken up by the CCRC. This situation demonstrates quite clearly that the right to appeal is neither automatic nor straightforward – a forensic scientist expressed "surprise" that glass fragments were not present amongst the fibres found on Mrs Albert's body – if the murderer had squeezed through such a small space in a broken pane of glass, it is almost inconceivable that he would do so without collecting a single fragment of glass. This suggestion leads to another, even more concerning possibility – that the fibres were not left by the murderer at all, but by someone who attended the scene as part of the investigation. (Remember, this is the crime scene where a pubic hair in the bathroom was found to belong to one of the investigating officers). However, as has already been shown, this could very easily be dismissed by appeal judges as not "new evidence," in that they could claim that such a suggestion could just as easily have been made before or during the trial as after it.

Once again, the precarious dependence on "expert" witnesses is exposed. Whilst we can accept that Professor Dennison's findings, or those of Peter Bull in Simon Hall's case *could* have been discovered prior to the trial, the defence would have had to have known, in advance, that these experts would come to different conclusions than the experts they employed. No matter how we look at it, the definition of "new evidence" is heavily weighted against the convicted person, in that virtually *anything* could, in theory, have been known in some form, prior to the trial. There is a general perception that repeated refusals of permission to appeal only demonstrate that the conviction was safe in the first place, the belief being that if permission to appeal has been rejected, there is no "new evidence" to support an appeal. As we can see, this is not the case, and indeed, many cases which, in the interests of justice *need* to be re-examined, cannot get through the barrier created by an over zealous application of the definition of "new evidence."

There is something of an irony in this very precise definition of the term which is central to the decision as to whether or not an appeal will be allowed, given that some of the most crucial terms in the original trial are left with no such definition – we have no definition of the "reasonable" in reasonable doubt, nor of the "burden of proof." That we can convict without these terms being adequately defined is surprising in itself, but becomes even moreso when we realise how tightly defined the term "new evidence" is.

Government reforms of the Criminal Justice System over the last five years have amounted to, according to the prime minister, Tony Blair,

> "a modernising and rebalancing of the entire criminal justice system in favour of victims and the community."

What this statement appears to miss is that the system is *already* weighted towards securing convictions, and ensuring those convictions stand, whether or not the defendant is actually guilty.

With so many reforms representing a complete overhaul of the system, it is sobering to realise that many of these reforms actually strengthen the existing anomalies in the system, and make it more likely that wrongful convictions will increase, as will the difficulties faced by those seeking to overturn wrongful conviction. For example, changes to the criminal justice system have progressed on the assumption that too many offenders were escaping conviction, and the system was not delivering "justice" for the victims of crime. According to the "Strategic Plan for Criminal Justice 2004 – 2008," which was presented to parliament in July 2004;

> "Too many offenders insist on the full judicial system, then plead guilty at the last minute, clogging up the courts when we should be encouraging them to plead guilty earlier."

This assumes that "suspects" and "offenders" are the same thing – how can we "encourage" a suspect to plead guilty early, if we are required by law to assume that suspect to be innocent until *proven* guilty? Rather than *improving* the system, this appears to be a step back to the "bad old days" of, for example, the discredited West Midlands Serious Crime Squad, whose numerous "encouraged" confessions led to a raft of wrongful convictions which were later overturned, at enormous cost to both the victims and the state.

The same document also states that

> "Too many avoidable mistakes are made at every stage of the criminal justice process."

Yet the mistakes to which it refers are those which result in cases not making it to court on time, or cases collapsing. At no point are any of the "mistakes" which have been highlighted in this book addressed, or even mentioned. Reform of the criminal justice system, it seems, will not involve a review of poor investigative procedures, mismanaged evidence, or collaboration between different agencies to secure convictions – indeed, collaboration between various sections of the prosecutory system is actively strengthened and encouraged:

"Prosecutors, particularly those prosecuting anti-social behaviour, will become more engaged with the community they serve"

and,

"In the past, cases have sometimes collapsed or got bogged down because a charge was chosen that wasn't backed up by sufficient evidence to prove it. The CPS's experience in court means they are well placed to judge what charges are supported by the evidence. We are now bringing the CPS in early to the process, so a trained prosecutor works alongside the police from an early stage, advising them on what charge to go for and on the evidence they need to assemble to bring a successful case."

The wording of this last paragraph is particularly worrying - "what charge to go for" and "the evidence they need to assemble" hardly ring harmoniously with an investigation to establish the facts of a case, and to examine all of the available evidence. Surely, for example, it is the crime itself which determines the charge? This particular paragraph appears to be encouraging the use of "technicalities" to ensure some sort of conviction is secured – a "top down" construction of a case, rather than allowing the evidence to build the case from the bottom up.

The aim of these reforms, it states, is

"to improve the delivery of justice by increasing the number of crimes for which an offender is brought to justice."

In other words, these reforms have been introduced to make it either easier, or more likely, that convictions will be secured, and "justice" is seen to have been done because a conviction has been secured.

Given the Home Office's own figures for conviction rates – 87% in the high courts, and 95% in magistrates courts, we are faced with the slightly sinister implication that almost *all* cases which come to court will result in a conviction. Whilst this may serve the ends of "efficiency" (what's the point in having a court case which doesn't result in a conviction), it hardly serves the ends of true justice. Justice is not, and never has been, defined by conviction. Justice demands that the guilty are convicted, and *the innocent acquitted.* The whole idea that cases will only be brought to court if there is enough evidence to secure a conviction, and that cases will be "assembled" or "constructed" to maximise the likelihood of securing a conviction appears to be in complete contradiction to what the majority of people believe is the purpose of the courts system in the first place – that is, to ascertain the innocence or guilt of the defendant. In the scenario outlined here, only those already deemed guilty by the prosecution team will make it to court.

The trial, in this respect, is nothing more than a sham – the important decisions have already been made, but to allow the public in general to feel that justice, as they understand it, is being done, the state will allow a "going through the motions" charade, continuing the illusion that the suspect has been found guilty by twelve ordinary citizens. The government's claim:

> "We have modernised the law both to update it and to tackle the abuses that undermine justice"

rings a little hollow in this respect, since, in fact, at least some of the proposed reforms actually reinforce the very abuses they claim to be tackling.

Further reinforcement is provided by the judiciary, who have been involved in:

> "developing, clarifying and applying the law for the benefit of society at large as well as in the cases that come before the courts,"

but that clarification does not extend to the most fundamental terms used in our criminal justice system.

When we take into account that:

> "The judges are independent of government and all other participants in the justice system. They occupy a unique position as guardians of fairness and impartiality,"

the enormity of their role becomes apparent.

Yet, as we have already seen in so many of the cases in this book, judges themselves have failed to understand evidence, or have given misleading advice to jurors, or have missed vital points, proving that, at least some of the time, they are not, perhaps, the best "guardians of fairness and impartiality."

The realisation that reforms to the justice system are making it more difficult for those wrongfully convicted to be heard, and to have their cases reviewed, is worrying.

There are other aspects of government intervention which also impact directly on case reviews and the possibility of appeal. In some cases, MPs actually support campaigns to have specific cases reviewed – in the cases of Susan May and Simon Hall, for example, MPs actively supported calls for their cases to be re-examined. However, this is very much a matter of personal opinion, and cannot be relied upon by everyone who is wrongfully convicted. When Derek Christian's brother wrote to MP John Townend for support, Mr Townend made it abundantly clear that his belief in the justice system was such that he could not even consider that it may have been wrong, going as far as to say "for the worse crimes, I have consistently voted to bring back the death penalty." His stance mirrored that of so many of the public in general – the jury had sat through all of the evidence, so they must have got it right, and the fact that an appeal was refused was used to support this notion. Yet, as has been shown in this chapter, refusal of permission to appeal does not necessarily mean that the original conviction was safe – a simple technicality such as the definition of "new evidence" can be enough to halt the process.

There has been a tradition of allowing Home Secretaries to intervene in certain cases – for example, in the case of Jon Venables and Robert Thompson, who were found guilty of the murder of Jamie Bulger, Home Secretary Michael Howard increased the original sentence handed down by the judge, because it was thought to be too lenient. The increase was later overturned by the European Court of Human Rights.

However, in the tragic case of Carol Hanson, who served twenty seven years in prison, wrongfully convicted, a Home Secretary, who has not been identified, decided that for Carol, and a handful of others, "life" was to mean exactly that – she would never be released. Carol was not told of this decision – after serving the twenty years handed down by the judge, she applied for parole, and was refused, without explanation. On April 28th 1997, Michael Howard, then Home Secretary, stated

> "for some prisoners, a life sentence would be exactly what it was – for life."

On May 2nd 1997, Carol Hanson committed suicide by drowning.

Such intervention by politicians introduces yet another dimension of uncertainty into the criminal justice system. We are supposed to accept that the justice system stands alone, unfettered by particular political persuasions, and immune to influence of a political nature. But in several high profile cases, particularly when public indignation is running high, there have been interventions of this sort, leaving the unanswered question, who is, ultimately, responsible for "justice" in the United Kingdom?

References:
"Unfair Legislation;" reproduced at www.portia.org. Chapter 6
Transcript: Appeal Before Lord Justice Kennedy, Mr Justice Dyson, Mr Justice Penry-Davey
December 21st 1999
Transcript: "Judgment," December 7th 2001
"Cutting Crime, Delivering Justice," HM Government: A Strategic Plan for Criminal Justice 2004-2008

"Lawyers Who Let You Down," Andrew Green, CONVICTION Newsletter No 16 reprinted 'Inside Time,' December 1996.

"Lawyers DID Let you Down," Andrew Green CONVICTION Newsletter No 18

"Grounds of Appeal in Criminal Cases", Peter Duff and Frazer McCallum, Crime & Criminal Justice Research Findings No 12 (1996), 1995/96.

Justice for All, JUSTICE's Response to the White Paper, October 2002

"Wrongful Convictions," The Observer Crime and Justice Debate, Michael Naughton, July 28th 2002

"Miscarriages of Justice and Court Reform," (Memorandum) Hazel Keirle, Miscarriages of Justice Organisation, November 7th 2003

Chapter Fifteen

Summary

THIS book has addressed some of the most brutal and horrific attacks on some of the most vulnerable members of our society – our young people, and our elderly. It is abundantly clear that the perpetrators of those attacks are extremely dangerous individuals, who need to be removed from our midst. But what has become frighteningly apparent is that, in many cases, those individuals are still living amongst us, free to strike again at any time, and at the same time, other, innocent individuals are locked away for crimes they did not commit.

Because crimes such as those examined in this book generate a highly emotional response, it is not surprising that mistakes are made – the need to apprehend those responsible is enormous, and waves of fear feed every passing day that the killer is still on the loose. Yet if we think about it logically, we should be much, much more fearful of the fact that dozens of overturned convictions mean that, during the whole time those wrongly convicted people were locked up, the real perpetrators were right here among us.

But it is not just the fear factor which is important. The reasons innocent people are routinely convicted for crimes they did not commit point to a much more institutionalised and embedded problem.

We expect, and, indeed, demand, that those responsible for such crimes are apprehended as quickly as possible, and held accountable before the full force of the law. It is probably fair to say that we are often, at best, ambiguous about exactly what we mean by that – do we lock people up to punish them for what they have done, to rehabilitate them, and teach them to be better human beings, to get them off the streets so that they are not a danger to anyone else, or a combination of all three? It is, however, critically important that we become very clear on this point, because it is one of the "unexamined assumptions" introduced at the start of this book, which drives certain decisions and behaviours, without us even being aware of it.

For example, Gordon Park, Sion Jenkins and Luke Mitchell were all portrayed as being "cold, emotionless and calculating" because they did not display the "necessary" degree of emotion or remorse either during the investigation or the trial. The Chief Investigating Officer in Derek Christian's case claimed that Derek did not "protest his innocence" enough!

The underlying assumption here is that there is an agreed, recognisable and measurable degree of displayed emotion or remorse which would somehow "prove" that the authorities had picked on the wrong man. Yet, if you are an innocent person, it is not humanly possible for you to show remorse, because you have done nothing to be remorseful about!

This flags up yet another ambiguity. For many years, the terms "emotion" and "remorse" have been used so interchangeably as to have come to provide an almost blanket cover concept, yet the two are quite distinctly separate. A guilty person may show varying degrees of emotion, from anger to despair (at being caught) to self pity, yet be completely unable to display remorse because they have no concept of the wrong they have done to another. One would imagine this would bypass the claim of "showed no emotion, remained emotionless throughout," yet it is nowhere near an indicator of innocence. However, if this person is displaying despair and anxiety, would this have an effect on our decisions as to whether they need to be *punished* whilst incarcerated, or whether they need more of a rehabilitation process? Are we more likely to inflict punishment on those who display no emotional connection to the crime for which they have been convicted?

It is this assumption that there is somehow a correct emotional response which either *everyone* or, at least, the vast majority of people would display in these circumstances, that leads us to come to generalised, and dangerously flawed conclusions.

Yet it is this very "human fallibility" alluded to by journalist Simon Regan, which allows the other faults and flaws in the system to become so ingrained and embedded as to be virtually invisible to us.

Our unquestioning acceptance of what we believe to be facts blinds us to the many problems and failings within our justice system.

Every person whose case has been highlighted in this book thought they knew what their rights were. They all believed that, because they had done nothing wrong, they had nothing to fear. They all imagined that they would have access to proper legal protection, and that the police would treat them fairly and honestly, within distinct and recognisable procedures. Between them, at the time this book goes to press, they have served a total of more than 50 years in prison *to date*. Only Sion Jenkins has been formally cleared of any wrong-doing – and even then, newspapers have continued to run stories portraying him as a violent, calculating, cold man, without a shred of evidence to back up their claims. Susan May was released on licence, and is still fighting to this day, some fifteen years after the event, and almost two years after her release, to clear her name. The others are still imprisoned, their fight to clear their names dependent on those of us on the outside ensuring that their plight is not forgotten.

It is bad enough that miscarriages of justice occur in the first place, but it is absolutely tragic that, having occurred, they are virtually impossible to have recognised and overturned.

It is almost as if it doesn't matter how much evidence to the contrary is found, the authorities cling tenaciously to the original findings, using some of the most ludicrous and unbelievable justifications for their actions.

The cases of Sion Jenkins, Luke Mitchell and Susan May are stark examples –claims by various judges that clear and compelling new evidence pointing away from Sion did not cast any doubt whatsoever on the safety of his conviction, or Lothian and Borders Police using the excuse that the case of the murder of Jodi Jones was closed (because Luke Mitchell had been convicted), as a reason not to pursue a credible new suspect, and the complete disinterest of judges as to the existence of another, more credible suspect in the Susan May case. In spite of the CCRC claims that police in Susan's case had *definitely* breached the rules of PACE (and even a cursory read over the available information shows this to be so), the judge decided that the police had not done anything wrong, and had not deliberately treated Susan unfairly!

Our judges are supposed to be impartial and unbiased. Yet time and time again, we see appeal judges, in particular, going out of their way to selectively interpret the information before them, in an effort to uphold the original conviction.

All the way through the system, from the moment the body is found, we see this repetitive pattern of events, whereby common sense and logic are sacrificed in order to secure a conviction, regardless of whether the right person is being convicted or not. This is propped up by a public which is fed a steady diet of fear that crime, especially violent crime, is on the increase, and that too many criminals are "getting away with it" – thumbing their noses at a system that they know how to manipulate to their own ends.

The lines between reality and fiction are blurred by media portrayals and so called "reality tv,' where ordinary people are encouraged to accept and believe that certain behaviours, reactions, and emotions are yardsticks and indicators of "normality" or otherwise.

Behind the scenes, the prosecution machine swings into action – on the one hand, people believe that an investigation is being carried out, and for so long as they can believe that to be the case, they are likely to accept that police and investigators will "do what they have to do" to get to the truth. There is an acceptance that, whilst this might not always be strictly by the book, it is *always* done with the best possible intention – to apprehend the criminal as quickly and effectively as possible. On the other hand, the police fulfill the public's expectation, and discharge their official duties by "securing a conviction," regardless of whether that conviction is safe, or has been fairly secured. Of course, not all cases follow this particular route, but those that do have devastating consequences for the innocent people, and their families, caught up in them. Worse still, if and when a case is finally proven to be unsafe, and the conviction overturned, the families of the murder victim face the appalling situation of having to start all over again, often many, many years later.

What is really required is a system whereby possible miscarriages of justice can be quickly, efficiently and impartially re-evaluated. The right to appeal, for example, where evidence arises following the original trial, but which was not led at that trial, should trigger an automatic right to appeal. Where it can be clearly demonstrated that a defence team has failed quite miserably in its duty to defend a client, once again, the right to appeal should be automatic.

In the long term, we need to look at why our police and prosecutors are so pressured to produce results that they feel compelled to sometimes construct cases, and why the system is being updated and amended in order to encourage and support cases where this has been the procedure.

Not only do the police themselves need to be more accountable (and preferably to independent investigators, and not other police forces), it is time we created an independent body to whom expert witnesses, solicitors, and even judges become accountable, especially where there are clear and blatant errors, misunderstandings, or breaches of duty.

The power held by these people cannot be underestimated, yet they are, as a general rule, both self-regulating, and supportive of one another. This book has given examples of judges backing up judges, prosecutors, and expert witnesses, prosecutors backing up shaky police procedures, dubious expert testimony, and so on. In this manner, juries can be duped into believing that what is being presented to them are the facts and evidence of a case.

It is not enough for us to throw our hands in the air, wondering what's to be done. It is not enough for us to carry on believing that our justice system gets it right "most of the time," and that this somehow justifies our turning a blind eye to the times when it patently does not get it right. It is not enough for us to convince ourselves that "they wouldn't get away with that," or that everyone who turns up at any place within the criminal justice system must have done something to get themselves there.

We are regularly and routinely locking up innocent people. As individuals, we take comfort from the knowledge that *someone* has been apprehended for a violent crime, and, having been removed from our midst, is no longer a danger to us, or to our loved ones. As long as that is as far as it goes, everyone, it seems, is happy – politicians will continue to get our votes because we feel safe, media owners will continue to get our money and our attention because they tell us what we need to hear.

It doesn't occur to us that the someone who has been locked up may never have been a danger to us in the first place. Indeed, the very suggestion seems ludicrous, so much so that it meets with robust resistance in most places. We have a need to maintain the illusion that all is well, because the alternative is just too unthinkable. The press plays a unique role in helping to maintain the illusion, by creating portraits of suspects which fit our unspoken expectations. Unfortunately, there is no requirement for the press to get it right – speculative, dishonest, negative and prejudicial reporting has been a significant factor in every one of the cases presented here, and those responsible were accountable to no-one.

Yet, as individuals, we must take some responsibility.

Rather than accepting information as it is presented to us, we need to be much more rigorous in our examination of that information. We need to become aware of our underlying assumptions and beliefs, and be willing to ask awkward questions. Above all, we must be prepared to demand that our justice system is based on a search for the truth, and insist that a system based simply on securing a conviction, no matter what, is unacceptable.

As the pace of modern life continues to increase, with its attendant pressures clamouring for our attention, it is too easy to claim that we don't have time, or that these occurrences are nothing to do with us. Fear plays its part also – people willing to speak out on behalf of those who have been wrongfully convicted are often seen as at best, misguided, and at worst, as bad as the people they are trying to defend.

It is almost impossible to convey the horrors faced by those wrongfully convicted, and their families and friends; lost years which can never be replaced, lost opportunities, relationships and experiences. Even if a wrongful conviction is overturned, the person remains branded, unable to return to normal life. The scars carried by those who are wrongly convicted may never heal.

The vast majority of us go about our everyday lives completely oblivious to the fact that this could happen to any one of us. The people in this book were just ordinary citizens, living ordinary lives, until they became caught up in a nightmare from which there was no escape. As hard as it is for us to believe, there was nothing in their lifestyles, background, or personalities which brought them into the criminal justice system as "suspects," quite aside from any consideration of evidence.

As has been shown in this book, there are far too many cases where the old maxim "there's no smoke without fire" simply does not apply – in these cases, there isn't even any smoke!

How You can Help

Throughout the researching and writing of this book, I was asked repeatedly, "What can ordinary people do about this?" The only way to bring about change is to put pressure on our politicians to have our justice system reviewed, and the necessary action taken to amend those areas most in need of alteration. If you would like to add your voice to the growing number of calls for change, you can send a copy of the following sample letter to your own MP, with a request that it be forwarded to the Home Secretary.

Sample Letter

Dear {MP's Name}
I was concerned to learn about the plight of several citizens whose convictions appear to be unsafe. I would like to add my support to those calling for review of the following cases:

Derek Christian, HMP Frankland, Brasside, Durham,
Simon Hall, HMP Swaleside,
John Taft, HMP Gartree
Gordon Park, HMP Strangeways
Luke Mitchell, HM YOI, Polmont, and
Susan May, released from HMP Askham Grange, April 26th 2005.

I also wish to add my support to calls for a review of the Criminal Justice System, with reference to the following areas in particular, in order to reduce the possibility of wrongful conviction in the future:

1. *Right of Appeal – a review of grounds for appeal, with relaxation of the requirement for, and definition of, "new evidence," and automatic right of appeal in certain circumstances.*
2. *Immediate availability of **all transcripts** to defence teams, in every case where conviction leads to sentence of five years or more.*
3. *Disclosure; an end to the system whereby evidence can be lost, suppressed, or destroyed by police and prosecutors. More stringent legislation to ensure that defence teams, juries and judges have access to all of the evidence.*
4. *The creation of an independent body to whom police officers, expert witnesses, and even judges become accountable.*

I would also request that you forward a copy of this letter to the Home Secretary on my behalf, and await your comments.

Yours sincerely, etc.

Sign the petitions

www.freegordon.com
www.justice4simon.co.uk
www.susanmay.co.uk

Details of all of the cases highlighted in this book can also be found at
www.innocent.org.uk

References
Websites

www.portia.org.uk
www.innocent.org.uk
www.lbp.police.uk
www.fitting-up.org/lawyers.htm
www.scotland.gov.uk
www.cabinetoffice.gov.uk/policy
www.freegordon.com
www.justice4simon.koncept07.net
www.lukemitchell.proboards41.com
www.crimeinfo.org.uk
www.justiceforsionjenkins.org.uk
www.sallyclark.org.uk
www.scandals.org/derekchristian
www.justice-for-john-taft.org
www.susanmay.co.uk
www.scotsman.com
www.scottishcourts.com
www.opsi.gov.uk
www.mojuk.org.uk

Articles

"A Murder Mystery: Why do some killings dominate the headlines?" **by Colin Wilson, The Times, January 28 2006.**

"The British Jury System – A conspiracy to convict?" **by Tom Watkins for** www.portia.org.uk **Chapter 6**

"Character Assassination," by **Ronnie Williams for** www.portia.org.uk **Chapter 9, March 15th 2006**

"Computers, hearsay, and the status of extradition proceedings," **by Ben Fitzpatrick BA, Faculty of Law, University of Leeds, 1998**

"Grounds of Appeal in Criminal Cases," **by Peter Duff and Frazer McCallum, Crime and Criminal Justice Research Findings No12 (1996) Scottish Office Central Research Unit.**

"Criminal Procedure (Scotland) Act 1995," **at** www.opsi.gov.uk

"Cutting Crime, Delivering Justice –A Strategic Plan for Criminal Justice 2004-2008," **HM Government, Office for Criminal Justice Reform (OCJR)**

"Detectives Learn Lessons from Shocking Murder," **by Craig Dobbie, Chief Constable's Electronic Newsletter 2005, Lothian and Borders Police at** www.lbp.police.uk

"DNA Evidence," article based on information from **"Crime Busting," by Jenny Ward (Chapter 20), Published by Blandford Press, ISBN 0 1737 2639 3 Printed at** www.portia.org **August 7th 2000**

"Eyewitness Testimony," **by Dr Amina Memon, Institute for Cultural Research, London, for ICR Seminar, February 2002**

"Expert Witnesses aren't what they seem, and I should know" **by Dr Theodore Dalrymple, Daily Telegraph, February 2nd 2003**

"False Result Fear over DNA Tests," by **Nick Paton Walsh, The Observer, February 2nd 2002**

"How big is the 'iceberg?' A Social Harm approach to quantifying miscarriages of justice," by **Michael Naughton, University of Bristol, published in 'Radical Statistics' Volume 81, Spring 2003**

"JUSTICE's response to the Auld review," by **the JUSTICE Organisation, Carter Lane, London, January 2002**

"JUSTICE FOR ALL – JUSTICE's response to the White Paper," by **the JUSTICE organisation, Carter Lane, London, October 2002**

"Justice Without Science Isn't Justice," by **Frank Ward, reproduced at** www.portia.org **Chapter 14, September 17th 2003**

"Lawyers who let you down," by **Andrew Green, first publication CONVICTION Newsletter No 16, second publication, Inside Time, December 1996.**

"Lawyers DID let you down," by **Andrew Green, CONVICTION Newsletter, No 18, 1997.**

"Life Sentence Review Commissioners, Annual report 2005," **ordered by the House of Commons to be printed Thursday 14th July 2005.**

"Media and Crime, Speech to Nacro Conference," by **Richard Garside, Director, Crime and Society Foundation, November 19th 2003**

"Miscarriages of justice," at www.crimeinfo.org.uk **March 17th 2006**

"Miscarriages of Justice and Court Reform," by **Hazel Keirle, Miscarriages of Justice Organisation, England, Wales and Scotland, November 7th 2003.**

"The Police and Corruption, by an ex police officer" at www.portia.org.uk **Chapter 6, March 15th 2006.**

"Rocks and a Hard Place," **Private Eye, January 20th 2006.**

"The role of juries in the British System," by **Dr Zakaria Erzinclioglu,** at www.justice4simon.koncept07.net **printed 09/04/06**

"Science and the Law," by **Zakaria Erzinclioglu, at** www.justice4simon.koncept07.net **printed 09/04/06**

"Scots Law and the Issue of Dock Identifications," by **Michael Bromby, Division of Law, Glasgow Caledonian University and Amina Memon, Professor of Forensic Psychology, University of Aberdeen, 2005**

"Tinkering or transformation? Proposals and principles in the White Paper, 'Justice for 'All?'" by **Ben Fitzpatrick, University of Leeds, published in Web Journal of Current Legal Issues, 2002.**

"Unbalanced newspaper coverage of homicide, teaching the public the wrong lessons," **Anna Hinds, Economic and Social Research Council, January 22nd 2003.**

"Unfair Legislation," reproduced at www.portia.org **Chapter 6, March 15th 2006.**

"Unreliable confessions and miscarriages of justice in Britain," by **Gisli H Gudjonsson, International Journal of Police Science and Management, Vol 4, No 4, August 1st 2002.**

"When science opinion outweighs science fact," by **Alex Ward, The Guardian, October 3rd 2004.**

"Why Experts Make Errors," by **Itiel E Dror and David Charlton, Journal of Forensic Identification, February 6th 2006**

"Convicted by Juries, Exonerated by Science; Case studies in the use of DNA Evidence to Establish Innocence after Trial," by **Edward Connors, Thomas Lundregan, Neal Miller, Tom McEwen, for National Institute of Justice (USA) June 1996**

"Wrongful Convictions," by **Michael Naughton, The Observer Crime and Justice Debate, July 28th 2002.**

"Police - Mitchell holiday plan led to Jodi's murder," **Kate Foster and Fiona MacGregor, Scotland on Sunday, January 23rd 2005.**

"My Luke Torment," by **Gordon McIlwraith, Daily Record, February 14th 2005**

Legal documents and transcripts

Transcript, Statement of Robin J Falconer 21/09/1995 (The Case of Derek Christian)

Transcript, Statement of Robin J Falconer 13/09/1996 (The Case of Derek Christian)

Transcript, Statement of Robin J Falconer 04/07/1997 (The Case of Derek Christian)

Transcript: Appeal Before Lord Justice Kay, Mr. Justice Silber and His Honour Judge Mellor October 2nd 2000 (The case of John Taft)

Excerpt: Written Application to Appeal, Oliver Blunt QC (The case of John Taft)

Transcript: Summing Up. Before; The Honourable Mr. Justice McCombe, Regina – V- Gordon Park, January 26th 2005. (The Case of Gordon Park)

Transcript: Jury deliberation. Before; The Honourable Mr. Justice McCombe, Regina –V- Gordon Park, January 28th 2005. (The Case of Gordon Park)

Transcript, Interview, ADS Fulton, DC Steven Quinn, Luke M Mitchell, July 4th 2003 (The Case of Luke Mitchell)

Transcript, Interview, DC George Thomson, DC Russell Tennant, Luke M Mitchell, August 14th 2003 (The Case of Luke Mitchell)

Transcript, Interview, DC George Thomson, DC Russell Tennant, DS David Gordon, Luke M Mitchell, August 14th 2003 (The Case of Luke Mitchell)

Report; Copy Psychiatric Report on Luke Mitchell, October 29th 2004 (The Case of Luke Mitchell)

Transcript: "Charge to the Jury", Lord Nimmo Smith, January 20th & 21st 2005 (The Case of Luke Mitchell)

Transcript: Note of Appeal, August 1ˢᵗ 2005 (The Case of Luke Mitchell)

Transcript; Report by Lord Nimmo Smith, Note of Appeal, February 7ᵗʰ 2006 (The Case of Luke Mitchell)

Transcript: Opinion of the Court, November 14ᵗʰ 2006 (The case of Luke Mitchell)

Transcript: Summing up, Before Justice Hutchison, Thursday April 22ⁿᵈ 1993 to Tuesday May 4ᵗʰ 1993 (The Case of Susan May)

Transcript: CCRC Statement of Reasons, referred April 1997, reported November 24ᵗʰ 1999. (The Case of Susan May)

Transcript: "Skeleton Argument," November 20ᵗʰ 2001 (The Case of Susan May)

Transcript: "Judgment," December 7ᵗʰ 2001 (The Case of Susan May)

Transcript: Appeal Before Lord Justice Kennedy, Mr. Justice Dyson, Mr. Justice Penry-Davey December 21ˢᵗ 1999 (The case of Sion Jenkins)

Other references

"Cognitive Psychology,
A Student's Handbook,
3rd Edition,"

Michael Eysenck & Mark T Keane
published by Psychology Press Ltd
1995.

"Criminal Law"

Jonathan Herring
published by Palgrave MacMillan
2005

"Criminological Perspectives
A Reader"

John Muncie, Eugene McLaughlin
and Mary Langan published by Sage
Publications 1996

"Textbook on
Criminology"

Katherine S Williams
published by Blackstone Press Ltd
1991.

"The Encyclopedia of
Forensic Science"

Brian Lane
published by Headline Book
Publishing plc. 1992.

"Human Memory
The Processing of
Information"

Geoffrey R Loftus & Elizabeth F
Loftus
published by Lawrence Erlbaum
Associates, Publishers, 1976.

"The Jigsaw Man"

Paul Britton
published by Bantam Press 1997

"Nutshells
Evidence
Fourth Edition"

Christina McAlhone & Michael
Stockdale
published by Sweet & Maxwell Ltd
2005

"Picking up the Pieces"

Paul Britton
published by Bantam Press
2000

"Psychology   Nicky Hayes & Sue Orrell
An Introduction"   published by Longman Group UK
Second Edition   1993

"Thinking and Deciding"   Jonathon Baron
Second Edition   published by Cambridge University
Press, 1994.

Printed in the United Kingdom
by Lightning Source UK Ltd.
120887UK00002B/235-246